Merry Christmas Dad
12-25-03
Love- Rhode, Kent
David

Merry Christmas Dad
12-25-03
Love- Rhode, Kent
David

WITNESS TO AN ERA

Gardner was a mighty good fellow—
also mightily my friend: he was always
loving: I feel near to him—always—
to this day: years, deaths, severances,
don't seem to make much difference
when you have once loved a man:
Gardner was a real artist—had the
feel of his work—the inner feel, if I
may say it so: he was not a workman—
only a workman (which God knows is
a lot in itself, too!)—but he was also
beyond his craft—saw farther than
his camera—saw more: his pictures are
an evidence of his endowment.[1]

—WALT WHITMAN

WITNESS TO AN ERA

THE LIFE AND PHOTOGRAPHS OF

ALEXANDER GARDNER

■

THE CIVIL WAR, LINCOLN, AND THE WEST

■

D. MARK KATZ

Rutledge Hill Press®
Nashville, Tennessee

ALSO BY D. MARK KATZ

Custer in Photographs

Published in Nashville, Tennessee, by Rutledge Hill Press, 211
Seventh Avenue North, Nashville, Tennessee 37219. Distributed in
Canada by H.B. Fenn & Company, Ltd., 34 Nixon Road, Bolton,
Ontario L7E 1W2. Distributed in Australia by The Five Mile Press
Pty., Ltd., 22 Summit Road, Noble Park, Victoria 3174. Distributed
in New Zealand by Tandem Press, 2 Rugby Road, Birkenhead,
Auckland 10. Distributed in the United Kingdom by Verulam Press,
Ltd., 152a Park Street Lane, Park Street, St. Albans, Hertfordshire
AL2 2AU.

First published in 1991 by Viking Penguin, a division of Penguin
Books USA, Inc.

Designed by Beth Tondreau Design / Mary A. Wirth

Library of Congress Cataloging–in Publication Data

Witness to an Era / Katz, D. Mark
       p.   cm.
    Includes bibliographical references.
    ISBN: 1-55853-742-2
    1. Gardner, Alexander, 1821–1882. 2. News
photographers—United States—Biography. I. Title
TR140.G35K38 1991
770'.92—dc20   89-40696
                                                      CIP

Printed in China.

1 2 3 4 5 6 7 8 9 — 07 06 05 04 03 02 01 00 99

TO
ABIGAIL
AND MY CHILDREN,
SHAUN, PHILLIP, BRIANNE, AND RORY

FOREWORD

Modern "fame" is ubiquitous. Anyone and everyone can achieve global—if fleeting—recognition. Daily, even hourly, we're pummeled by a media onslaught ballyhooing the latest "superstar," and also giving us intimate glimpses of players in the great dramas of life and death around the planet.

But before mass media, fame and recognition were more elusive, and often (too often) the contributions of deserving figures were eclipsed by more flamboyant peers.

So it was in the early days of photography. The clear, prevailing public perception of the Civil War is that Matthew Brady was the most important photographer, if not the *only* photographer.

But there were others, certainly as capable, perceptive, and courageous, who pioneered the American tradition of taking photojournalism into war. Alexander Gardner was one of these. While Brady's name has become synonymous with the Civil War, many of the most memorable images were actually taken by Gardner.

Alexander Gardner is a photographer generally unknown to history, perhaps, but familiar to those of us who followed his footsteps onto fields of battle armed with the same weapon he carried: a camera.

Gardner's war was between America's North and South; mine was also between North and South, but occurred in Vietnam, more than one hundred years later and half a world away.

As a combat photographer in 1971, all I needed were a couple of Nikons and a few rolls of 35mm film. In 1861 Gardner needed a darkroom on wheels, draft horses to pull it, and a camera the size of a soapbox.

Besides covering war, Gardner and I had another thing in common. He made some historical photos of President Abraham Lincoln, and more than a century later I was official photographer to President Gerald Ford.

Gardner's pictures of Lincoln were formal and posed, for the most pragmatic of reasons: the exposure took more than a minute! High-speed film, lightweight cameras, and an understanding president gave me unprecedented access and provided the public with candid, behind-the-scenes glimpses of the White House.

Despite the primitive restrictions of his chosen art form, however, Gardner's images—if not his name—remain etched in history, bringing into sharp focus the faces of war.

Witness to an Era sets the record straight, documenting the life and impact of one of America's most important photographers. It is gratifying to know that work that has inspired generations of other war photographers may now be appreciated by the wider audience Gardner deserves.

David Hume Kennerly
Los Angeles, California

CONTENTS

PREFACE

It seems fitting that in this 125th anniversary year of the end of the Civil War and the assassination of Abraham Lincoln the name and work of Alexander Gardner, so intimately involved in those events, should be brought to public attention. In 1883, Gardner's obituarist wrote:

> There are always men who seem to be made for the times in which they live; men who are generic forces, who originate thought, create circumstances and stamp their own impress upon the community. Men whose plans command confidence, whose approbation is a guarantee of success, and whose word with those who know them has the force of law. Alexander Gardner was such a man.

It has been my purpose to bring together in this volume all that is known about Alexander Gardner and present the best of his work, assembled for the first time. It was Gardner's misfortune to have had his name and memory overshadowed by that of Matthew Brady, synonymous for many with Civil War photography. Gardner had a long association with Brady, opening and running his Washington studio before the war, and indeed worked for Brady through the Battle of Antietam. Like that of other Brady operatives, Gardner's work was published under the Brady name. Gardner photographs used as models for newspaper illustrations were thus identified for the public as "Brady photographs," as if Brady himself had taken the pictures. *The Photographic History of the War*, published in 1910, carried this misconception over into book form. To this day, history and photography books perpetuate the error. Unfortunately, this has led to Gardner's remaining an obscure figure, with many of his most powerful images being credited to others.

Gardner's career was truly extraordinary: gallery work with Brady, photographing soldiers and public figures; work with Pinkerton and the infant Secret Service; battlefield coverage, and portrayal of camp life; numerous sessions with President Lincoln. These various photographic situations prepared him for and put him in the middle of some of the most wrenching historical events of his era: the assassination of Lincoln, the apprehension and execution of the conspirators, and the execution of Confederate Captain Henry Wirz, commander of Andersonville Prison. His photography in the West with the expanding railroad and at the Fort Laramie Treaty Council, as well as his studio portraits of Indian delegations in Washington, contributed additional significant and memorable images to an already impressive body of work. Technically, Gardner's images are remarkable. Many of them have only been seen by the public poorly reproduced, usually from copy prints. In this volume I have been able to reproduce many images directly from original prints made by Gardner himself, making every attempt to convey the quality of the originals themselves.

But it is not technical expertise that is ultimately Gardner's accomplishment—rather it is in extending the power of the photographic image in affecting public awareness. The photographic coverage of the Civil War by Gardner and others sent authentic images of the horrors of the battlefield directly to the public for the first time. In November 1988, the twenty-fifth anniversary of the assassination of President Kennedy, CBS newsman Dan Rather noted that television coverage of that tragic event, including the televised killing of Lee Harvey Oswald, "marked the coming of age of television." Gardner's photographic coverage of the execution of the Lincoln conspirators marked a similar transition point—the birth of photojournalism as we now know it.

It was these photographs, some of which were published in Jim Bishop's book *The Day Lincoln Was Shot*, that mesmerized me and drew me to Gardner's work.

William A. Frassanito's epic 1975 study *Gettysburg: A Journey in Time* critically dissected Gardner's role as a Civil War photographer, shedding new light on his story.

Donald K. McCoo, of Paisley, Scotland, Gardner's birthplace, wrote a wonderfully revealing dissertation on Gardner, called *A Rare Specimen Found: Alexander Gardner, Scots American Photographer*. This paper is a primary source of information on Gardner and his family in Scotland.

In 1958 Josephine Cobb, an iconographer for the National Archives, wrote the first detailed biographical sketch of Alexander Gardner. Unfortunately, she did not include footnotes or complete sources. When I visited Ms. Cobb shortly before her death I discovered that one of her main sources on Gardner had been his daughter-in-law, Elizabeth Keating Gardner, the wife of Gardner's son, Lawrence. Elizabeth Gardner passed away in 1940.

Without the works of William A. Frassanito, Donald K. McCoo, and Josephine Cobb, *Witness to an Era: The Life and Photographs of Alexander Gardner* would not exist, and I am grateful to them for their work and the inspiration it provided me.

Frustratingly little is known about Alexander Gardner the man. By tracking down documents in the government archives and correlating references in various journals and accounts, I have been able to trace the course of his career, especially his movements during and just after the Civil War, when he was involved in so many pivotal events. But most important, I have been able to assemble Gardner's work, which speaks eloquently and powerfully for itself. It is my hope that the body of his work, published as a whole at last, will bring him the recognition he deserves as one of America's great photographers.

There has been some difference of opinion about the spelling of Matthew Brady's name. I have chosen the spelling that Brady seems most likely to have used. He always went by "M. B. Brady," so it has proved impossible to definitively confirm his spelling, but New York and Washington business directories from the time list it as "Matthew." And in fact "Matthew" was the common spelling of the name until the late nineteenth century, at which point "Mathew" became the predominant form.

I am particularly grateful to David L. Hack and Lloyd Ostendorf, friends and colleagues who have loaned me original Gardner photographs and materials for this book, and who have given me steadfast encouragement as well. This book is a testament to our friendship.

I am also grateful to the other people who graciously offered me the use of photographs from their private collections, all of which contributed to the richness of this volume: Marshall Pywell, Plater T. Gedney, Lawrence T. Jones III, George Nas, David R. O'Reilly, James Lowe, and Salvatore Alberti.

I would like to thank the following people and organizations for their help and cooperation: Mr. George Hobart at the Library of Congress; the Smithsonian Institution; the National Portrait Gallery and the Bureau of Ethnology, with special thanks to Paula Fleming; the National Archives; Gettysburg College, Special Collections; Acacia Life Insurance Company, Special Collections; the Kansas State Historical Society; and the Western Reserve Historical Society.

I also appreciate the efforts of others who selflessly contributed their time and efforts in support of this project: John Brennan, Robert L. Kessler, Jack Torres, William A. Frassanito, Karl Sundstrom, Philip B. Kundhardt, Donald K. McCoo, and especially Marie Verrelman Melchiori (whose tenacity and skill in genealogical research helped track down numerous leads in attempting to follow the movements of Gardner and his family). Thanks as well to my agent, Ralph Vicinanza, to my editor, David Stanford, to Mary Wirth of Beth Tondreau Design, and to Cindy Achar, Roni Axelrod, Roger Devine, Kate Griggs, Amy Hill, Lisa Pliscou, Todd Radom, Neil Stuart, and Karen Zilversmit at Viking, all of whose efforts on behalf of the book I appreciate.

And special thanks to Ryan and Chad.

—D. MARK KATZ
AUGUST 1990

THE
EARLY YEARS

1821—1856

*A*lexander Gardner, the first child of
James Gardner and Jean Glenn, was born on October 17, 1821, in Paisley, Scotland,
five months after his parents were married. His mother had been raised in an affluent
Renfrewshire family of eminent clergymen, prominent physicians, and well-to-do
landsmen. Shortly after Alexander's birth, the family relocated to Glasgow, where,
according to parish records, his twin sisters, Agnes and Catherine, were born in 1826
and his brother, James, was born in 1829.[1] Nothing further is known about his sisters.
A cholera epidemic struck the Glasgow region about this time, probably causing the
death of his father.[2]

Young Alexander's mother encouraged and cultivated his scholastic studies. The
boy excelled in his schooling, particularly in astronomy, botany, and chemistry. At the
age of fourteen he was apprenticed to a jeweler in Glasgow, where he served faithfully
until 1842.[3] His position as jeweler's apprentice and craftsman gave him a privileged
station in a status-conscious society, and he became partial to the company of educated
people. However, Gardner early developed an interest in the plight of the working
class. His Calvinistic upbringing advocated "reward through industrious effort,"[4] and
Gardner was also undoubtedly influenced by his study of the ideals of Robert Owen,
the early-nineteenth-century Welsh Socialist, who founded a utopian society in New
Harmony, Indiana.[5]

In 1847 Gardner became manager of the Clydesdale Discount and Loan Company. Why he changed professions is not known, but it apparently became clear to him
that his future was in the world of business and finance. In his new position he also acted
as a "bill broker," buying and selling bills of exchange and promissory notes.

In December of that year Gardner became a charter member of the Glasgow
Atheneum and established intimate contacts with a cross section of influential Glasgow
citizens, including social and political reformers. His Atheneum membership afforded
him access to its reading rooms and reference library, as well as admission to the
scientific lectures delivered at the Atheneum every Monday and Thursday evening.[6]

Deeply disturbed by the exploitation of the working class, Gardner fully supported the early cooperative movements forming in Scotland. In 1848 he conceived
the idea of establishing a group of liberal-minded fellow citizens in the United States.
This venture was given the official name of the Clydesdale Joint Stock Agricultural
and Commercial Company. The bylaws reveal that Gardner's socialistic plans were

> for the purpose of acquiring land in some suitable locality in the United States
> of America in which to establish by means of the united capital and industry of

its partners a comfortable home for themselves and families where they may follow a more simple useful and rational mode of life than is found practicable in the complex and competitive state of society from which they have become anxious to retire.[7]

In June 1850 Alexander Gardner's future brother-in-law, Robertson Sinclair, left Scotland with eight friends and relatives to establish a cooperative community in Clayton County, Iowa. Among them were James Gardner, Alex's twenty-year-old brother, listed as a laborer; James Love and James Shant, both farmers; and Jesse Stevens, who would soon become the wife of Robertson Sinclair.[8] Alexander Gardner attended to every detail in the formation of the settlement, even scheduling duties for its individual members. He wanted to be sure that the association could handle any emergency that might arise.[9]

The Clydesdale company was incorporated in Iowa with fixed capital in the amount of $20,000 divided into 800 shares of $25 per share. Each resident member who owned four shares was entitled to occupy a house with two acres of land for himself and his family. During this period they would also receive a small allowance for subsistence. Five percent was paid on the capital stock and twenty-five percent of the profits was diverted as shares. The balance of the profits was divided among the members of the company in proportion to the time and labor they provided the association.[10]

The settlement was located close to the township of Monona, five miles west of McGregor's Landing on the Mississippi River. Within two years of settling, the cooperative had elected its administrators. Gardner, still in Glasgow, maintained and safeguarded the colony's business interests and investments and recruited new members.

In April 1851 Gardner became the proprietor of the *Glasgow Sentinel* newspaper. Continuing his concern for the rights of the working class, he advocated those rights in his editorials. Robert Buchanan and William Love had launched the *Sentinel* in 1850, with an editorial policy aimed at supporting liberal social reform. As a weekly newspaper, the *Sentinel* published three editions every Saturday, with coverage of international, national, and rural news. After only three months, the circulation averaged 6,500 copies weekly, more than any other paper in town except the *Glasgow Saturday Evening Post.*

In his editorial for the first-anniversary edition, Gardner wrote:

> The present proprietor who had long felt the necessity of an efficient and independent Democratic newspaper in Scotland was induced to become the purchaser April last not as mere speculation in the usual sense of the term but as a means of enlightening the public on the great political, educational, and social questions of the times and of guiding right the popular mind of this country on all matters of state policy whatever advice was necessary or important.[11]

Although Charles Dickens had lectured at the inauguration of the Glasgow Atheneum in 1847, the organization did not thrive—in fact, membership decreased steadily. Gardner commented on the situation in an editorial:

An institution of this kind can only be kept in a healthy state by the members generally taking an interest in its welfare and management . . . it does not speak well for our city that her literary and educational institutions should have so many difficulties to contend with. . . . We call then upon the working classes and upon all those of every class who sincerely desire to see mankind progressing—become really civilized—to see to it that while seeking to reform old or to obtain new they fail not to work to the best advantage of our existing educational agencies.[12]

On May 1, 1851, Queen Victoria officially opened the Crystal Palace Exhibition at Hyde Park in London. The theme of this internationally important event was "Industry of All Nations." It ran for five months and offered many valuable lessons for the craftsmen and merchants who visited or exhibited there. New production methods were revealed, design deficiencies were overcome, and certain trading prejudices were discovered. On May 10 Alexander Gardner published a sullen editorial about the exhibition:

The scene was typical of the world's condition—a vast assemblage of powers as yet unmeasured in their capacity but half reduced to order, armed force still watching to supply the defeat in the organization of society; society half starved by its own toil, some rolling in luxury some weary and afoot, dusty, hungry, envying and dangerous; yet in that crystal edifice was great work done. . . .[13]

Among the thirty classes of exhibits at the Hyde Park extravaganza were displays on paper, printing, and book binding, as well as of precious metals, jewelry, and scientific instruments. Outstanding were photographs—including those of the American Matthew B. Brady, who was awarded the Grand Prize Medal for the best daguerreotypes. It is quite possible that while attending the exhibition, Alexander Gardner met Brady. In any case, the futures of both men were destined to be intertwined.

Alex Gardner withdrew from active association in publishing the *Glasgow Sentinel* early in 1852. Although his reasons for leaving are unclear, they appear to relate to the termination of the Clydesdale company and the breakup of the experimental colony of Scotsmen in Iowa.

The Clydesdale colony had decided by unanimous resolution on March 29, 1853, to dissolve its company. It is impossible to know why the colony failed, but in any case, the proceeds from the sale of its effects scarcely covered expenses. Gardner's abrupt departure from the *Sentinel* indicates that his presence was urgently needed in Iowa since he was an experienced businessman, and the one who had conceived the utopian experiment. Following the dissolution of the colony, many members merged into other outlying communities in Clayton County; Robertson Sinclair moved to McGregor's Landing, and James Gardner returned with his brother to Scotland, in the summer of 1853.[14]

It was Alexander Gardner's interest in chemistry and science that led him to experiment with photography. Professional daguerreotype studios were operating in Glasgow as early as the mid-1840s. In October 1850 the *Sentinel* had reviewed the opening of the gallery of Stephen A. McLeod Young, from Paisley, who'd previously been a printer.

The main contributors to the photography exhibit at the Crystal Palace Exhibition had been England, France, Italy, Germany, Austria, and the United States. Scotland was represented by Ross & Thompson and David Octavius Hill, both from Edinburgh. In the years that followed, the art form flourished. The first meeting of the Glasgow Photographic Society was held in 1854 at McClure's Gallery on Buchanan Street. Although its charter members remain unidentified, the very existence of such a society attests to the spreading popularity of photography.

The British Association for the Advancement of Science staged its annual seminar in Glasgow, in September 1855, and as part of the proceedings, a photographic exhibit was presented at the gallery of Wylie & Lockhead. Only one individual still exhibited the by-then-outmoded daguerreotype—an indication of the progress being made. The more advanced technical achievements included the calotype, the waxed-paper process, the albumen print, the collodion print, and photolithography. The *Sentinel* gave the exhibition an enthusiastic review:

> Nothing of the kind has ever been seen before in this city. The art of "Sun Picturing" seems to be making rapid strides. Everytime almost that we are called upon to inspect the exhibited specimens of this art we are more struck with its wondrous capabilities. Here we have not only the human face divine but architectural objects of the highest interest and landscapes of the most astonishing truthfulness. . . . We can only recommend that as many of our readers as have a shilling to expend on the beautiful exhibit visit the gallery for themselves, and we have at the same time to beg the committee that before closing they will afford the working classes an opportunity of seeing their fine collection at a nominal price.[15]

That December, the *Sentinel* reviewed Roger Fenton's historical photographs taken during the Crimean War:

> The portraits of the heroes who have done so much for the honor of the allies are most vividly portrayed. We can hardly commend any of the photographs more than another, but we would suggest to the visitor to pay particular attention to the one on the "Council of War" held on the night previous to the taking of Mamelon.[16]

Alexander Gardner undoubtedly had frequent opportunities to review, assess, and practice this new art. His access to the reading rooms of the Atheneum might well have provided him with opportunities to read Frederick Scott Archer's articles on the new wet-plate collodion process. He could have learned the process from either Stephen A. McLeod Young or John Urie. In any case, he was actively pursuing the art of photography by the end of 1855, for on December 26 the *Dumbarton Herald* advertised that "Mr. Gardner offered his services from the photographic Gallery which had been erected in Mr. Buchanan's Woodyard, near the church on High Street in Dumbarton." Gardner's enticement for customers was the gift of a gold watch with the purchase of a calotype portrait, and a portrait brooch with each collodion portrait. The free jewelry was a final remnant from his apprenticeship trade. The editorial section of the *Dumbarton Herald* confirmed that Gardner's gift offer was legitimate:

> It will be seen from an advertisement in another column that Mr. Gardner is practicing among us as a photographic artist and the portraits he has turned out of several well known townsmen entitle him to be considered among the foremost professors of this beautiful art. The branch of the art to which he confines his chief attention is the Calotype discovered by Mr. Talbot and the first process ever announced for taking sun pictures. Not the least valuable part of the process is the power by which any number of copies can be reproduced at a cheap rate after the first copy is taken and being on paper they can be sent through the post without any fear of having been destroyed. To congregations who wish a faithful portrait of their minister having all the breadth and vigor of a steel engraving combined with the delicacy and minuteness of the finest daguerreotype, the present opportunity ought not to be lost sight of, as it will entirely depend upon the encouragement Mr. G. gets how long he may remain a guest amongst us. The watch and brooch which he purposes making a present of to his finest subscribers we have seen and can truly say they are no sham.[17]

By March 6, 1856, Gardner was advertising without the inducement of free gifts, and by April 24, he ceased advertising altogether. It was clear that in this span of four months, he began to realize there was a lack of interest in his work. Fortunately for history and photography, Gardner, now married, decided to leave Scotland and emigrate to America.[18]

In the spring of 1856, Alexander; his mother, Jean Glenn; wife, Margaret; brother, James; nine-year-old son, Lawrence; and infant daughter, Eliza, sailed from Scotland to join the remnants of the Clydesdale colony. Upon their arrival in Newfoundland, Gardner received news from Iowa that most of their family and friends had fallen victim to the dreaded "galloping consumption," later known as tuberculosis. His brother-in-law, Robertson Sinclair, was gravely ill, and Sinclair's wife, Jesse, was dead. Under those circumstances, Gardner decided to leave his family in New York and travel alone to Iowa to oversee the welfare of his infant niece, Margaret "Robbie" Sinclair.[19] In Iowa he found Robertson Sinclair alive, though gravely ill. (In 1858 Sinclair died from the effects of tuberculosis.) Gardner ensured the welfare of his niece by arranging her adoption with John T. Stoneman, a local attorney from McGregor's Landing, who would later become a judge in Cedar Rapids, Iowa.[20] Throughout his lifetime, Gardner held a special affection for his niece, named after his wife, Margaret Sinclair Gardner.

Upon his return to New York, Gardner faced the perplexing choice of returning to Scotland or staying in America to seek his fortune. Providentially, the thirty-five-year-old skilled jeweler, proficient journalist, and experienced businessman and photographer decided to initiate contact with Matthew Brady, the premier American photographer, whose work he had seen at the Crystal Palace Exhibition in London five years before.

2

THE YEARS WITH MATTHEW B. BRADY

1856–1861

*F*renchmen Joseph Nicéphore Niepce and Louis Jacques Mandé Daguerre experimented for years with the camera obscura in the hope that their work would lead to securing a permanent photographic image. They formed a partnership in 1829. Niepce died in 1833, but the partnership continued through his son, Isidore. In the fall of 1835, a French publication announced that Daguerre had succeeded in obtaining a permanent photographic image. Three years later Daguerre was ready to promote his new discovery. The French Government granted Daguerre and Niepce pensions so that their invention, called the daguerreotype, could be placed before the world.[1]

One of the first Americans to embrace the new art was Samuel F. B. Morse. While in Europe promoting his new telegraph system, Morse read about the daguerreotype and, being an accomplished artist, contacted Daguerre for personal instruction in the new art. They met in March 1839. Morse later declared the daguerreotype "Rembrandt perfected." Upon his return to the United States, Morse brought a camera provided by Daguerre and became an enthusiastic supporter of the daguerreotype. Daguerre formally revealed his secret in August 1839, and the next month the process was introduced to America.[2]

Matthew Benjamin Brady was born in 1823. His early life is shrouded in mystery and uncertainty. He was born either in Cork, Ireland, or in Fort Warren, New York, and professed to having no knowledge of his parents, who were supposedly Irish immigrants. However, on his death certificate they are identified as Andrew and Julia Brady and listed as having been born in the United States. When Brady was sixteen years old, he left home to seek employment in Saratoga, New York, where he met and became good friends with the young and struggling portrait artist William Page. "Giving him a bundle of his crayons to copy," Page encouraged young Brady to sketch, while he sought commissions to paint.[3]

In either 1839 or 1840, both Brady and William Page left Albany for New York City. Brady was soon employed as a jeweler at A. T. Stewart's, on the corner of Chambers Street and Broadway; Page continued to paint portraits. One day Page visited his old friend Samuel F. B. Morse, then president of the National Academy of Design. Brady accompanied Page on the visit, which turned out to be the turning point in his life. After meeting with Morse, Brady felt his life "was inextricably enmeshed with the infant art of photography." Some time in 1840, Morse opened what could be described as the first school of photography. His first students were Edward Anthony,

Samuel Broadbent of Philadelphia, Albert S. Southworth of Boston, and his new friend, Matthew Brady. Morse charged between $25 and $50 for his course on photography. Although a fortune at that time for young Brady, he willingly worked hard as a clerk and jeweler's helper to be able to afford it. He also received additional instruction in photography from the eminent chemists Professor John W. Draper of New York University and Professor Robert Ogden Doremus.[4]

Brady's First Gallery

Four years later, feeling that he had achieved some proficiency in the new art, Brady opened what was to be his first daguerreotype studio at 207 Broadway. The directories list him as both a "Daguerrian miniature gallery" and a "jewel, miniature, and surgical case manufacturer."[5] In the spring of 1844, the American Institute held its first photographic exhibition. Brady won a silver medal for first honors. He repeated his achievement for the next four years. In 1849 *Humphrey's Journal* (one of the earliest daguerrian trade journals) glibly announced, "Mr. B. has won again."[6]

In 1845 Brady conceived the idea of photographing for posterity distinguished Americans, and publishing the portraits under the title *The Gallery of Illustrious Americans*. With the enticement of a complimentary sitting, Brady induced many prominent "men and mothers of America" to appear before his camera. Statesmen, politicians, scientists, writers, actors, and actresses were all lured by vanity or curiosity into his studio. One of Brady's great achievements was to acquire a daguerreotype of the dying ex-president, Andrew Jackson. The picture was actually taken on April 15, 1845, by photograher Dan Adams of Nashville, Tennessee. However, Brady was not above taking credit and used it as the foundation for his "Gallery of American Presidents." Proud of his surrogate achievement, he exhibited this famous daguerreotype in his gallery for all to see.[7]

Brady made the first in a series of unsuccessful attempts at operating a second gallery in 1847, in Washington, exhibiting photographs of President James K. Polk and General Zachary Taylor. In 1849 and 1850, he took portraits of three of the most honored Americans: Henry Clay, Daniel Webster, and John C. Calhoun. These portraits formed the nucleus of his exhibits throughout his long career and always had a special meaning and importance to him.

The year 1850 was a milestone in Brady's rapidly developing career. First he married his sweetheart, Juliet Elizabeth Handy, the daughter of Maryland attorney Colonel Samuel Handy. Then his *Gallery of Illustrious Americans* was published in a handsome leather-bound album that sold for $300. The engravings in the collection, based on his daguerreotypes, were published by F. D. D'Avignon, and the accompanying text was written by C. Edwards Lester, a leading New York art critic. Although this venture was a critical success, it proved to be a financial failure.[8] Apparently none of the volumes have survived.

Another opportunity to display his work came when Queen Victoria announced

Matthew Benjamin Brady, Juliet Handy, and Mrs. Haggerty, c. 1851. This portrait is believed to have been taken prior to Brady's trip to London to attend the Crystal Palace Exhibition by his manager, George S. Cook. From the original daguerreotype.

a "Great Exhibition," the Crystal Palace Exhibition, to be held at Hyde Park in London in the spring of 1851. Since one of the announced categories was photography, Brady, like others in New York, began to prepare his finest work for exhibition. The competing participants naturally planned to enter their most unusual and noteworthy daguerreotypes. Some of them even offered complimentary sittings in a quest for unusual or freakish subjects. Brady, to avoid anything crass or sensational, chose not to advertise or try to attract customers, relying on the photographs that were already in his files or in his *Gallery of Illustrious Americans*. He submitted forty-eight of his finest daguerreotype portraits to the Photographic Committee in London.[9]

Brady was ambitious and hardworking, and his grueling schedule began to take its toll. In 1851 the *Photographic Art Journal* declared:

> Mr. Brady is not operating himself, a failing eyesight precluding the possibility of his using the camera with any certainty. But he is an excellent artist, nevertheless, understands his business perfectly, and gathers about him the finest talent to be found. . . . Brady's proverbial enterprise is not to be questioned and his gallery is the most fashionable in the city.[10]

In July of that year, Brady and his wife sailed from New York to London. In his absence, George S. Cook, a South Carolinian, was placed in charge of his New York gallery. The Great Exhibition opened as scheduled on May 1, 1851, but of the twenty-four nations represented, only six (England, France, Italy, Germany, Austria, and the United States) exhibited photography. Of the five medals awarded for photography, three were won by Americans: John A. Whipple and Martin M. Lawrence of Boston and Matthew Brady, who was honored for the "general excellence of his entire collection."[11] The European press commented on America's contributions: "America stands alone for stern development of character. . . . After a very minute and careful examination we are inclined to give America first place. . . . The likenesses of the various distinguished Americans by Mr. Brady are notable examples of this style of art. . . . The American daguerreotypes are pronounced the best which are exhibited."[12] At the close of the Great Exhibition, Brady and his wife remained in Europe, traveling throughout the winter of 1851 and into the spring of 1852.

The Brady-Gardner Partnership

In early 1855 Frederick Scott Archer announced his new wet-plate collodion process. The wet plate made it possible for unlimited reproduction, which resulted in the obsolescence of the daguerreotype, a single, nonreproducible image. Photography was no longer seen as "a new art," and was now ready to be considered big business. Brady realized that his future success depended on his ability to adapt to this and other innovations. With his eyesight continuing to worsen, he began to seek an assistant with the energy and genius for detail that he had once possessed. Alexander Gardner was that man.

The illustrated *London News* set a clear precedent in the use of engraved illustrations, an example followed in 1855 by the first American illustrated newspaper, *Frank Leslie's*, which featured woodcuts. *Harper's Weekly* followed, in January 1857. Gardner undoubtedly saw the tremendous potential for illustrated newspapers in America. What better way to break into this field than to work in close alliance with the premier American photographer, Matthew Brady? The May 2, 1857, issue of *Harper's Weekly* was the first to use a woodcut based on a Brady photograph. Appropriately, the image used was copied from a portrait of Samuel F. B. Morse. Thirteen more woodcuts based on Brady photographs appeared throughout that year.[13]

Gardner's publishing experience and administrative ability enabled him to help Brady fulfill his commercial commitments while Brady personally attended to studio clientele. An experienced businessman, Gardner was appalled at the condition of Brady's bookkeeping. He immediately instituted proper recording procedures, insisting that a professional bookkeeper be employed. Brady had little patience for these office formalities, but came to understand that, because of them, his business was running smoother and more profitably.

The Imperial photograph was an Alexander Gardner innovation. Made by the Woodward Solar Camera, these enlargements, measuring 17 × 21 inches, were introduced into Brady's New York studio and subsequently featured in his new Washington gallery as well.[14] The life-size images were copied from daguerreotypes and usually finished in india ink. Brady loved the Imperial, which proved very profitable for the studio. Prices ranged from $50 to $750, depending on the amount of retouching required. Brady hired professional artists to do the work, which essentially transformed a photograph into a painting. A local critic and rival photographer, Augustus McCarty, described them as "the pantaloon photographs, eclat Imperials, and have nothing imperial about them except the price."[15]

Matthew Brady came to realize his good fortune in having found someone capable of successfully managing all aspects of his Washington gallery. Gardner; his brother, James; and Timothy H. O'Sullivan, a young apprentice, were given the responsibility of developing and protecting Brady's burgeoning Washington interests. On January 26, 1858, Brady formally announced the opening of his new gallery in the *Washington Daily National Intelligencer*:

> M. B. Brady respectfully announces that he has established a Gallery of Photographic Art in Washington. He is prepared to execute commissions for the Imperial Photograph, hitherto made only at his well-known establishment in New York.
>
> A variety of unique and rare photographic specimens are included in his collection, together with portraits of many of the most distinguished citizens of the United States.
>
> Mr. Brady brings to his Washington Gallery the results of fourteen years' experience in Europe and America, and the choicest products of his art during that period. He feels confident that the resources at his command and the artistic quality of his works will commend his Gallery to the attention of the Washington public.

Mr. Gardner's Counterfeit Check

Another example of Gardner's inventiveness is the story of his counterfeit check. Before he left New York, Gardner used his inventive talent in an extraordinary experiment. While testing ways of copying documents, he decided to make a photographic copy of a check so perfect that it would fool a banker. After many hours of work, he made a perfect copy and brought it to the local bank. The teller cashed it without question.

Gardner asked: "Is the check good, sir?"

The teller smiled and replied, "It's perfect, Mr. Gardner."

"Very well, please summon the president." The surprised clerk called for the president of the bank and Gardner asked for his check.

"Is anything wrong with this check, sir?" Gardner asked.

The president examined it. "If it isn't genuine, Mr. Gardner, I'll eat it."

"You had better start eating then," Gardner said. "This is a photographic copy and here is the real check."

That afternoon the bank president called a meeting of other New York bankers to demonstrate Gardner's technique. The bankers soon devised a formula "to produce a check that could not be photographed," and in a short time no check issued in New York could be photographically reproduced.[16] In his own way, Gardner was the nation's first check counterfeiter, and he helped make it difficult for less honest souls to use photographic techniques for illicit gain.

Gardner in Washington, D.C.

Gardner had arrived in Washington in February 1856 and the excellence of his work soon attracted the public's attention. He "was always the experimentalist, never hesitating to spend time and money to secure any device that might enable him to reach the best results and therefore elevate the taste of the public in behalf of photography, which he ever held to be one of the fine arts along with painting and sculpture."[17] As long as Gardner's management remained efficient, Brady allowed him complete freedom of operation.[18] He paid his employees fairly, at the same time permitting them the opportunity to fulfill photographic assignments elsewhere; however, he insisted on retaining possession of their negatives. His prices to the public were justifiably expensive. He opposed Brady's policy of luring prospective clients into the gallery under the guise of a complimentary sitting and discouraged this practice at all times. He was also adamant in his disdain for the composite photograph, which was difficult to produce, quite expensive to print, and popular only for a short time. Gardner was in complete charge of Brady's Washington gallery and under those circumstances was quite content to work for him.[19]

Brady's Washington gallery, located at 352 Pennsylvania Avenue, was quite an elegant showcase. The reception room on the second floor was outfitted to attract the

The earliest known portrait of Alexander Gardner, possibly taken on his arrival in Washington, D.C., in 1858. From an original unpublished carte de visite.

Matthew B. Brady, c. 1856. From an original unpublished salt print.

attention of patrons as well as the general public. Fourteen Imperial portraits were displayed, among them famous statesmen—including Webster, Clay, and Calhoun—and men of the arts like James Fenimore Cooper, Washington Irving, and Daniel Drew, the financier. Other Imperials finished in india ink portrayed Amos Kendall, the retired postmaster general; and the industrialists George Peabody and William Wilson Corcoran. Current commissions were displayed in a sidewalk case that stood on C Street, at the rear entrance to the gallery. On the third floor, immediately above the reception room, were the finishing and mounting rooms. All artwork took place in these rooms, with full-time artists employed to retouch and finish in either oil or water color the magnificent Imperial prints.

The camera operators worked on the top floor, where the skylight was located. The hours for producing portraits were limited to the morning, between 8 A.M. and noon. Appointments were canceled on rainy or cloudy days. James Gardner and Timothy O'Sullivan were regularly employed as apprentice photographers at the gallery. The special artists were the highest-paid employees, earning from $11 a day to $16.66 for working on Sundays. The women employees who handled the delicate mounting and framing of pictures were paid $8 a week.[20]

Although Brady's Gallery proved to be an outstanding success under his management, Gardner had to contend with resolute competition from other Washington photographers—chief among them Francis H. Bell, Bryant and Smith, Henry Ulke, Augustus McCarty, and Selmer Seibert. But Gardner's reputation for quality portraits, coupled with his innovations, such as the Imperial photograph, set him apart from others in the capital.[21]

In 1859 the carte de visite, or visiting card, became popular in the United States. Measuring approximately 2½ × 4 inches, they were used as calling cards. Alexander Gardner accurately foresaw that these small, easily produced, and inexpensive photographs would bring repeat customers into his gallery for reorders or updated versions. Instinctively he felt that the carte de visite format had the potential for mass merchandising photographs of the famous, alive and dead, foreign and domestic. Gardner ordered special four-lens cameras that could make multiple exposures on a single glass plate, thereby quadrupling the number of prints from a single pose.[22]

Brady personally found the carte de visite distasteful. He felt that its size and price debased the art of photography. Most cards were produced directly from the negative, which precluded any retouching. The rule of thumb at Brady's Gallery was that "if you were somebody, you might get retouched considerably; if you were nobody, your picture would most likely remain unblemished by the painter's brush."[23]

On February 27, 1860, the Republican candidate for the presidency, Abraham Lincoln, visited Brady's Gallery in New York. Lincoln had been overwhelmed by requests for a photographic likeness of himself. On that Monday morning he was scheduled to give his now famous Cooper Union speech. Members of the Republican Club escorted him to Brady's Gallery, where his portrait was taken. Later, thousands of carte de visite copies of this portrait were sold to the public.[24] This was the first of the many photographs of Lincoln taken by Matthew Brady or his assistants. At a later date, when Brady met Lincoln at the White House, Lincoln remarked that "in his ready way, Brady and the Cooper Institute made me President."[25]

The first Japanese delegation ever to visit this country arrived in Washington in May 1860 to ratify Commodore Perry's treaty of March 1854. The photographs taken of the delegation carry the Brady imprint, but they were in fact taken by Alexander Gardner. Some of the photographs were reproduced in *Harper's Weekly*, with the credit line given to Brady.[26] Although there is no evidence to indicate how Gardner felt about the practice, it was customary in the 1860s to give credit to the photographic proprietor rather than the cameraman. It is interesting to note that in later years Gardner was scrupulous about always giving credit to the cameramen under *his* employ.

Preparing for War

The South had threatened to leave the Union if Lincoln were elected to the presidency, and on December 20, 1860, six weeks after his victory, the Southern states, beginning with South Carolina, seceded. War was imminent. Lincoln was inaugurated on March 4, 1861. On April 12, Fort Sumter, in Charleston harbor, South Carolina, under the command of Major Robert Anderson, was fired upon, and soon capitulated.

During this tense period, Alexander Gardner began to prepare for the changes war would inevitably bring to Washington and the photographer's trade. He ordered additional four-tube carte de visite cameras in anticipation of the tremendous influx of soldiers who would be clamoring to have their photographs taken in uniform. Major Anderson's surrender of Fort Sumter made him an instant celebrity in the North. The demand for card photographs of him was sudden and unprecedented. As other military leaders gained prominence, the demand for their portraits made it necessary to mass produce their photographs. No photographic gallery of the day was quite prepared to meet that demand. However, the previous March Gardner had wisely entered into a contract with Edward Anthony, the owner of E. & H. T. Anthony, a major commercial photographic establishment in New York. Under the terms of their contract, Anthony agreed to make and distribute thousands of card photographs of major personalities of the day from negatives furnished by M. B. Brady & Company. Anthony would pay Brady a fee and credit him on the card mounts.[27]

Gardner's business acumen resulted in a profit of over $12,000 for Brady the first year the agreement was in effect and approximately $4,000 a year for the remainder of the war.[28] Within a few weeks of the outbreak of hostilities, Gardner began purchasing negatives from other photographers to transmit to E. & H. T. Anthony, one of the first being a portrait of the Union's first hero, Major Anderson.

On February 8, 1861, photographer George S. Cook of Charleston was allowed to photograph Anderson and his staff inside the impenetrable Fort Sumter. Shortly thereafter, Cook sold his negatives to photographers Thomas Faris and Edward Anthony for $25. Upon their receipt in New York, Anthony printed the following facetious broadside:

IMPORTANT FROM CHARLESTON
MAJOR ROBERT ANDERSON TAKEN!
ENTRANCE OBTAINED UNDER A FLAG OF TRUCE
NEW YORKERS IMPLICATED!
GREAT EXCITEMENT.
WHAT WILL THE SOUTHERN CONFEDERACY DO NEXT?

On the 8th inst., at about 12 hours before midnight under cover of a bright sun, Col. George S. Cook, of the Charleston Photographic Light Artillery, with a strong force, made his way to Fort Sumter. On being discovered by the vigilant sentry, he ran up the flag of truce. The gate of the fortress being opened, Col. Cook immediately and heroically penetrated to the presence of Maj. Anderson, and levelling a double barrelled Camera, demanded the unconditional surrender in the name of E. Anthony and the Photographic community.

Seeing that all resistance would be in vain, the Major at once surrendered, and was borne in triumph to Charleston, forwarded to New York, and is now for sale in the shape of exquisite Card Photographs at 25cts per copy.

E. ANTHONY, 501 Broadway[29]

Walter Dinmore, a Philadelphia photographer, had already written to Cook in January, offering to purchase some of his negatives and thus "cash in on Anderson's popularity," even proposing to split the profits with Cook. At the height of Anderson's popularity, Anthony made upward of one thousand prints a day of this photograph.[30]

Another potential source of photographs for the Gardner/Brady operation was amateur photographer Montgomery C. Meigs, who was soon to be named quartermaster general of the War Department. A March 23rd letter from the Brady Gallery to Meigs confirms that the gallery would publish a carte de visite he had sent them, and confirms their interest in any other pictures he may have to offer.

President Lincoln issued a call for 75,000 volunteers on April 14, 1861, and on May 3 asked for an additional 42,034. Washington was soon swollen with troops in many types of uniforms. As Gardner had foreseen, Brady's Gallery was filled to capacity with soldiers wanting photographs. Some of the first regiments to patronize the gallery were the 7th, 8th, and 12th New York State Militia. Brady and Gardner traveled to campsites on the outskirts of Washington to solicit and secure photographs of the men. Everyone thought the war would be short and wanted to have his photograph taken in uniform to send to loved ones. That is, while there still was a war!

Both Brady and Gardner claimed the idea of photographing the Civil War. In 1869 each petitioned Congress offering to sell the government their negative collections. Brady's petition was submitted on February 17 by Senator Henry Wilson of

Massachusetts. Gardner's was filed four days later by Senator Samuel C. Pomeroy of Kansas. Congress referred each of the petitions to the Joint Committee on Library, which had jurisdiction to purchase works of art for the government.

Brady's petition claimed:

> That, at the very commencement of the Rebellion, with a view to the collection and preservation of valuable historical material, he organized, at great expense, an efficient corps of Artists for the production of photographic views illustrating prominent incidents of the War.

In his petition Gardner claimed:

> that at the outbreak of the Rebellion he conceived the idea of furnishing of it, a consecutive Photographic History.

In their own words they seem to clarify the proper allocation of credit: It was Gardner who "conceived the idea" and Brady who "organized" and implemented it.

On the other hand, records show that on June 10, 1861, Professor John W. Draper, president of the American Photographic Society, appointed a committee to discuss the importance of photographing the Civil War with the Secretary of War. Draper's committee filed their suggestion with the War Department, although it was reported that "little progress had been made in the matter owing to the extraordinary preoccupation of the department."[31] So it is possible that Gardner may not have been the first or the only person to conceive the task of photographing the war. In any case, he was clearly the prime mover of its ultimate accomplishment.

Major Robert Anderson, photographed at Fort Sumter on February 8, 1861, by George S. Cook. Edward Anthony of New York purchased the negative and sold more than 1,000 prints a day at the height of Anderson's fame as the war's first hero. From an original carte de visite.

MAJOR ANDERSON, U. S. A.
TAKEN AT FORT SUMTER FEB'Y 8, 1861,
PUBLISHED BY E. ANTHONY, 501 BROADWAY,
Entered according to Act of Congress, in the year 1861, by E. ANTHONY, in the Clerk's office of the District Court of the United States for the Southern District of New York.

C H A P T E R

THE
CIVIL WAR

1861—1865

Brady,   Washington.

Exceedingly rare unpublished carte de visite portrait of Alexander Gardner in the buckskin outfit of Judge Arney, c. 1861.

*N*either the photographic community nor the public took the threat of war too seriously. As John W. Draper, editor of the *American Journal of Photography*, declared: "A battle scene is a fine subject for an artist-painter, historian, or photographer. . . . We hope to see a photograph of the next battle. . . . There will be little danger in the active duties, for the photographer must be beyond the smell of gunpowder or his chemicals will not work."[1] Draper certainly underestimated the dangers and hardships ahead for the intrepid combat photographers.

Matthew Brady was adamant in his desire to photograph the war. Through the intercession of Allan Pinkerton, head of the intelligence operation that became known, in the course of the war, as the Secret Service, Brady presented his plan to President Lincoln, who did not object, provided all expenses would be borne by Brady. As he was wishing him luck, Lincoln scrawled on a piece of paper, "Pass Brady."[2] On Tuesday morning, July 16, 1861, Brady, dressed in his linen duster and broad-brimmed hat, left Washington for Virginia in two black-hooded wagons. Accompanying him were Ned House, his assistant; Dick McCormack, a newspaper reporter; and Alfred Waud, a sketch artist for *Harper's Weekly*. They arrived at Fairfax Court-house on Wednesday and at Centerville on Thursday, where they rested and waited for the anticipated action.

The authorities in Washington had exerted considerable pressure on the Federal army to attack the Confederate forces of General P. G. T. Beauregard, who was now massing his troops at a vital railroad junction near Manassas, Virginia. A large percentage of the Federal army consisted of ninety-day militia units whose terms of enlistment were near expiration. However, General Irvin McDowell, commander of the Union forces, was protesting to the powers that be that his troops were ill-prepared to attack or engage the enemy. On Sunday, July 21, despite his fears, McDowell ordered his forces to attack the numerically inferior Confederates.[3] In Centerville, on a hill overlooking Bull Run, Brady prepared his equipment for the morning's engagement.

By 4 P.M. an apparent Federal withdrawal from the battlefield had turned into an obvious rout. Brady followed the army to the high ground around the Matthews' House, where, for a time, he was totally engulfed by the retreating army. Although his wagons were overturned, Brady managed to retrieve some of his wet plates before following the troops back to Washington. Late the next day, July 22, he arrived in Washington and immediately had a portrait of himself taken in his soiled linen duster.[4]

During the Battle of Manassas (Bull Run), Alexander Gardner was on duty in

Brady,   Washington.

An unidentified captain and his child, c. 1861. Taken
by Gardner, published by Brady. From an original carte
de visite.

Autographed portrait of Allan Pinkerton, 1863. From an
original unpublished carte de visite.

Washington, managing Brady's Gallery. However, it was undoubtedly through Gardner's influence with Allan Pinkerton that Brady had been allowed access to the Union troops. Pinkerton, a Scotsman like Gardner, was born in Glasgow in 1819. He fled his native land in 1842, following a violent civil demonstration.[5] Emigrating to the United States, he settled in Illinois, where he became a deputy sheriff. In 1850 he worked as a city detective in Chicago and later that year opened his own detective agency. Initially his assignments were to help escaped slaves obtain their freedom, but he later became the first U.S. Mail agent in Chicago, protecting the mail from robbers.[6]

Pinkerton accompanied President-elect Lincoln in February 1861 on the trip from Springfield, Illinois, to Washington, foiling on the way a suspected assassination attempt in Baltimore. Upon his arrival in the capital, Pinkerton took steps toward instituting the Federal Secret Service. After the Battle of Manassas, he had been serving under General George B. McClellan as his chief detective and head of his intelligence network. Brady's access to the battlefields, then, is attributable to Pink-

OPPOSITE PAGE: *Matthew Brady upon his return from the*
Manassas Battlefield, July 22, 1861. Copied from an original photograph.

erton's friendship with Gardner and Pinkerton's familiarity with many members of the military command. Following his appointment to McClellan's staff, Pinkerton (also known as "Major E. J. Allen") recommended Gardner for the position of chief photographer under the jurisdiction of the U.S. Topographical Engineers. According to William A. Pinkerton, Allan's son:

> It was during the winter of 1861–1862 that Gardner became attached to the Secret Service Corps, then under my father. I was then a boy, ranging from seventeen to twenty-one years of age, during all which time I was in intimate contact with Gardner, as he was at our headquarters and was utilized by the Government for photographing maps and other articles of that kind which were prepared by the secret service. . . . I used to travel around with Gardner a good deal while he was taking these views and saw many of them made.[7]

Gardner and the Secret Service

For all intents and purposes, Gardner's *active* management of Brady's Washington gallery ceased in November 1861 upon his appointment to General McClellan's staff, with the honorary rank of "captain." However, this did not mean that he disassociated himself from Brady or the studio. He was able to use his continuing management of Brady's Gallery as a front for his covert operations within the Secret Service. Through his contacts with McClellan, again thanks to Allan Pinkerton, Gardner was allowed complete access to troops and their encampments within the Army of the Potomac. This arrangement was certainly approved and encouraged by Brady. What better way to obtain exclusive photographs than from within the army itself? Brady was spending more time in his Washington gallery, which allowed Gardner the freedom to pursue his Secret Service assignments; through his studio, Brady controlled exclusive publishing rights to all of Gardner's work. Under "Captain" Gardner's immediate supervision was a corps of excellent photographers: Timothy H. O'Sullivan, James F. Gibson, George N. Barnard, John Wood, David B. Woodbury, William R. Pywell, David Knox, James Gardner, and John Reekie.

Gardner, Spies, and Military Planners

Initially, Gardner and his associates were assigned to copy maps and charts for the Secret Service, photographic prints of which were distributed to both field and division commands. Gardner became so trustworthy in this assignment that McClellan allowed him unlimited access to troops in the field.[8] Pinkerton foresaw the special value of Gardner's photographs in helping to detect and identify military spies among the troops. Whenever there was a suspicion of spying activities, Pinkerton instructed

OPPOSITE PAGE: *Confederate spy Rose Greenhow and her daughter in Old Capitol Prison, Washington, 1862. Taken by Gardner, published by Brady. From an original direct-contact albumen print.*

BRADY.   WASHINGTON.

Entered according to act of Congress, in the year 1862, by M. B. BRADY, in the Clerk's Office of the District Court of the District of Columbia.

INCIDENTS OF THE WAR.

No. 212.

MRS. GREENHOW AND DAUGHTER,

Imprisoned in the Old Capitol, Washington.

Secret Service Headquarters, Army of the Potomac, c. 1862. One of the two individuals is probably Allan Pinkerton's son, William, and the other may be Gardner's son, Lawrence, who accompanied his father in the field and was a friend of Pinkerton. From an original direct-contact albumen print.

Gardner to enter the campsites and take random group photographs. It is quite possible that Pinkerton's agents would use Gardner's prints to identify spies, based on intelligence provided either by Federal agents or Union scouts operating in southern territory. Those photographs allowed the Secret Service to recognize a spy by sight, without his being aware that he had been identified. "Avoid the camera" thus soon became the rule among enemy agents on both sides. But few if any of the thousands of Union soldiers in the hundreds of photographs taken by Gardner, knew that their pictures were being taken for the basic purpose of seeking out spies.[9]

Photography was being utilized as a covert tool by the War Department for still another purpose. Photographs of potential battle sites were needed so that commanders could familiarize themselves with the terrain and military planners could know exactly where to place their field hospitals, mess areas, and barracks. The Corps of Engineers also requisitioned photographs—of bridges, railroad tracks, and other installations related to their combat responsibilities. The photographs of probable battle sites were frequently taken by commercial civilian cameramen, few of whom, if any, had official status either by rank or salary.[10] With Gardner and his staff already in the field, many commissions were obtained by him for Brady's Gallery in Washington.

Photographic Coverage of the War

Brady's definition of a photograph identifiable as a "Brady photograph" was ambiguous at best. Any exposure made by an operative or employee certainly fell within this category, and if Brady was present at the scene or provided the photographic materials, he assumed he owned the rights to the picture. Another common practice of the period was to acquire the negatives of another photographer and print and publish them as your own. Although this custom was generally considered acceptable at the time, Gardner viewed the practice as unethical and made a concerted effort to identify the origin of each image submitted to him.

On August 1, 1861, the *American Journal of Photography* reported on Brady's sojourn in Virginia:

> Brady, the irrepressible photographer, who like the war horse, sniffs the battle from afar. He got as far as the smoke of Bull Run and was aiming his never-failing tube at friends and foe alike, when with the rest of our Grand Army they were completely routed and took to their heels, losing their photographic accoutrements on the ground, which the Rebels no doubt pounced upon as trophies of victory. Perhaps they considered the camera as an infernal machine. The soldiers live to fight another day, our special friends to make again their photographs . . . when will photographers have another chance in Virginia?[11]

Even before the Union fiasco at Manassas, Brady and Gardner had recruited additional teams of photographers for their planned photographic coverage of the war. The North's anticipatory sweep into Richmond evolved into a cautious rationalization that the war was a much more serious affair than had been previously envisioned and

Mr. Toller's house, Cumberland Landing, Virginia, May 1862. Taken by James F. Gibson and published as plate no. 385 in Gardner's catalog. Allan Pinkerton, seated, is in the middleground of the image. Copied from an original photograph.

would last for at least another few months. In August 1861 General George Brinton McClellan was appointed commander of the Army of the Potomac, and three months later was promoted to general-in-chief of the Armies of the United States. The climate was ideal for Gardner's ascendancy within the U.S. Secret Service as "Photographer, Army of the Potomac." For the remainder of the year, both Gardner and Brady prepared for the upcoming spring offensives.

In November and December 1861 Timothy O'Sullivan accompanied Captain Samuel F. Du Pont in his actions against two South Carolina forts, Walker and Beauregard. From there O'Sullivan became attached to the forces of General Thomas W. Sherman in Port Royal, South Carolina, photographing maps and charts for the Secret Service. In March and April 1862 he traveled to Hilton Head and Beaufort, South Carolina.[12]

Scouts, guides, and Secret Service agents. The three men seated are, from left, John Irving; Lieutenant Robert Klein, 39th Indiana Cavalry; and Dan Cole, all Secret Service agents. Copied from an original photograph.

Portrait of Major General George Brinton McClellan, c. 1863. From an original unpublished carte de visite.

Credit Where Credit Was Due

In the first quarter of 1862, Brady began a campaign to photograph celebrities in and around Washington. On January 6 he copyrighted a group portrait of Generals McClellan and George W. Morell at Headquarters, Minor's Hill, Virginia; on January 11 he copyrighted seven portraits of first lady Mary Todd Lincoln, two portraits of General Fitz John Porter, and a series of photographs taken in and around Washington, Fort McHenry, and Federal Hill, Baltimore; on March 12 he copyrighted portraits of Generals Winfield Scott Hancock, Joseph Hooker, Charles Dana, James W. Denver, Henry W. Slocum, and Abner Doubleday, as well as ten group portraits taken in Washington, D.C., Georgetown, and Fairfax, Alexandria, and Arlington Heights in Virginia, which he titled "Brady's Incidents of the War"; on April 12, he copyrighted portraits of General McDowell and Senator John Sherman of Ohio; and on May 5 Brady sought copyright protection for four views: no. 296, Taylor's Tavern; no. 297, Falls Church; no. 298, Baileys Cross Roads; and no. 301, Centerville. Each of these views was published under the newly coined title "Brady's Album Gallery."[13] In March George Barnard and James Gibson returned to the battlefields of Manassas and Centerville, where they took twenty-eight stereoviews and large-format photographs. Those were also copyrighted on May 5, with the numerical sequence 300 to 327.[14] These listings are significant. Some historians have harbored the incorrect notion that Gardner and his employees left Brady solely because he did not credit them as camera operatives. In fact, Barnard and Gibson were copyrighting their own material along with and on the same day that Brady copyrighted his. The only accommodation made to Brady in those instances was that Barnard and Gibson annotated the information that the listed photographs were to be *published* under "Brady's Album Gallery." It is clear therefore that, as early as May 5, 1862, all camera operatives in Brady's employ (including Gardner) were free to claim credit for their own work.

On May 7 Brady copyrighted eleven views in and around Manassas with the numerical sequence 201 through 211. Again, on May 7, Barnard and Gibson copyrighted twelve more pictures of Manassas with the numerical sequence 226 through 237. These photographs were published as "Incidents of the War"—which suggests that they were the larger-format views.[15]

The Peninsula Campaign

After the Battle of Manassas, the Confederacy and the Union viewed each other's capital as their main objective. Upon General Joseph E. Johnston's withdrawal from Manassas to the Rappahannock, General McClellan advanced toward Richmond. On March 17, in command of twelve divisions, McClellan left Alexandria and was transported down the Potomac River into the Chesapeake Bay to Fortress Monroe, on the banks of the James River across from Norfolk, Virginia. On April 4, McClellan met with resistance from General John B. Magruder at a defensive position along the

Warwick River. McClellan withheld any action for two days while conducting recon-
naissance. Meanwhile, also on April 4, General Robert E. Lee, then military advisor
to President Jefferson Davis, foresaw McClellan's action and reinforced Magruder.
Two days later, McClellan faced his opposition along the Yorktown line. The Confederates held an eight-mile front with no more than 17,000 men, while the Union
forces numbered 60,000.

By May 3, McClellan's inactivity had enabled the Confederates to mass over
60,000 troops, commanded by General Johnston, to face 112,000 Union troops under
McClellan. They clashed on May 5 at Williamsburg in an indecisive action. Johnston
abandoned Norfolk and withdrew to Petersburg on May 9, a retreat that opened the
James River seven miles below Richmond. When, on May 15, the Federal Navy was
repulsed at Drewry's Bluff, McClellan's command was forced to operate north of the
Chickahominy River. On May 27 General Fitz John Porter skirmished with the Confederates at Hanover Courthouse, and on May 31 the Battle of Fair Oaks and Seven
Pines was fought. At that encounter, the Confederates failed to take advantage of

*Gibson's Battery (Companies C and G), 3rd U.S. Artillery, near Fair Oaks, Virginia, June 1862. Taken
by James F. Gibson and published as plate no. 431 in Gardner's catalog. Copied from an original
photograph.*

Federal weaknesses. Lee assumed command of the Army of Virginia when Johnston was wounded, and on June 25, the Seven Days' Battle ensued. Although the Union forces failed to achieve a victory, they did forestall further Confederate advancement and remained at Harrison's Landing into July.[16]

In early April Gardner dispatched Gibson, Barnard, and John Wood to accompany General McClellan on the Peninsula campaign, in and around Williamsburg, Yorktown, Norfolk, and Richmond. Some time in May, David Woodbury was sent to assist Gibson in the field.

Although the Peninsula campaign failed to generate a Northern victory, it played a vital role in the maturation of documentary war photography in the United States. During the first week in May, Gibson and Wood began their work in the vicinity of Yorktown. Some of the views they produced were of fortified gun emplacements, the encampment at Camp Winfield Scott, and group portraits of Union officers and foreign military observers.[17] As the Federal army moved toward Richmond, Gibson and Wood joined McClellan at his various headquarters.

Because of inclement weather and poor lighting conditions after the Battle of Fair Oaks (Seven Pines), Gibson was unable to photograph the battlefield.[18] However,

Captain John C. Tidball and staff, near Fair Oaks, Virginia, June 1862. From left: Lieutenant Robert Clarke, Captain Tidball, Lieutenant Dennison, and Lieutenant A. G. M. Pennington, all members of Horse Battery A, 2nd U.S. Artillery. Taken by James F. Gibson and published as plate no. 435 in Gardner's catalog. From an original stereoview.

Entered according to the Act of Congress, in the year 1862, by Gardner & Gibson, in the Clerk's Office of the District Court of the District of Columbia.

he did take a poignant study of then 2nd Lt. George Armstrong Custer seated with his old friend and classmate Lt. James Barroll Washington. Washington, a member of George Washington's family and of General Johnston's staff, had been captured earlier that day at the Battle of Fair Oaks. Upon discovering that his friend had been taken prisoner, Custer, a lowly member of the 2nd U.S. Cavalry, saw to all of Washington's needs. "A camp photographer [Gibson] seeing the two seated on a log, chatting, was preparing to photograph them, when young Washington called out to a small darkey standing near and placed the child between them, saying the picture ought to be called 'Both sides, the cause.' And so it appeared in *Harper's Weekly*."[19] Gibson took two separate views of the pair, one with the black child (no. 428) and one without. Around June 1 Gibson was on hand to photograph freshly dug graves and Northern artillery batteries positioned behind newly finished gun emplacements. What made these photographs unique was the fact that they were taken during an active campaign, the photographers never knowing when the Confederates might attack again.

Lieutenant James Barroll Washington, 2nd Lieutenant George Armstrong Custer, and a young black child, May 20, 1862. Taken by James F. Gibson and published as plate no. 428 in Gardner's catalog. From an original gallery card.

The Wounded and the Dead

On June 28, during the Seven Days' Battle, Gibson was at Savage Station at a field hospital near McClellan's headquarters and took numerous photographs of soldiers wounded at the Battle of Gaines' Mill the day before. The Confederates attacked the next day, causing the Federals to retreat and leave behind over five hundred of their wounded. Gibson's photographs are quite poignant when one realizes that some of the unfortunate men shown were destined to die in Confederate prisons or hospitals. Although Gibson failed to secure any actual death scenes, he did obtain some of the most immediate and effective battlefield photographs thus far achieved. Important lessons learned from this series of photographs would become evident within three months, at the Battle of Antietam. Gibson had proved that war photographs could be obtained. Gardner and others would soon follow his lead.[20]

On May 9 Barnard, or a representative, copyrighted thirty-one photographs, no. 350 through no. 380, taken from May 1 to May 7. Like the prior ones, they were identified as "Brady's Album Gallery." These views were published rapidly: Brady released them for publication a mere two days after they were taken; time was of the essence.

The Brady Myth

With Brady's rapid release and sale of the Peninsula campaign views, the public's perception of the war through photography became more acute. The *New York World* wrote:

> Mr. Brady's "Scenes and Incidents" . . . are inestimable chroniclers of this tempestuous epoch, exquisite in beauty, truthful as the records of heaven. . . . Their projector has gone to his work with a conscientious largeness becoming the acknowledged leader of his profession in America. . . . "Brady's Photographic Corps," heartily welcomed in each of our armies, has been a feature as distinct and omnipresent as the corps of balloon, telegraph, and signal operators. They have threaded the weary stadia of every march; have hung on the skirts of every battle scene; have caught the compassion of the hospital, the romance of the bivouac, the pomp and panoply of the field review—aye, even the cloud of conflict, the flash of the battery, the afterwreck anguish of the hard-won field.[21]

On July 21 the *New York Times* reported:

> Brady was the first to make photography the Clio of war. . . . His artists have accompanied the army on nearly all its marches, planting their sun batteries by the side of our Generals' more deathful ones, and taking towns, cities, and forts with much less noise, and vastly more expedition. The result is a series of pictures christened "Incidents of the War," and nearly as interesting as the war itself: For they constitute the history of it, and appeal directly to the great throbbing hearts of the north.[22]

The Commercial Possibilities of War Photos

Gardner had of course been aware all along of the commercial possibilities of these early war views. On July 18 he entered into a formal partnership with Gibson. Under the terms of the arrangement, each would share in the proceeds from sales of all prior and future photographs taken by Gibson. Gardner would be responsible for marketing and publishing them. The title of this partnership was "Gardner and Gibson."[23] Three days later, Gardner copyrighted forty-seven exposures numbered 446 through 492. These had been taken in June and July and were published under "Brady's Album Gallery." Their final picture was copyrighted on August 13, an image titled "Photograph, Camp Winfield Scott, Yorktown, Virginia." Although the partnership ended the next day, it was not the breakup of their association. They worked well with each other, but not as partners. This fact was evident within the month, in their unprecedented coverage of the Battle of Antietam.

Gardner and Woodbury joined Gibson and other battlefield photographers in late July and early August. Gardner took numerous views of officers and men at Harrison's Landing and Westover Landing, fulfilling his obligation to the Secret Service. Brady remained in Washington without visiting the battlefields for almost a year. In early July, O'Sullivan returned from his assignment in South Carolina and immediately set about covering General John Pope's Virginia campaign in and around Manassas, prior to his active military operations. Accompanying the army in its move southwest, O'Sullivan produced numerous pictures of military bridges, railroad depots, and various other scenes in and around Warrenton, Sulphur Springs, and Culpeper. On August 9, the day of the Battle of Cedar Mountain, O'Sullivan photographed an artillery battery crossing a tributary, with the horses and guns stopped at midstream. This view was captioned "Battery fording a tributary of the Rappahannock, on the day of the battle of Cedar Mountain." Although it could have been taken a few miles from Cedar Mountain, it was significant in that it was the first time a photograph of a battle scene was taken the same day as the battle.

Another major achievement was a series of thirteen photographs taken of the Cedar Mountain battlefield a few days after the conflict. The dead had been buried, but O'Sullivan did, on at least one occasion, photograph the bloated carcasses of horses. On August 29 and 30, at the Battle of Second Manassas, Pope's forces were again routed and driven back to Washington. O'Sullivan was forced to flee along with the troops, as Brady had the year before, unable to secure any pictures. To quote historian William A. Frassanito, "Despite occasional setbacks, photographic coverage of the war had still managed to make tremendous strides during the first eight months of 1862. And yet, though cameramen were rapidly increasing the immediacy of their war views, no one thus far had been presented with the opportunity of recording the stark horrors of a battlefield strewn with human dead. By the beginning of September, that opportunity would not be far off."[24]

Field Hospital, Savage Station, after the Battle of Fair Oaks, June 28, 1862. Taken by James F. Gibson and published as plate no. 479 in Gardner's catalog. Copied from an original photograph.

Lee Brings the War into Maryland

After Pope's defeat at Second Manassas, Lee implemented his strategy for invading the North. Although he was not in a position to defeat the Army of the Potomac, Lee realized that the momentum of the war was with him and that he was in a strategic position to take the initiative. He theorized that taking the war into Maryland might provide the catalyst in maneuvering that state into the Confederacy. By strengthening the antiwar movement in the North and drawing Federal troops away from locations surrounding Richmond, Lee felt his invasion would result in a significant step toward a Confederate victory.

On September 9, Lee captured Frederick, which resulted in his pursuit by General McClellan. In order to secure his line of communication for his invasion in the North, the Confederate general decided to split his force into two wings. General Thomas "Stonewall" Jackson was dispatched with six divisions to capture Harpers Ferry, while General James Longstreet, with his three divisions, moved against Hagerstown. These tactics would allow Lee to shift his supply lines east of the Blue Ridge mountains and into the more protected Shenandoah Valley. While in pursuit of Lee's Army of Northern Virginia, McClellan fortuitously secured a copy of Lee's plans upon his arrival at Frederick. Ever the skeptic, McClellan proceeded cautiously, thinking it might be a trap, and that Lee might actually be planning to attack Washington from south of the Potomac.

Antietam: America's Bloodiest Day

On September 14, in an attempt to relieve Harpers Ferry, General William B. Franklin engaged the Confederates under General Lafayette McLaws at the Battle of Crampton's Gap. The result of this action was the loss of the important crossroads, with the Federal forces under Colonel D. S. Miles surrendering Harpers Ferry on the morning of September 15. But on the 14th, the Federal cavalry under General Alfred Pleasonton engaged General D. H. Hill at the Battle of South Mountain. Through sheer aggressiveness, the Federals succeeded in capturing the high ground overlooking Turner's Gap. Receiving news of this victory, Lee decided to take up a defensive position at the small village of Sharpsburg, Maryland. His audacious plan was amazing when one considers that he had only 19,000 men under his immediate command and stood with his back against the Potomac in opposition to an army twice his size. McClellan again failed to seize the initiative, not arriving on the field until the evening of the 16th.

The next morning, McClellan launched an uncoordinated attack, first against the Confederate left flank, then against the center, and finally the right flank. General Ambrose E. Burnside's delay in arriving at the right flank permitted Lee to shift his positions in opposition of generals Hooker, Mansfield, and Sumner. The fighting around Bloody Lane, the Corn Field, West Woods, East Woods, and Dunkard Church

*Autographed portrait of photographer
Timothy H. O'Sullivan. From an original
unpublished carte de visite.*

Battery fording a tributary of the Rappahannock on the day of the Battle of Cedar Mountain, Virginia. Taken by Timothy H. O'Sullivan and published as plate no. 520 in Gardner's catalog. Copied from an original photograph.

OPPOSITE PAGE: *Photographer James F. Gibson. Taken by Timothy H. O'Sullivan and published as plate no. 651 in Gardner's catalog with the caption "Our Special Artist at Manassas, July 4, 1862." Copied from an original photograph.*

Dead horses on the Battlefield of Cedar Mountain, at the Confederates' first position, from which they were dislodged. Taken by Timothy H. O'Sullivan and published as plate no. 510 in Gardner's catalog. Copied from an original photograph.

was savage and bloody. The Confederates managed to secure the left flank and center of the line. Burnside was able to push back the Confederate right flank over a stone bridge; however, Hill arrived from Harpers Ferry in time to push Burnside and the Union forces back, thus saving Lee's right flank. Among the 75,316 Federal troops, there were 12,410 casualties (2,108 killed, 9,549 wounded, and 753 missing). The Confederates had a force of 51,844 with an astounding 13,724 casualties (2,700 killed, 9,024 wounded, and approximately 2,000 missing).

The Battle of Antietam would thereafter be known as "America's Bloodiest Day." Lee successfully withdrew into Virginia on the evening of September 18. President Lincoln was furious with McClellan for not having followed through and preventing Lee's forces from escaping. The Federals had 24,000 fresh troops held in reserve, with an additional 12,000 arriving on the morning of the 18th.[25]

It is not known specifically what day Gardner and Gibson arrived at the Antietam battlefield. A caption on one of their photographs reads, "View of Battle-field of Antietam, on day of battle, Sept. 17, 1862." Frassanito makes a convincing argument that it was actually taken on September 18; he leads us to assume that both Gardner and Gibson arrived at the battlefield on that day.[26]

Gardner was not in Washington preparing for the battle, but was with McClellan and Pinkerton at their headquarters in Rockville, Maryland, as early as September 9. Sensing the proximity of the impending engagement, Gardner wired O'Sullivan that morning: "Come right away to Rockville there make for headquarters. Bring Cmdr of Telegraphic Corps one horse."

By September 18 Gardner was on the battlefield preparing to photograph the carnage. Within hours of the Confederate withdrawal, he and Gibson were exploiting this opportunity to the fullest extent. They began photographing the dead soldiers along the Hagerstown Pike and in Bloody Lane on the 19th. During the 21st and 22nd they concentrated on the right flank of the battlefield along the Antietam Bridge. From here, they photographed McClellan's headquarters near the village of Sharpsburg. In all, seventy photographs were taken between September 18 and 22: fifty-five stereoviews and eight large-format views by Gardner and seven stereoviews by Gibson.[27] On the 21st Gardner wired the good news to David Knox back at the gallery: "Send four by ten glass got forty five negatives of battle. . . . Tell Jim please deliver as soon as possible."

The news of the dead at Antietam had a profound impact on the course of war photodocumentation. They sold well and created the incentive for photographers to reach the battlefield as soon as possible—prior to the burial of the dead.[28]

Perpetuating the Brady Myth

Rave reviews of Gardner's and Gibson's graphic, morbid photographs were issued by the press. On October 20, the *New York Times* enthusiastically praised Brady and his works:

> Mr. Brady has done something to bring home to us the terrible reality and earnestness of war. If he has not brought home bodies and laid them on our derrieres and along the streets, he has done something very much like it. . . . It seems somewhat singular that the same sun that looked down on the faces of the slain, blistering them, blotting out from the bodies all semblance of humanity, and hastening corruption, should have thus caught their features upon canvas, and given them perpetuity for ever. But it has.[29]

The irony in this assessment is that Brady's name became synonymous with the series, though his only real contribution was that his name was used in its publication.

After viewing the photographs of Antietam, Oliver Wendell Holmes, the well-known author and father of a future Supreme Court Justice, remarked:

Entered according to the Act of Congress, in the year 1862, by ALEX. GARDNER, in the Clerk's Office of the District Court of the District of Columbia.

Dead horse of a Confederate colonel, possibly Henry B. Strong of the 6th Louisiana Infantry, Antietam, September 20, 1862. Published as plate no. 558 in Gardner's catalog. From an original stereoview.

Entered according to Act of Congress, in the year 1862, by Alex. Gardner, in the Clerk's Office of the District Court of the District of Columbia.

Scene of Sedgwick's advance and the grave of Lieutenant John A. Clark, 7th Michigan Volunteer Infantry, Antietam, September 19, 1862. Published as plate no. 551 in Gardner's catalog. From an original stereoview.

Let him who wishes to know what war is look at this series of illustrations. . . .
It is so nearly like visiting the battlefields to look over these views that all the
emotions excited by the actual sight of the stained and sordid scene, strewed with
rags and wrecks, came back to us, and we buried them in the recesses of our
cabinet as we would have buried the mutilated remains of the dead they too
vividly represented. The sight of these pictures is a commentary on civilization
such as the savage might well triumph to show its missionaries.[30]

During the first week of October, Gardner returned to Antietam in anticipation
of President Lincoln's visit to the battlefield. On October 3 and 4 he took twenty-five
exposures—twelve stereoview negatives and thirteen large-format views.

The reason for Lincoln's visit on October 3 and 4 was to prod the general into
pursuing Lee into Virginia. McClellan felt that a serious shortage of equipment and
horses existed. Without being provided these supplies, he arrogantly refused to consider
making any advance. Finally, on November 7, in desperation, Lincoln removed
McClellan from command, making General Ambrose E. Burnside his successor.
McClellan's downfall signaled the end of Pinkerton's control over the Secret Service,
and Pinkerton's removal resulted in a reduction of Gardner's duties as "Photographer,
Army of the Potomac."

On October 7 Gardner copyrighted eighteen of his ninety-five Antietam negatives. The significant aspect of this copyright application is the conspicuous absence
of Brady's name as publisher. The success of Gibson's earlier Peninsula views undoubtedly suggested to Gardner that his Antietam series could serve as the nucleus
for his own collection. On October 11 Gardner deposited prints of the eighteen photographs for copyright protection.

Gardner's Antietam series was initially offered for sale through Brady's Gallery
and was published under the heading "Brady's Album Gallery." This was to be the
last of Gardner's work to be published in association with Matthew B. Brady. Since
Brady's name was on the label of this highly visible and commercially successful
venture, he continuted to be publicly recognized as *the* premier Civil War photographer.

As already pointed out, it is a misconception that Gardner left Brady's employ
because he and his associates were not given proper credit. Brady's employees were
actively copyrighting their own materials as early as May 5, 1862—freely assigning
their own titles and negative numbers. It is a fact that Brady, more than any other
person with the possible exception of Gardner, was *the* prime factor in the establishment
of this corps of Civil War photographers. Brady's name, coupled with his financial
backing of other cameramen, resulted in the excellent photographic coverage of the
Civil War—up to and including the Battle of Antietam. Brady deserves all the credit
due him for the service and contribution he made to the art of photography. However,
it was Alexander Gardner and his associates who paved the way for the future of war
photography, by braving the elements in the field while producing such memorable
images.

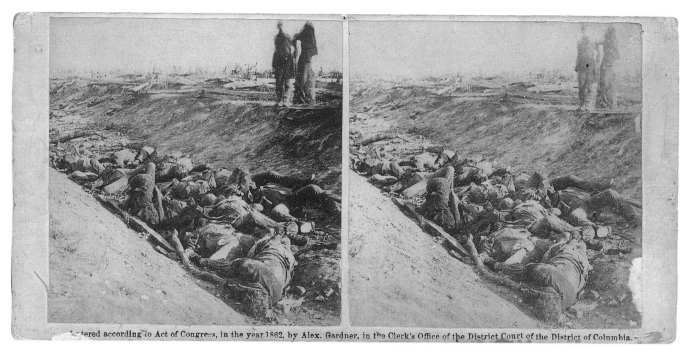

Confederate dead in Bloody Lane, Antietam, September 19, 1862. Published as plate no. 553 in Gardner's catalog. From an original stereoview.

Colonel Crocker, Lt. Colonel Butler, and Adjutant of 93rd New York Volunteers, Antietam. Published as plate no. 630 in Gardner's catalog. From an original stereoview.

GARDNER, Photographer.   M. B. BRADY, Publisher.

GEN. McCLELLAN'S HEADQUARTER GUARD,

93d Reg. N. Y. S. V.

At Antietam. September 16. 1862.

*McClellan's Headquarters Guard, 93rd New York
Volunteers, September 16, 1862. Taken by Alexander
Gardner, published by Matthew Brady. From an
original direct-contact print.*

Brady   New York

*Matthew B. Brady, c. 1864. An
unpublished portrait.*

The Separation: Gardner's Photographic Gallery

Gardner's reduced responsibility within the Secret Service allowed him to re-consider his future as Brady's employee. Some time after McClellan's dismissal on November 7, Gardner decided that the time had come to disassociate himself from Brady and create his own legacy for the future. He well knew that it was his leadership and foresight that were behind the successful marketing of his war views, and he was confident that the contacts he had established within the government could help assure him the success he deserved. He resigned his position with Brady. The exact date of his departure is not known, but it was most likely in early November 1862. On leaving

GARDNER, PHOT'R.   Entered according to act of Congress, in the year 1862, by ALEX. GARDNER, in the Clerk's Office of the District Court of the District of Columbia.   WASHINGTON

INCIDENTS OF THE WAR.

Allan Pinkerton near the Antietam Battlefield, October 4, 1862. From an original direct-contact albumen print.

the gallery, he took with him all the negatives from the Peninsula campaign, First and Second Manassas, O'Sullivan's South Carolina views, General Pope's campaign, and Antietam. It must be assumed that the separation was amicable. Throughout their lifetimes these famous photographers retained a genuine respect for each other, both as artists and as leaders in their field.

As the war continued, Gardner and his associates abandoned Washington for the field. Gardner and Gibson attached themselves to General Burnside's command, where they photographed numerous views of officers on his staff in and around Warrenton. In December and January, Gibson and David Woodbury were working in Fredericksburg and Falmouth, Virginia. In February 1863, Gardner, Gibson, and O'Sullivan were shadowing General Hooker in and around Aquia Creek, Falmouth, and Fredericksburg.

At about that time, Gardner closed his home in Kendallsville, Maryland, and sent his wife and infant daughter to live in McGregor's Landing, Iowa. His fifteen-year-old son, Lawrence, was enrolled at Mount Saint Mary's boarding school in Emmitsburg, Maryland, near Gettysburg, Pennsylvania.[31]

Alex and his brother James began making plans for opening their own photographic studio. The location they chose was at 511 Seventh Street, a large building at the corner of Seventh and D streets. The studio was on the top floor of the building, above Shepard & Riley's Bookstore and opposite the *Washington Daily National Intelligencer*. As manager of Brady's Gallery, Gardner had become acquainted with the book publishers Franklin Philp and Adolphus S. Solomons. These two men constituted the firm of Philp & Solomons, at 332 Pennsylvania Avenue, where Gardner had briefly operated his studio under the name of Philp and Solomons Metropolitan Gallery before opening his own establishment. His own gallery completed, Gardner announced its grand opening in the *Washington Daily National Intelligencer* on May 26, 1863:

> Having had these premises expressly fitted up as a Photographic Gallery, it has been stocked with the newest and most improved apparatus, and every arrangement has been adopted which could in any way facilitate the production of "Beautiful Pictures"
>
> To avoid the fault so generally and justly complained of, the "Light" has been constructed so as to obviate all heavy and unnatural shadows under the eyebrows and chin. And the chemical department has been brought to such perfection that the sitting for a Carte de Visite rarely exceeds five seconds! Oftener not more than one or two!
>
> The great difficulty which has heretofore existed of taking fine Photographs of Children and Family Groups is now at this Gallery a comparatively easy task
>
> The operating room will be open for sitters from eight am till 6 pm. Excellent pictures are on exhibition taken as late in the evening as 6:20

Upon opening his own gallery, Gardner obtained the services of most of his old associates at Brady's—Timothy O'Sullivan, James Gibson, William Pywell, David Knox, John Reekie, W. Morris Smith, and, of course, his brother James.

Gardner's Gallery, corner of 7th and D streets, Washington, D.C. Copied from an original photograph.

Interior view of Gardner's Gallery; possibly Gardner's son, Lawrence, seated in chair, May 1863. From an original unpublished stereoview.

Alexander Gardner, May 1863. Taken at the time his gallery opened, this portrait shows Gardner in the ubiquitous Congressional chair. From an original carte de visite.

Photography in the Field

The process of making a photograph in the field was a long and arduous one. The wagon utilized was humorously called a "What-is-it wagon." This portable dark-room was described as "an ordinary delivery wagon of the period . . . with a strong strap attached at the rear and below the level of the wagon floor. A door was attached to the back, carefully hung so as to be lightproof. The door came down over the step, which was boxed in at the sides, making it a sort of well within the wagon rather than a true step. The work of coating or sensitizing the plates and of developing them was done from this well, in which there was just room enough to work. As the operator stood there, the collodion was within reach of his right hand in a special receptacle. On his left also was a holder of one of the baths. The chief developing bath was in front, with the tanks of various liquids stored in front of it again, and the space between it and the floor filled with plates."[32]

The process of securing an image on the battlefield was recalled in great detail by George Rockwood, a Civil War photographer:

First, all the plain glass plates in various sizes, usually 8 × 10, had to be carefully cleaned and carried in dustproof boxes. When ready for action, the plate was

Alexander Gardner, c. 1864. From an original unpublished carte de visite.

James Gardner. From an original unpublished carte de visite.

*Brigadier General Rufus
Ingalls. From an original
direct-contact albumen print.*

OPPOSITE PAGE, TOP:
*Colonel Charles B. Norton at the
Antietam Battlefield, October
1862. From an original direct-
contact print.*

OPPOSITE PAGE, BOTTOM:
*Captain Henry Page, Assistant
Quartermaster. From an
original direct-contact print.*

*Lt. Colonel Albert V. Colburn,
2nd U.S. Cavalry,
November 1862. Colburn was
killed the following June 17.
From an original direct-
contact print.*

carefully coated with collodion, which carried in solution the excitants—bromide and iodine of potassium, or ammonia, or cadmium. Collodion is made by the solution of gun-cotton in about equal parts of sulfuric ether and 95-proof alcohol. The salts above mentioned are then added, making the collodion a vehicle for obtaining the sensitive surface on the glass plate. The coating of plates was a delicate operation even in the ordinary well-organized studio. After coating the plate with collodion and letting the ether and alcohol evaporate to just the right degree of stickiness, it was lowered carefully into a deep bath holder which contained a solution of nitrate of silver about 60 degrees for quick field work. This operation created the sensitive condition of the plate and had to be done in total darkness, except subdued yellow light. When properly coated (from three to five minutes) the plate was put into a slide or holder and exposed to the action of the light of the camera. When exposed, it was returned to the darkroom and developed. . . . On exceptional occasions in very cold weather, the life of a wet plate might be extended to nearly an hour on either side of the exposure, the coating or the development side, but ordinarily the work had to be done within a few minutes, and every minute of delay resulted in loss of brilliancy and depth in the negative.[33]

J. Pitcher Spencer, a photographer during the war, made the following observations from his experiences in the field:

We worked long with one of the foremost of Brady's men. . . . When I made some views, there came a large realization of some of the immense difficulties surmounted by those who made war pictures. When you realize that the most sensitive of all the list of chemicals are requisite to make collodion, which must coat every plate, and that the very slightest breath might carry enough poison across the plate being coated to make it produce a blank spot instead of some much-desired effect, you may perhaps have a faint idea of the care requisite to produce a picture. Moreover, it took unceasing care to keep every bit of the apparatus, as well as each and every chemical, free from contamination which might affect the picture. Often a breath of wind, no matter how gentle, spoiled the whole affair.[34]

The War Moves North

After two failed Federal attempts at penetrating the Confederate defensive positions at Fredericksburg, and the march on Richmond, Lee felt that another invasion of the North would benefit the Southern cause. Lee convinced the powers in Richmond that a Southern victory on Northern soil would strengthen the growing peace movement within the North and also encourage England to intervene on the South's behalf. In addition, moving the war into the North could very well relieve the pressure being put on Vicksburg and Chattanooga.

Lee's Army of Northern Virginia was reorganized after the death of Stonewall Jackson at Chancellorsville on May 10, 1863. General James Longstreet still commanded the I Corps, and Jackson's old corps was divided between General Richard S. Ewell commanding the II Corps and General Ambrose P. Hill commanding the III Corps. By June 4 General Joseph Hooker, then in command of the Army of the

INCIDENTS OF THE WAR.

General Hooker and his staff, June 1863. Taken by Timothy H. O'Sullivan and published by Gardner in Incidents of the War. *From an original unpublished direct-contact albumen print.*

Potomac, was aware that Lee was preparing to march. On June 10 Lee instructed Ewell to proceed toward the Shenandoah, thereby forcing Washington to pull back the Army of the Potomac to defend the capital. On June 14 Hill departed Fredericksburg, following Ewell's corps into the valley. The next day Longstreet moved east of the Blue Ridge mountains in order to confuse Hooker as to Lee's objectives (Washington or Pennsylvania?).

As soon as Hooker learned that the Army of Northern Virginia had crossed the Potomac into Maryland, he concentrated his forces in Frederick, hoping to cut Lee's line of communication. Upon General Henry W. Halleck's countermanding his orders, Hooker resigned. General George Gordon Meade took over command of the Army of the Potomac on June 28. Meade's plan was to maneuver through Frederick toward Harrisburg, Pennsylvania, threatening Lee's line of communication, while continuing to protect Washington. On July 1 an advance division of Federal cavalry under General John Buford encountered a Confederate brigade under General James J. Pettigrew in the town of Gettysburg. After holding back this brigade, Buford was reinforced by

Staged roughhousing among members of General Hooker's staff, June 1863. From left: unidentified, Colonel Benjamin C. Ludlow, Lt. Colonel Joseph Dickinson, Captain Ulric Dahlgren, Lieutenant Ronald S. Mackenzie (back of head), Lt. Colonel Edward R. Warner, Major Daniel Webster Flagler, Captain Henry Russell, and Captain John R. Coxe. From an original direct-contact print.

OPPOSITE PAGE, FROM LEFT TO RIGHT: *Major General Joseph Hooker; Major General George Gordon Meade, Commander of the Army of the Potomac at Gettysburg, Pennsylvania; and Major General Alexander Stewart Webb. At Gettysburg, Webb commanded the 2nd Brigade, Gibbon's Division, II Corps. His four regiments were positioned at the "clump of trees," focal point for Pickett's Charge. Webb was wounded in the face and received the Congressional Medal of Honor for his valor. The scar from the wound is visible in this portrait. All from original unpublished cartes de visite.*

Members of General Hooker's staff, June 1863. From left: Colonel Benjamin C. Ludlow, Captain Ulric Dahlgren, Lt. Colonel Joseph Dickinson, Captain Zeppalin of Prussia, and Lieutenant Frederick Rosencranz of Sweden. Published as plate no. 45 in Gardner's Photographic Sketch Book of the War *and captioned* "Studying the Art of War." *From an original direct-contact albumen print.*

General John Reynolds's I Corps and General O. O. Howard's XI Corps. Later that day, the I and XI Corps were forced to withdraw to Cemetery Hill, where they were joined by General Dan Sickles's III Corps and General Henry Slocum's XII Corps. Reynolds had been killed earlier in the day by a Confederate sharpshooter, and the I Corps was being commanded by General Abner Doubleday.

Gettysburg: High Tide of the Confederacy

General Meade, still located in Maryland, sent General Winfield Scott Hancock into Gettysburg, a place he determined to be as good as any to confront Lee's advancing troops. However, the Union position was bottlenecked on Cemetery Hill, and Lee failed to attack it there. Thus ended the first day's events.

Hancock ordered troops to occupy Culp's Hill, while Meade was concerned with Lee, breaking his line of communication along the Baltimore Pike. On the morning of July 2, Meade's forces were positioned in the form of a fishhook, with the tip at Culp's Hill on down through Cemetery Hill along Cemetery Ridge and ending at the Round Tops. Lee positioned himself around the outside of this fishhook with Ewell on the northern barb, Hill along the center, and Longstreet at the southern portion. Lee ordered Longstreet to hit the Union position and drive the enemy northward along the Emmitsburg Pike. Hill and Ewell were ordered to launch a secondary attack to prevent Meade from shifting his troops to defend against Longstreet's attack.

After many delays, the second day's battle began at 4 P.M., with Hood's attack directed toward the Round Tops. General G. K. Warren foresaw this threat and rushed his troops in defense of Little Round Top. The Union forces repulsed Hood at a fearful cost. Hill's failure to attack on time allowed Meade to shift his forces from his front to support his left flank. Ewell waited until 6 P.M. to attack the Union north flank, thus failing to take advantage of Meade's weakened northern position.

Despite Longstreet's objection, Lee was determined to take the offensive on the third day. Lee's plan was to hit the center of Meade's line with ten brigades, supported by 159 guns. Since Lee had previously attacked both flanks, Meade correctly guessed that Lee would next attack his center. Longstreet relayed Lee's command to his subordinate, General George Edward Pickett, and at 1 P.M. Lee commenced his artillery attack against Meade's line. At 1:45 P.M., 15,000 Confederate infantrymen crossed a half mile of open field in a steady formation. Within a few hundred yards of the Federal position along the Emmitsburg Pike, the Confederates regrouped and charged toward the "little group of trees" located in an area known as the Angle.

Within a short time, the "high tide of the Confederacy" had ebbed and the Union had successfully thwarted Lee's invasion of the North. The next day, July 4, aided by a torrential rainstorm, Lee and the remnant of the Army of Northern Virginia retreated into Virginia. As had been the case after the Battle of Antietam, the Army of the Potomac was again too shattered to pursue Lee. The carnage of this battle was catastrophic. The Confederates' 75,000 troops sustained more than 28,000 casualties, including 3,903 killed, 18,735 wounded, and 5,425 missing. Federal forces of 88,289 men sustained casualties totaling 23,049, with 3,155 killed, 14,529 wounded, and 5,365 missing. This, the bloodiest battle of the Civil War, consumed 51,112 lives.[35]

Gardner's movements during the Gettysburg campaign are uncertain. However, on June 24 he was still accompanying the Army of the Potomac, and he wired his brother: "Will not leave until tomorrow." Between June 19 and June 24, the Army of the Potomac was spread out between Manassas and Leesburg. On June 25 General Ewell began his march from Chambersburg to Carlisle, Pennsylvania, which compelled Hooker to give chase.[36]

Gardner at Gettysburg

Understanding the importance of Lee's maneuvering, Gardner must have realized that a major battle would soon be fought. While it is possible that his statement about his leaving on June 25 meant he intended to stay with Hooker's command, it more likely indicated his intention to leave the field and return to his gallery in Washington. The first notification of the battle didn't reach Washington until July 3. On alert and fully prepared, Gardner, accompanied by O'Sullivan and Gibson, left immediately, hoping to arrive in time to document it. Undoubtedly alarmed and concerned for his son's safety at Mount Saint Mary's in Emmitsburg, Maryland, some 10 miles from the reported battle site, Gardner hastened toward Gettysburg—a distance of seventy-seven miles. In the early morning of July 5, retreating General J. E. B. Stuart and his cavalry entered Emmitsburg, capturing a number of Union soldiers and obtaining desperately needed medical supplies. One of the prisoners taken was Alexander Gardner. A few days later, Gardner and Gibson returned to the town and photographed the location of his arrest. The original caption for this stereoview read: "Farmer's Inn and Hotel, Emmitsburg, where our Special Artist was captured, July 5, 1863." As the title indicates, only one of the photographic trio was detained by the Confederates, suggesting that the others were elsewhere when the raid occurred.[37] Fortunately, Gardner's detention was brief, and he was on his way to the battlesite on the morning of July 5.

At around noon he and his associates arrived on the field via the Emmitsburg Road, located at one of the last areas to be cleared of the dead—near the Rose Farm. Gardner and the others took approximately twenty negatives within this area, which completed their first day's work. On July 6 the trio concentrated their efforts around Devil's Den and at the base of Big Round Top. As most of the dead had been buried by July 6, the rest of Gardner's photographs were views of breastworks and battlefield locations. On the final day of photographing, the 7th, they concentrated on places in the town and the cemetery.[38]

Gardner was euphoric because he had scooped all his competitors, namely Matthew Brady. However, his elation was short-lived. In his haste to photograph the scenes of the dead, he had completely overlooked important landmarks of the battle, including

Entered according to Act n and Hotel, Emmittsburg, where our special Artist was captured, July 5th, 18a.

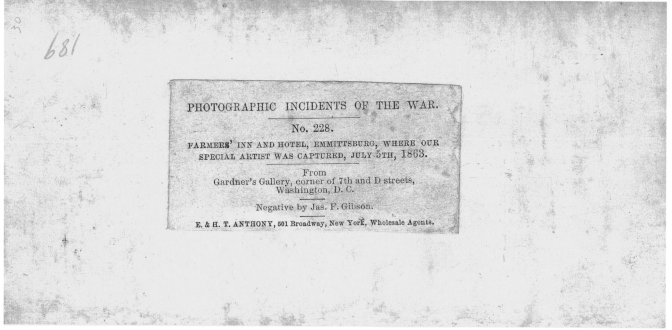

Front and back of an original stereoview of Farmer's Inn and Hotel, Emmitsburg, Maryland, where Gardner was captured on July 5, 1863.

Pennsylvania College, Lee's headquarters, the Lutheran Seminary, and the Union breastworks on Culp's Hill. The reason for the omissions was that he had arrived *too* *soon* after the battle to acquire a competent guide, who would have identified all the vital landmarks for him. Gardner's group, however, was the only one to secure the highly desirable photographs of the dead on the battlefield. They captured the true horror of Gettysburg and the images of war held in the memory of the soldiers who fought there.[39]

The views taken during the Battle of Antietam proved to Gardner that photographs of the dead commanded the public's attention and translated into sales and profits. Of the approximately sixty negatives secured by him and his team at Gettysburg, three quarters are of bloated corpses, dead horses, open graves, or other incidents detailing the wholesale carnage.[40] Considering the sheer number of "death views," and the amount of time Gardner and the others spent using them as subjects, it is apparent that Gardner was well aware of the commercial value of those pictures.[41]

Having completed their photographic coverage on July 7, Gardner and Gibson began their return trip to Washington. Briefly stopping over once more in Emmitsburg, Gardner took seven photographs, including one already mentioned, of the Emmitsburg Inn, where he had been captured two days before. His apprehension about his son's safety is undoubtedly what caused Gardner to pick the boy up at Mount Saint Mary's for the return trip to Washington. At Gettysburg, Gardner, O'Sullivan, and Gibson each took an equal number of stereoviews, with O'Sullivan doing the bulk of the large-format photographs. Gardner utilized two darkroom wagons, and all three helped prepare and develop the plates.[42]

O'Sullivan did not accompany the group on its return to the capital, as is indicated by the following message:

> T H O Sullivan
> Head Quarters
> Army of the Potomac

> I have just got back from Gettysburg. Woodbury & Berger were there. if they come your length I hope you will give them every attention. tell Jim that McGraw is dead   I will write.

> Alex Gardner

As this telegram is not dated, Gardner's exact date of return is not known. However, the message does provide important information: it identifies Brady's operatives at Gettysburg as David B. Woodbury and Anthony Berger, and also indicates the kind of consideration the community of photographers showed one another. The McGraw mentioned in this note could be Lieutenant Hugh McGraw of the 140th New York Infantry who was killed at Gettysburg.[43]

Within a week after Gardner left Gettysburg, Brady appeared on the scene to photograph the aftermath of the devastating battle. Brady took advantage of the fact that the landmarks of the battle were, by then, known to a myriad of guides, all offering

Entered according to Act of Congress, in the year 1863, by Alex. Gardner, in the Clerk's Office of the District Court of the District of Columbia.

Alexander Gardner and either Timothy H. O'Sullivan or James F. Gibson on the Gettysburg Battlefield, July 1863. Gardner is carrying the "prop gun," which he placed alongside bodies in numerous photographs. This appears to be plate no. 268, referred to in Gardner's catalog as "View near the Emmitsburg Road on the Battle-field of Gettysburg." From an original stereoview.

Entered according to Act of Congress, in the year 1863, by Alex. Gardner, in the Clerk's Office of the District Court of the District of Columbia.

Confederate dead on the Rose Farm, Gettysburg, July 5, 1863. Published as plate no. 260 in Gardner's catalog. From an original stereoview.

Entered according to Act of Congress, in the year 1863, by Alex. Gardner, in the Clerk's Office of the District Court of the District of Columbia.

Confederate dead gathered for burial at the edge of the Rose Woods, Gettysburg, July 5, 1863, with Gardner's darkroom wagon in the background. Published as plate no. 256 in Gardner's catalog. From an original stereoview.

Entered according to Act of Congress in the year 1863, by Alex. Gardner, in the Clerk's Office of the District Court of the District of Columbia.

Dead Confederate soldier, Devil's Den, Gettysburg, July 6, 1863. Taken by Timothy H. O'Sullivan and published as plate no. 263 in Gardner's catalog. From an original stereoview.

Entered according to Act of Congress, in the year 1863, by Alex. Gardner, in the Clerk's Office of the District Court of the District of Columbia.

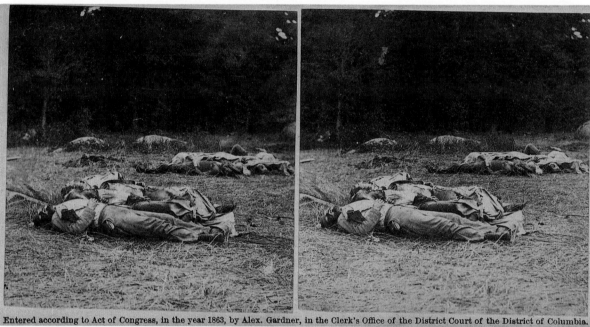

Entered according to Act of Congress, in the year 1863, by Alex. Gardner, in the Clerk's Office of the District Court of the District of Columbia.

TOP: *Unidentified Confederate grave, probably on the Rose Farm, July 5, 1863. Wagon in the background is used to gather arms and equipment on the battlefield. Taken by Timothy H. O'Sullivan and published as plate No. 233 in Gardner's catalog. From an original stereoview.*

ABOVE: *Dead Confederates at edge of the Rose Woods, Gettysburg, July 5, 1863. Published as plate no. 235 in Gardner's catalog. From an original stereoview.*

OPPOSITE PAGE, BOTTOM: *"Alfred R. Waud, Special Artist of Harper's Weekly." Taken on July 6, 1863, at Devil's Den, Gettysburg, by Timothy H. O'Sullivan and published as plate no. 254 in Gardner's catalog. From an original stereoview.*

Negative by T. H. O'SULLIVAN.   *Entered according to act of Congress, in the year 1865, by A. Gardner, in the Clerk's Office of the District Court of the District of Columbia.*   Positive by A. GARDNER, 511 7th St., Washington.

Union dead on the Gettysburg Battlefield. Titled "A Harvest of Death," this was taken by Timothy H. O'Sullivan and published as plate no. 36 in Gardner's Photographic Sketch Book of the War. *From an original direct-contact albumen print.*

Entered according to Act of Congress, in the year 1863, by Alex. Gardner, in the Clerk's Office of the District Court of the District of Columbia.

Dead Confederate soldier in a field along the Rose Woods, Gettysburg, July 5, 1863. Gardner composed this scene, adding his prop rifle, a canteen, and a severed hand. An identical stereoview published by Gardner as plate no. 258 was captioned "A Confederate sharpshooter who had been killed by a shell at Battle of Gettysburg," though it seems more likely the body was mutilated by wild pigs after the battle.

their services. He photographed McPherson's Woods, Lee's headquarters, the Lutheran Seminary, Pennsylvania College, Little Round Top, and John Burns, a veteran of the War of 1812 who had fought alongside the Union troops, and who was at his home recuperating from his wounds. Although Brady's pictures lacked the dramatic impact of Gardner's death views, they did show subjects of general historical interest.[44] In an August 1863 issue of *Harper's Weekly*, Brady's, not Gardner's, images were illustrated. Although Gardner was the first on the field and the only photographer to obtain death views, he had in fact failed to obtain exposures of any of the battle's highlights. By August 22 the press had already reported the story of the engagement, and certain locations had become generally known. Brady's photographs of those locations were thus widely copied and circulated as engraved illustrations. Furthermore, the two heroes of the battle, John Burns and John Reynolds, appeared in Brady's photographs. Brady captured Burns on his porch convalescing, and also provided an illustration of "The wheatfield in which General Reynolds was shot."

In an attempt to make up for his omissions, Gardner arbitrarily changed one item in his 1863 catalog to amplify "View on the field on the right wing" by adding "Where General Reynolds fell." In 1865, when he issued his sketchbook, he further modified this caption to make it read, "Field where General Reynolds fell." Ironically, General Reynolds never fell in a field at all, but was killed inside the eastern edge of McPherson's Woods. Therefore both Brady's and Gardner's captions were flawed.[45]

Another misidentification by Gardner was the view he captioned in 1863 as "Slaughter pen foot of Roundtop." In 1865 Gardner changed the title to read "Slaughter pen foot of Little Round Top"—undoubtedly influenced by the press's extensive descriptions of this famous location. One of Gardner's most interesting fabrications involved his famous "Dead Confederate sharpshooter at the Battle of Gettysburg." He came upon the body of a soldier from either the 1st Texas or 17th Georgia Infantry lying beside a large boulder on the southern slope of Devil's Den. He took six photographs of this soldier in an attempt to obtain a "sentimental composition." Three were taken at the spot where the Confederate died before Gardner noticed a stone wall forty yards away. It had been constructed by Southern soldiers the night of July 2. Struck by the artistic potential of the scene, Gardner, with the help of others, dragged the body to the wall and positioned him with his knapsack underneath his head and his rifle against the rocks. This view Gardner captioned "Home of a Rebel sharpshooter." In reality the rifle was Gardner's prop—it appears in numerous photographs—so we know he was not above stretching the truth. In 1865, while preparing the captions for his sketchbook, he wrote this explanation to accompany the print:

> Two of the large rocks in front of round top came near each other. The space
> between two large rocks was walled up & loop holed so that he could take
> deliberate aim at any one who showed himself on round top, he had been wounded
> on the head with part of a shell. As the canteen & surrounding indicates that he
> had lain sometime before he died. When passing over the field in November

Home of a Rebel Sharpshooter

~~Two of the large rocks in front of round top~~
~~came near to each other~~ The space between two
large rocks was walled up & loop holed ~~so~~
that he could take deliberate aim at any one
who showed himself on round top, he had been
wounded in the head with part of a shell, as the
canteen & surrounding indicated that he had lain
some time before he died When passing over the field
in November afterwards when the Monument was dedicated
I took a friend to see the place and there the bones
lay in the clothes he had evidently never been buried

afterwards when the Monument was dedicated I took a friend to see the place and there the bones lay in the clothes he had evidently never been buried.

Later, he wrote a flowing and sentimental passage for inclusion in his sketchbook. Gardner also claimed authorship for the postmortem photograph in his 1865 publication; but in 1863 he had given credit for it to O'Sullivan.[46]

Finally, Gardner came upon the decomposed and dismembered body of a Confederate soldier. In order to increase the impact of this composition, Gardner placed a spent artillery shell on the ground above the soldier's right knee and a rifle on his legs, keeping a dismembered hand in front of the rifle. Gardner captioned this view "War effect of a shell on a Confederate soldier at the Battle of Gettysburg."[47] In reality the dead soldier had probably been used as a meal by the wild pigs that gorged themselves at night on the dead during and after the battle.

A telegram sent by Gardner on July 31st indicates that O'Sullivan was still accompanying the Army of the Potomac almost a month after the Battle of Gettysburg, not languishing in Washington.

"Photographer to the Army of the Potomac"

On December 31, 1863, Gardner copyrighted twenty-one of his Gettysburg series. While he claimed authorship in the application for copyright, his catalog gives credit to O'Sullivan and Gibson. Also on December 31 Gardner copyrighted a wonderful composite of Senator Charles Sumner of Massachusetts and Henry Wadsworth Longfellow, titling it "The Politics and Poetry of New England." As was the case with most other views, both his carte format and the large-plate view were identically captioned and thus protected under his copyright application.

In September 1863 Gardner issued his *Catalogue of Photographic Incidents of the War*. This catalog marked the first time that he referred to himself as "Photographer to the Army of the Potomac." The catalog was printed by E. Polkinhorn of Washington and was furnished to photographic customers for ordering purposes. The twenty-eight-page document is rich in information, both biographical and descriptive. In it Gardner divided his photographs into two groupings: (1) folio-size prints and (2) stereoviews and album gallery cards. Gardner's prices ranged from $1.50 for the folio image (7 × 9 inches mounted with title on 13 × 18 plate paper), to 50 cents for stereographs and 25 cents for album cards. He also offered sets of 50 folio pages, bound in morocco, for $75 each.

OPPOSITE PAGE: *Dead Confederate soldier at Devil's Den, Gettysburg, July 6, 1863. This image, one of the most famous photographs of the war, was composed by Gardner, who dragged the body of the dead soldier forty yards to make a "sentimental composition." Published as plate no. 41 in* Gardner's Photographic Sketch Book of the War. *From an original direct-contact albumen print. Gardner's fictional caption for the photograph, below, written in his own hand on the back of a print of the composition he titled "Home of a Rebel Sharpshooter." In his published* Sketch Book, *the caption differed from this version.*

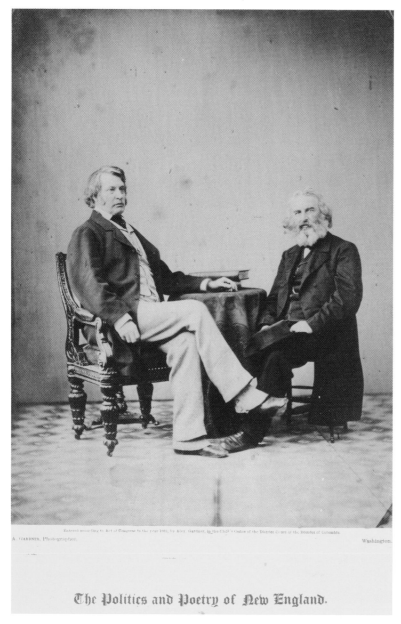

The Politics and Poetry of New England.

A. GARDNER, Photographer.

Washington.

The Politics and Poetry of New England.

Entered according to Act of Congress in the year 1863, by A. Gardner, in the Clerk's Office of the District Court of the District of Columbia.

LEFT: *"The Politics and Poetry of New England": Massachusetts Senator Charles Sumner and poet Henry Wadsworth Longfellow. One of three similar views taken by Gardner. From an original direct-contact albumen print.*

ABOVE: *Variant view identically captioned. From an unpublished original carte de visite.*

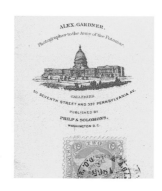

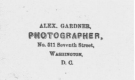

Gardner's issuance of his Gettysburg series marked a transition in his association with E. & H. T. Anthony as his exclusive wholesale agent. Although Anthony was the first to distribute his Gettysburg series, within a short time Gardner transferred the rights of publication solely to Philp & Solomons with Anthony continuing to act as his wholesale agent. But by 1864 Anthony was no longer acting as his wholesale agent. Since Philp & Solomons were already in the business of publishing and bookselling, it seemed natural for them to take over the publishing as well as the distribution of his photographs. Because Gardner's September 1863 catalog made no mention of Philp & Solomons, we can assume that his association was activated after that date. In early 1864 Gardner began using his famous "gold dome" backmark on his carte de visite photographs. He indicated that they were published by Philp & Solomons, and he provided his address at 511 Seventh Street and 332 Pennsylvania Avenue, the location of Philp & Solomons.

Gardner's "official" status within the army was becoming more ambiguous. The high point of his association with the U.S. Topographical Engineers (alias the Secret Service) was during McClellan's Maryland campaign. After McClellan's termination, Gardner's affiliation diminished substantially, though he was still frequently called upon to serve as their photographer. In November 1862 General Burnside utilized Gardner's services prior to the Fredericksburg campaign. On January 26, 1863, Burnside was relieved of his command of the Army of the Potomac and replaced by General Joseph Hooker. Since Fredericksburg and Chancellorsville were clear Union defeats, and since the battlefields remained in enemy hands, Northern photographers were unable to reach the field.[48] In February Gardner, along with O'Sullivan and Gibson, was with Hooker in and around Aquia Creek, Virginia. O'Sullivan remained with Hooker well into June, photographing in the area of Brandy Station and Falmouth, Virginia. After the Gettysburg campaign, O'Sullivan remained with the army in its winter quarters at Brandy Station. On March 12, 1864, General Ulysses S. Grant, appointed General of the Armies, took personal control over Meade's Army of the Potomac.

Grant's Virginia Campaigns

By the time Grant initiated his spring campaign in May, O'Sullivan was in charge of Gardner's field operations. As such, it was he who was granted permission to photograph Grant's crossing the Rapidan River on May 4.[49] Grant's unprecedented authorization to O'Sullivan was obviously brought about through Gardner's influence. However, Gardner was directed to submit an application for a pass, which until that time had not been required.

OPPOSITE PAGE, BOTTOM: *The reverse of Gardner cartes de visite, showing various studio addresses and imprints. Top row: 1862–63, 1863, 1864–66, 1867–68; bottom row: 1869, 1870, 1871–79, 1871–79.*

Entered according to Act of Congress, in the year 1864, by Alex. Gardner, in the Clerk's Office of the District Court of the District of Columbia.

May 1864
Headquarters Army of the Potomac
Brandy Station

Requesting permission "for taking views on the march." The following named photographers were submitted for consideration. T. H. O'Sullivan; Samuel Ott; John Reekie; S. F. Denny; James Gardner. Associated with Mark Cohen.

Alex Gardner[50]

That spring Gardner and his associates enjoyed privileges shared by no other photographic firm. In mid-April orders were issued from army headquarters instructing all "civilians to vacate the camps by April 16." Included in this order would be the sutlers, traders, and camp photographers.[51] Despite this order Gardner's men stayed with the army.

On May 4 O'Sullivan and James Gardner covered the crossing of the Rapidan. On May 16 or 17, James Gardner photographed a grouping of Confederate prisoners awaiting transportation at Belle Plain, and on May 19 he was in Fredericksburg photographing hospitals and landmarks. Meanwhile, O'Sullivan was still attached to Headquarters, Army of the Potomac, and by May 19 he was with V Corps in Spotsylvania. The next day O'Sullivan came upon Confederate dead near Mrs. Alsop's house; he photographed them where they had fallen and also their subsequent burial.[52]

May 21 proved fortuitous for young O'Sullivan. Around noon, he happened upon Grant's Council of War at Massaponax Church. Undoubtedly with the permission of the general, O'Sullivan set his camera on the second-story front window, within the church itself, and took three sequential stereoview photographs.[53]

Entered according to Act of Congress, in the year 1864, by Alex. Gardner, in the Clerk's Office of the District Court of the District of Columbia.

Entered according to Act of Congress, in the year 1863, by Alex. Gardner, in the Clerk's Office of the District Court of the District of Columbia.

OPPOSITE AND ABOVE: *This series of three views records General Ulysses S. Grant's council of war at Massaponax Church, Virginia, on May 21, 1864. In the first photograph, Grant, on the left, leans over the shoulder of General George G. Meade, as they examine a map just completed by the U.S. Topographical Engineers. In the second view, Grant is writing a dispatch. Taken by Timothy H. O'Sullivan, the photographs were published by Gardner as plates 730, 731, and 732. From original stereoviews.*

Between May 24 and May 26, O'Sullivan was photographing along the North Anna River. June 3 marked the Battle of Cold Harbor, and the next day he was on the outskirts of the battle area. On June 14 O'Sullivan and James Gardner were together again at Charles City Courthouse. By June 15 O'Sullivan, Gardner, and Brady's cameramen were on the banks of the James River photographing the Union advance on Petersburg.[54]

On the morning of June 20, O'Sullivan and Brady's operatives came upon the execution of Private William Johnson, a black soldier of the 23rd Regiment of the United States Colored Troops. Johnson stood accused of raping a white woman on June 8 outside Cold Harbor. According to *Harper's Weekly:*

> William Johnson, a colored soldier from the Twenty-third United States Colored Troops . . . attempted to commit an outrage on a white woman. Considerable importance was given to the affair, in order that the example might be made more effective. Johnson confessed his guilt, and was executed within the outer breast-works about Petersburg, on an elevation, and in plain view of the enemy, a white flag covering the ceremony.[55]

The fact that Brady's and Gardner's firms traveled and worked together would not be considered out of the ordinary. Most of the operatives had at one time or the other worked together under Brady's employ and, of course, shared common experiences and acquaintanceships. As civilian professionals, these cameramen "transcended commercial competition" for the benefit of their art.[56]

Final Months of the War

O'Sullivan's presence at Petersburg is unrecorded after June 24. It is therefore conceivable that he was summoned back to Washington to resupply his equipment and deliver his negatives to Gardner. After all, O'Sullivan had been in the field continuously for more than three months.

Gardner's expense in keeping cameramen with the military was becoming prohibitive. In the past he had always sent them to the field in direct response to a battle or conflict. His current policy of allowing O'Sullivan to travel and stay with the army was not producing dividends commensurate with expenditures. This would help explain O'Sullivan's subsequent absence from the battlefield for such a prolonged period.[57] By June 20 it had become apparent that Grant intended on laying siege to the city of Petersburg.

O'Sullivan did return to the field early in July. He and Gardner must have discussed Gardner's leaving Washington and joining him in Petersburg. O'Sullivan dissuaded Gardner, wiring him on July 11, "I do not need you at present."

In August and September, O'Sullivan and another Gardner operative, David Knox, were stationed in the Petersburg area. Knox took numerous pictures of the Mortar Dictator, manned by members of Company G, 1st Connecticut Heavy Artillery, a mile northeast of City Point Railroad. During the month of September, O'Sullivan

Execution of Private William Johnson, Petersburg, Virginia, June 20, 1864. Taken by Timothy H.
O'Sullivan and published as plate no. 783 by Gardner. From an original print.

produced many pictures of soldiers and officers in the vicinity of Meade's headquarters well behind the Union lines. Subsequent to this series, Gardner decided to suspend for a time his primary field operations in Virginia with the Army of the Potomac.[58]

After the Battle of Gettysburg, Gardner felt compelled to stay in Washington to oversee his business interests and had named O'Sullivan his "Superintendent of Field and Map Work for the Army of the Potomac,"[59] confident that his interests were being well served in the field. In late December he dispatched O'Sullivan to document the Federal expedition against Fort Fisher, North Carolina. Shortly after Fort Fisher fell, on January 13, 1865, O'Sullivan went ashore and took numerous photographs of the Confederate gun positions.

Since Gardner's field operations with the Army of the Potomac were on indefinite hold, there was no reason for him to be on or near any battlefield until the final assault on Petersburg. The night of April 1, Federal forces began a tremendous artillery bombardment on Petersburg. By April 3 Petersburg capitulated. It was Thomas C. Roche, the contract photographer in the employ of E. & H. T. Anthony, who was present when the successful IX Corps entered Fort Mahone. Much to his surprise and delight, he walked right into an array of Confederate dead in the trenches of Fort Mahone. Roche was undoubtedly aware of Gardner's commercially successful Antietam and Gettysburg series.

Confederate dead in the trenches of Fort Mahone, the morning after the storming of Petersburg, Virginia, April 2, 1865. Taken by T. C. Roche.

OPPOSITE PAGE: *O'Sullivan's photographic wagon outside Petersburg, c. 1865. From an original print.*

Graves of Union soldiers on Belle Isle, a Confederate prison, Richmond, Virginia, April 8, 1865,
published by Gardner as plate no. 890. The man inspecting the grave is photographer John Reekie.

According to historian Frassanito, Roche realized "the inordinate difficulties involved in securing actual photographs of a freshly scarred battlefield, because to do so required a rare combination of motivation, fortitude, connections, patience, ability, experience, financial backing, timely information, and, at times, just plain luck." For the first time, Gardner had been scooped by another photographer in obtaining death views. Roche took full advantage of his "chance of a lifetime opportunity,"[60] taking twenty-two pictures of the Confederate dead over most of the day on April 3.

Within a week after the fall of Petersburg, on April 9, Lee surrendered his Army of Northern Virginia to Grant at Appomattox Courthouse, Virginia. Alexander Gardner was concerned not with Grant's final operation, but with the fallen city of Richmond, the capital of the Confederacy and the geographic location that had eluded him and the Union forces for more than four long years. The fall of Richmond was the impetus that brought him personally back to the battlefield and to his place behind the camera. He left Washington immediately after learning of the evacuation of Richmond, arriving there on April 6. He immediately began photographing the city, documenting the widespread destruction enacted by the fleeing Confederates. Gardner took over fifty of the one hundred photographs made in Richmond between April 6 and April 15. Accompanying him was his employee John Reekie, who also took photographs of Richmond and Petersburg between April 12 and April 16. Gardner's extensive collection of Richmond views was published under the title *Memories of the War*.[61]

On April 17 Reekie went to Lee's Franklin Street residence in Richmond hoping to obtain a portrait of the defeated general. He had to settle for a photograph of the house. In late April, after Reekie completed his series on Richmond, Gardner dispatched O'Sullivan to Appomattox Courthouse to photograph the location of the final surrender. In early May, O'Sullivan arrived in Petersburg to photograph structures along the Appomattox River. O'Sullivan then took forty exposures of Union positions on the deserted IX Corps front, including views of forts Sedgwick, Stedman, Meikle, Rice, and Morton. Some of O'Sullivan's scenes show his darkroom wagon, which bears the identification "Photographic Wagon, Engineer Department." Although Gardner commercially published these pictures, there is an indication that O'Sullivan at the time was employed in an "official" capacity. Perhaps the government was again utilizing Gardner's services or was financing his Petersburg series.

On June 4 Henry L. Abbot, captain of engineers and brevet brigadier general, made the following report to the Chief of Engineers, General Richard Delafield:

> I have retained command of my regiment and brigade during the month [May 1865]. The latter has been engaged in removing the heavy water bearing guns from the rebel James River batteries. I have prevailed upon a photographer [William Frank Browne], who has a fine stereoscopic instrument, to take a series of views of these batteries, with a view of preserving an invaluable record of their wonderful completeness. General [Peter Smith] Michie may take a few sets, but I think the [Engineer] Department should order several more. I will vouch for their excellence and importance.[62]

On May 8, O'Sullivan sent the following to Gardner:

> Petersburg, May 8, 1865
> A. Gardner, 511 7th St, Washington
>
> Lt. Col. [Nathaniel] Michler wishes you to send the original drawings and copies of the work in front of Petersburg immediately he wants the [sic] them to work from. Send to this city.
>
> T. H. O'Sullivan

Nathaniel Michler was breveted brigadier general on April 2, 1865, for meritorious service and gallantry at Petersburg. General Michler was also a member of the U.S. Topographical Engineers.[63] One can only speculate as to the meaning of the foregoing cryptic message. As nothing is known of Gardner drawings, it seems safe to assume O'Sullivan was in fact referring to photographs.

Libby Prison, Richmond, April 6, 1865. Published as plate no. 89, Gardner's Photographic Sketch Book of the War. *From an original direct-contact albumen print.*

Negative by J. REEKIE.   Entered according to act of Congress, in the year 1865, by A. Gardner, in the Clerk's Office of the District Court of the District of Columbia.   Positive by A. GARDNER, 511 7th St., Washington.

Burial party, Cold Harbor, Virginia, April 15, 1865. Taken by John Reekie and published as plate no. 94, Gardner's Photographic Sketch Book of the War. *From an original direct-contact albumen print.*

OPPOSITE PAGE, BOTTOM: *Castle Thunder Prison, Richmond, April 7, 1865, published by Gardner as plate no. 859. From an original stereoview.*

Appomattox Courthouse, Virginia, April 1865, by Timothy H. O'Sullivan. From an original direct-contact albumen print.

Lt. Colonel Nathaniel Michler, a member of the U.S. Topographical Engineers, was breveted Brigadier General for his meritorious service during the siege of Petersburg, Virginia. From an original unpublished carte de visite.

The Gardner-Brady Rivalry

Brady's extensive battlefield coverage of the Petersburg campaign helped to expand his reputation. In a number of photographs taken on the front lines, he made sure that he personally was included in the photograph. He wanted the public to know that he had been *there,* at the front. Gardner, on the other hand, rarely ever appeared in his own photographs. Although on cordial terms, the two men did in fact share a deep rivalry. At the end of the war, their competitiveness manifested itself in a variety of ways.

On May 5, 1865, the Washington *Daily Morning Chronicle* printed the following announcement:

> The first picture taken of Andrew Johnson as President of the United States was taken by Brady, of 352 Pa. Ave., near 6th St., and a picture of such excellent points is rarely seen. A physiologist unacquainted with the antecedents of this extraordinary man could from this life-like picture write not only the past, but the future of the subject thereby. Like all of Brady's works, it is easy in position, bold in outline, clear in finish, and true as life itself. Copies of this gem photographic can be had, all sizes, at the gallery as above.

However, it was Alexander Gardner's imposing portrait of President Andrew Johnson that graced the May 13 issue of *Harper's Weekly.* After reading about Brady's coup, Gardner no doubt prevailed upon Johnson to sit for his camera. Or it is possible that Gardner secured his portrait of then–Vice President Johnson prior to Lincoln's assassination. In any case, Gardner's majestic Imperial portrait was copyrighted by him on May 17, 1865, and was captioned: "Andrew Johnson, President U.S."

The Grand Review of May 23 and 24 was Washington's official celebration of the end of the war. Thousands of troops paraded through the city past grandstands packed with citizens and dignitaries. Gardner dispatched his operative W. Morris Smith to photograph the historic event. Smith's photographs served as models for the engravings that put the event on the cover of *Harper's.*

Gardner's Photographic Sketch Book of the War

After Appomattox, Gardner decided to publish a definitive bound photographic compendium of war photographs. This was not his maiden attempt, as his September 1863 catalog had offered fifty images "beautifully bound in morocco with title page," titled *Incidents of the War.* As no copy of this 1863 set is known to exist, it must be assumed that all copies were eventually broken up. The 1865 book, *Gardner's Photographic Sketch Book of the War,* drew on photographs from his various cameramen. Gardner selected one hundred pictures that best represented his interpretation of the war. Beginning with negatives from as early as March 1862, Gardner organized his book chronologically. Each of the one hundred original tipped-in photographs was accompanied by a title page of descriptive text. In the foreword, Gardner made the following comments:

In presenting the Photographic Sketch Book of the War to the attention of the public, it is designed that it shall speak for itself. The omission, therefore, of any remarks by way of preface might well be justified; and yet, perhaps, a few introductory words may not be amiss.

As mementoes of the fearful struggle through which the country has just passed, it is confidently hoped that the following pages will possess an enduring interest. Localities that would scarcely have been known, and probably never remembered, save in their immediate vicinity, have become celebrated, and will ever be held sacred as memorable fields, where thousands of brave men yielded up their lives, a willing sacrifice for the cause they had espoused.

Verbal representations of such places, or scenes, may or may not have the merit of accuracy; but photographic presentments of them will be accepted by posterity with an undoubting faith. During the four years of the war, almost every point of importance has been photographed, and the collection from which these views have been selected amounts to nearly three thousand.

Gardner's *Sketch Book*, priced at $150, was published in two volumes and in two editions: in 1865 and 1866. The first edition was bound in red leather, and the second edition in blue leather. There were also special brown morocco-bound editions with ivory tabs in the front covers. The mounts of the 1865 edition were captioned "Incidents of the War." Below this caption line was the notification "Published by Philp & Solomons, Washington." In the lower-left portion of the mount was the date of the photograph. Gardner's 1866 edition lacked both the caption line "Incidents of the War" and the publishing information. This edition did include the individual plate numbers in the lower-right-hand portion of the mounts. Both editions were published by Philp & Solomons in Washington.

Gardner's *Sketch Book* remains to this day the finest photographic documentary of the Civil War ever produced. It is regarded by some as the most significant photographically illustrated book published in the United States. Nonetheless, it is not without errors. As discussed before, Gardner was not averse to stretching the truth in his dates and captions. In addition, the text accompanying the photographs displayed his resolute disdain for everything the South represented. Gardner's obituarist stated his position best:

A lover of liberty, he was an abolitionist from the earliest recollection, and remained an enemy of slavery until it was destroyed.[64]

In promoting the sale of *Gardner's Photographic Sketch Book of the War*, Alexander Gardner, through his agents Philp & Solomons, circulated an extensive advertisement titled "Photographic History of the War."

Photographic History of the War

At once superb and unique, and an intensely National work, none more so, entitled Gardner's Photographic Sketch-Book of the War. It is complete in two large volumes, imperial elongated quarto, handsomely and solidly bound in morocco.

We have in this magnificent work a collection of one hundred "photographic sketches of the war"—each portraying, with the graphic truthfulness which can be attained only by the photographer's art, some scene made memorable by the momentous struggle through which our country has recently passed. With what curious interest every reader of Grecian history would gaze upon a photograph of the "Pass of Thermomopylae," taken on the morning of August 8 in the year 480 B.C., one day after the struggle which had strewed its defiles with Spartan and Thespian dead, buried beneath heaps of slaughtered Persians! What we would not give for a faithful picture of "gray Marathon," as it lay before the eyes of Miltiades, on the day when, with ten thousand Greeks, he had put to flight the myriad host of Mardonius! We should like to see a vivid sketch of the stricken field of Cannae, littered with the remains of Roman chivalry, on the disastrous day when the star of Rome paled before the genius of Hannibal; or of the plain of Pharasalia, reddened with the blood shed in the fratricidal struggle between the adherents of Pompey and Caesar.

Or could the scenes of the war for American independence be gathered by photography? Could the minute men of Lexington as they were drawn up before the Court-House sullenly listening to the insolent orders of Pitcairn? Could the sturdy resistance of the Concord farmers at the Old North Bridge, where the shot for liberty was first fired, "which was heard round the world"? Could Bunker Hill have been portrayed as it was, when for the third time the confident troops of England reeled back to the water's edge unable to stand against the deadly fire of New England yeomen? Could Dorchester Heights, bristling with the guns that sent every red coat out of the old Bay State? Or the plains of Saratoga, where the chosen general of the mother country surrendered the flower of the British army to an American command? The rush of British and Hessian foes when the Delaware had been crossed and Trenton delivered, saving by one act of peerless strategy the disheartened forces of Washington. Could the bitter scenes of the dreary and doubtful winter at Valley Forge, and the final victory of Yorktown, which won the liberties of a people and added a nation to the world, have been garnered with unerring fidelity for immortal preservation, with what patriotic delight would our eyes now behold these faithful records of the revolution, and with what sacred care and love would they be forever regarded by the American heart?

What we would desire to have for the elucidation of scenes made famous in the annals of past history we here possess for the perpetual memorial of localities and events connected with the Titanic contest that recently shook our continents. The eye rests upon these pictured pages with the happy consciousness that they are no fancy sketches, drawn "out of the artist's head" for the sensational adornment of some pictorial newspaper. They are true to nature in a manner and to a degree which no pencil of the pre-Raphaelite school have dreamed of reaching. And if the art of which they are the fruits affords in itself an infallible guarantee for their fidelity, it is equally needless to say that the name of the eminent artist under whose auspices they were taken carries with it the best possible assurance of skill in the finish and of taste in the execution of his photographic products.

The price, $150, may seem a large amount for a book, but it is put within very reasonable limits for such a work as this, which contains one hundred admirable photographs of places which have become known to the world as scenes of memorable events in the great civil war now ended—many of these places being known, indeed, solely on the account, and will ever be held sacred as memorable fields, where thousands of brave men yielded up their lives a willing sacrifice for the cause which they had espoused. During the four years of the war Mr. Gardner photographed about three thousand views—the contents of the two volumes under notice are the best and most striking out of the collection. Each view is accompanied with letter-press, in which a sufficiently full and always accurate description is given. The date is affixed to each view, and the name of the locality is engraved. These photographs are mounted on tone paper, which makes them resemble India proofs. The price comes to $1.50 for each mere photograph—mounting, letter-press, lithographed title-pages, and rich binding, being thrown in for nothing. As an addendum to every History of the Rebellion it will be found invaluable. Another advantage is, the whole arrangement of these views has been strictly according to time. The first view

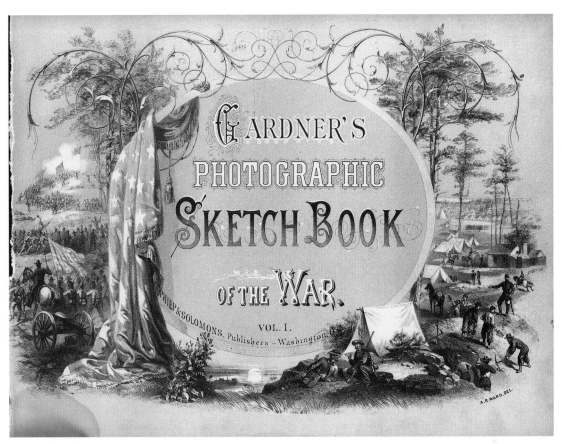

Title page of the original 1866 edition of Gardner's Photographic Sketch Book of the War.

represents the Marshall House, Alexandria, where Colonel Ellsworth was murdered by the proprietor, Jackson, in May, 1861, and the last shows the dedication of the Monuments, on Bull Run battle-field, so late as June, 1865. The whole course of the War is traced, pictorially, in the ninety-eight photographs which intervene between the first and the hundredth. We believe that photography has never been so employed so extensively in any published work, and the letter-press descriptions are sufficiently explicit and graphic to assist the memory of American citizens, who may spend a few hours tracing the war through these volumes, without the necessity of referring to any history whatever.

On March 6, 1866, Philp & Solomons submitted a two-volume set of the *Sketch Book* to the quartermaster general's office for inspection and purchase. On March 10 Major John C. McFerran, attached to the quartermaster general's office, authorized the purchase of this book and recommended payment. This demonstrates Gardner's relentless business acumen: his access to the battlefield was through the cooperation of the government, which he then charged for the very document that had been compiled through its collaboration.

No more than two hundred sets of *Gardner's Photographic Sketch Book of the War* were ever produced. No more than twenty remain intact. These beautifully produced volumes, and the powerful images they have passed down to us, are a tribute to the talent and foresight of a great American historian with a camera. A great legacy was left us by Alexander Gardner, Matthew B. Brady, Timothy H. O'Sullivan, James F. Gibson, and other unsung heroes—men with a camera and a dream, whose efforts to capture the truth about war influenced and inspired the work of those who came after them.

The Grand Review, May 24, 1865. From an original print attributed to Gardner.

2080

Theron E. Hall, Quartermaster, Army of the Potomac,
c. 1863. From an original unpublished direct-
contact albumen print.

Butterfield

General Daniel Butterfield, Chief of Staff under
General Meade, 1865. Butterfield composed the now-
traditional bugle call "Taps" and was wounded at
Gettysburg. From an original unpublished carte de
visite.

OPPOSITE PAGE, BOTTOM, FROM LEFT
TO RIGHT: General William Tecumseh Sherman,
c. 1865; General Philip Henry Sheridan, Cavalry
Commander, Army of the Potomac, 1865; and
Admiral David Glasgow Farragut, c. 1865. All from
original unpublished cartes de visite.

Major General Henry Jackson Hunt, Chief of Artillery, Army of the Potomac, 1865. From an original unpublished carte de visite.

Major General Ethan Allen Hitchcock, Commissary General of Prisoners, 1865. From an original unpublished carte de visite.

Major General Francis Preston Blair, Jr., 1865. Blair was successful both as a politician and as a military man. From an original carte de visite.

Major General Nathaniel Prentiss Banks, who served as governor of and later congressman from his native state of Massachusetts. From an original unpublished carte de visite.

Major General James Brewerton Ricketts, recovering from a bullet wound received at the Battle of Cedar Creek, Virginia, October 1864. From an original unpublished carte de visite.

Major General Benjamin Henry Grierson, "The Horse Soldier." Grierson led a successful raid behind Confederate lines in April 1863, the basis for the John Wayne movie The Horse Soldiers. *From an original unpublished carte de visite.*

Major General Rufus Ingalls. From an original unpublished carte de visite.

Brigadier General Marsena Rudolph Patrick, c. 1863. From an original unpublished carte de visite.

Brigadier General William Farquhar Barry. From an original unpublished carte de visite.

Major General Andrew Atkinson Humphreys, who commanded II Corps, Army of the Potomac. From an original unpublished carte de visite.

Major General Alfred Pleasonton, who commanded the Cavalry Corps, Army of the Potomac, October 1863. From an original carte de visite.

Major General Emory Upton. He commanded three branches of the army during the war (artillery, infantry, and cavalry) and became a brevet major general before the age of 26. Upton was commandant of West Point and later commanded the Presidio in San Francisco, where he shot and killed himself on March 15, 1881. From an original unpublished carte de visite.

Admiral Joseph Smith. From an original unpublished carte de visite.

Captain George N. Bliss, Congressional Medal of Honor winner. From an original unpublished carte de visite.

Frederick Rosencranz, a Swedish officer who served in the Union Army and was breveted lieutenant colonel for faithful and meritorious service. From an original unpublished carte de visite.

Captain E. Boliano, a Romanian officer on the staff of General Alexander Webb, 1865. From an original unpublished carte de visite.

Lt. Colonel John B. Howard, right, and an unidentified officer, 1863. Taken by Alexander Gardner in 1863 at the studios of Philp & Solomons. From an original unpublished carte de visite.

Two brothers. From an original unpublished carte de visite.

Assistant Secretary of the Navy
Gustavus Fox; Henry A. Wise,
U.S.N.; Wise's son; and Captain
Percival Drayton, U.S.N. From an
original carte de visite.

Thomas Fayles Maury, surgeon
for General Longstreet.
From an original carte de visite.

A paroled Confederate prisoner
from J. E. B. Stuart's command,
1863. From an original
unpublished carte de visite.

Major General George
Armstrong Custer, January 2,
1865. From an original
stereoview.

General Sheridan and staff, January 2, 1865. From an original Imperial print.

General Philip H. Sheridan and staff, January 2, 1865. From left: Major General Wesley Merritt, Brigadier General James W. Forsythe, Major General George Crook, General Sheridan, and Major General George Armstrong Custer. From an original unpublished carte de visite.

Admiral David Dixon Porter on deck of his flagship Malvern, *after the victory at Fort Fisher, North Carolina, January 1865. From an original direct-contact albumen print.*

Three unidentified officers. From an original direct-contact albumen print.

James Gardner standing beside a battery wagon outside of Petersburg, Virginia, 1864. Taken by David Knox and published as plate no. 73 in Gardner's Photographic Sketch Book of the War. From an original direct-contact albumen print.

General William Tecumseh Sherman and staff, April 1865. From an original Imperial print.

Dr. Jonathan Letterman, medical director, Army of the Potomac, and his staff, Antietam, October 1862. From left: Henry Francis Clarke, Albert V. Colburn, John Buford, James Chatham Duane, Dr. Letterman, unidentified, Albert James Myer, George Suckley, Delos Bennet Sackett, and John Gibbon. From an original unpublished direct-contact albumen print.

OPPOSITE PAGE, TOP TO BOTTOM: *General Ulysses S. Grant and staff, April 1865, and Major General George G. Meade and staff, April 1865. From original Imperial prints.*

General John Gibbon and selected officers and enlisted men preparing to present the captured colors of General Robert E. Lee and the Army of Northern Virginia to Secretary of War Edwin M. Stanton, May 1, 1865. From an original direct-contact albumen photograph attributed to Alexander Gardner.

OPPOSITE PAGE, TOP: *Company I, 6th Pennsylvania Cavalry (Lancers). Illustrator Alfred Waud is seated at front of photograph. From an original direct-contact albumen print.*

OPPOSITE PAGE, BOTTOM: *Guardsmen's mess. From left: Captain A. H. G. Richardson, Captain J. S. Crawford, unidentified, Captain G. W. Bratton, unidentified, and Captain H. E. Rulon. From an original print.*

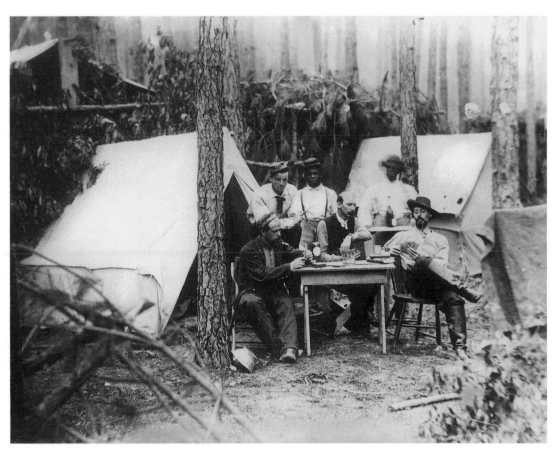

THE PHOTOGRAPHS OF ABRAHAM LINCOLN

1861–1865

Abraham Lincoln was one the most pho-
tographed presidents of the nineteenth century. He sat for thirty-three photographers
on sixty-one occasions, resulting in one hundred twenty-seven portraits.[1] Lincoln's
first portrait was a daguerreotype taken in Springfield, Illinois, in 1846, by N. H.
Shepard. The final photograph was a postmortem view taken in New York's City Hall
on April 24, 1865, by Jeremiah Gurney.

Of those one hundred twenty-seven photographs, Alexander Gardner took
thirty-seven, more than twice that of his closest competitor, Anthony Berger, who
took only thirteen views.[2] It is no wonder Gardner has been called "Mr. Lincoln's
Cameraman."

Gardner's seven distinct Lincoln sittings were, in chronological order,

1. A series of five carte de visite portraits at Brady's Studio, Sunday,
   February 24, 1861.
2. One portrait of Lincoln's inauguration, Monday, March 4, 1861.
3. Six photographs of Lincoln visiting the Antietam Battlefield, October 3–4,
   1862.
4. Seven photographs of the president taken at Gardner's studio, August 9, 1863.
5. Five portraits at Gardner's studio, November 8, 1863.
6. Five portraits at Gardner's studio, February 5, 1865.
7. Eight photographs of Lincoln's second inauguration, March 4, 1865.

February 24, 1861

Gardner's first meeting with Abraham Lincoln took place on Sunday,
February 24, 1861. *Harper's Weekly* had commissioned Brady to photograph Lincoln
upon his arrival in Washington from Springfield. George H. Story, a portrait artist
and friend of Brady's, made the following observations: "A day or two after the President's arrival, Mr. Gardner, Mr. Brady's representative in Washington, came to my
room and asked me to come and pose Mr. Lincoln for a picture. When I entered the
room, the President was seated in a chair wholly absorbed in deep thought.[3]

"Lincoln seemed absolutely indifferent to all that was going on about him, and
he gave the impression that he was a man who was overwhelmed with anxiety and
fatigue and care."[4] Brady asked Story to model Lincoln in an artistic pose. Story
continued: "I said in an undertone to the operator [Gardner], 'Bring your instrument

here and take the picture.' "[5] Gardner proceeded to take a sequence of five carte de visite photographs. On April 27 *Harper's Weekly* noted: "We publish herewith, from a photograph just taken expressly for this paper, a portrait of the President."

March 4, 1861

Lincoln's inauguration was scheduled for Monday, March 4, 1861. During the first week of February, Brady sent for his two best New York operatives, J. F. Coonley and George N. Barnard, to help with his and Gardner's preparations for the event. In light of evidence from Allan Pinkerton that there was a plot afoot to assassinate Abraham Lincoln, General Charles P. Stone, who was in charge of security, had stationed sharpshooters along Pennsylvania Avenue and a battalion of troops near the steps of the Capitol. On the morning of Lincoln's inauguration, General Stone received a report "from a reliable informant" that a bomb had been placed below the wooden platform upon which Lincoln and President James Buchanan would be standing later that morning.[6] Stone sent an additional battalion of armed soldiers to encircle the platform, while plainclothesmen and uniformed officers were stationed within the crowd when Brady and Gardner arrived early that morning to set up their cameras; stringent security measures forced them to take a position off to the side of the stand.[7]

Another photographer was present at the inauguration. Colonel Montgomery C. Meigs, an amateur photographer who would later be appointed quartermaster general of the army, took at least two views with his small stereoview camera.[8] The next day a newspaper reported: "A small camera was directly in front of Mr. Lincoln, another at a distance of a hundred yards [Meigs], and a third, of huge dimensions, on the right, raised on a platform built specially for the purpose [Brady-Gardner]."[9]

George Story's Portrait

In June Gardner asked George Story to undertake a portrait commission based on a photograph of Lincoln. Story accepted the offer but said that he'd need more recent photographs. Lincoln was too busy to pose for Gardner, but did allow Story to visit the White House to complete his painting. Lincoln's secretary, John Nicolay, noted: "Graphic art was powerless . . . before a face that moved through a thousand delicate gradations of line, contour, light, and shade, sparkle of the eye and curve of the lip, in the long gamut of expression from grave to gay, and back again from the rollicking jollity of laughter to that serious, faraway look with prophetic intuitions. There are many pictures of Lincoln; there is no portrait of him." As Lincoln was constantly in motion, his face frequently in shadow, Story was unable to make any preliminary sketches for his oil. But with the help of Gardner's earlier photographs, he was able to execute his commission.[10]

ABOVE AND RIGHT: *Five views of Abraham Lincoln, Sunday, February 24, 1861. From original cartes de visite.*

Brady's note to Gardner advising him that Lincoln would be coming to the gallery to be photographed.

Feb. 22, 1861

Mr Gardner—

President Elect Lincoln will visit the gallery on the 24th. Please ready equipment.

M.B. Brady

ABRAHAM LINCOLN.

Lincoln's first inauguration, March 4, 1861. From an original photograph.

FAR LEFT: *Major General Montgomery Meigs. From an original unpublished carte de visite.*

LEFT: *Lincoln's secretary John Nicolay. From an original unpublished carte de visite.*

October 3–4, 1862

After the Battle of Antietam, on September 17, 1862, Lincoln decided to pay General McClellan a personal visit to learn why he had not pursued Lee into Virginia. The president left Washington for Harpers Ferry on October 1 accompanied by General John A. McClernand, an acquaintance and a staunch Democrat; his bodyguard Ward Hill Lamon; Joseph C. G. Kennedy, an expert on munitions production; Ozias M. Hatch, the secretary of state of Illinois and an old friend; and John W. Garrett, president of the Baltimore and Ohio Railroad. On the afternoon of October 1, General McClellan arrived at Harpers Ferry to meet with the president and to review the Union troops stationed at Bolivar Station. Later that afternoon McClellan returned to his headquarters at Antietam. The next morning, Lincoln left Harpers Ferry for Antietam,[11] after sending the following telegram to his wife:

Mrs. A. Lincoln

General McClellan and myself are to be photographed tomorrow by Mr. Gardner if we can sit still long enough. I feel General M should have no problem on his end, but I may sway in the breeze a bit.

A. Lincoln[12]

This telling statement sets the sardonic tone for his meetings with General McClellan. It also points to Alexander Gardner being with either Lincoln or McClellan on October 1, having possibly accompanied Lincoln from Washington.

Gardner took two group photographs of Lincoln and McClellan with his officers. The first was a stereoview portrait numbered 605 and titled "President Lincoln, Generals McClellan, McClernand, and Marcy, and Messers. Garrett, Hatch, Lamon, Kennedy, and others, previous to reviewing the troops on Battle-field of Antietam, October 3, 1862." Shortly after the photograph was taken, Lincoln accompanied McClellan and others to General Fitz John Porter's headquarters, a mile west of Sharpsburg. After the presidential party reviewed troops from the V Corps, Gardner accompanied them to General Porter's headquarters, where one large-format 8 × 10 photograph was made.[13] Gardner titled this view "President Lincoln, Generals McClellan, Porter, Morrell, Hunt, Humphrey, Colonel Sackett, Lieutenant Colonels Swietzer, Webb, Locke, Doctor Letterman, Captain Custer, &c., at Headquarters Fitz John Porter, Antietam, October 3, 1862." Gardner's catalog noted that a duplicate was available only as an album gallery card and was numbered 606. However, that caption no. 606 seems to be a copy of the large-format view, not a separate or distinctly different photograph. In 1865 and 1866 Gardner would issue this same view as plate no. 23 in his *Photographic Sketch Book of the War*. Shortly after this plate was developed, it fractured. At least one print of it has survived with the telltale crack. Gardner must have masked the cracked negative from which all further prints, including the ones utilized in his *Sketch Book*, were reproduced. This conclusion is based on the evidence that a large portion of the emulsion was removed to mask the crack.[14]

The next morning Gardner recorded two 8 × 10 views of President Lincoln posed between Allan Pinkerton and General John McClernand. Gardner captioned these views "President Lincoln, General McClernand, and E. J. Allen [aka Allan Pinkerton], Chief of S.S. [Secret Service], U.S.A., at Secret Service Department, Headquarters Army of the Potomac, October 4, 1862." As in the case of his group portrait of General McClellan, Gardner issued an album gallery card numbered 604 as one of his views. This was either a copy of the large-format view or simply a captioning error.

The final exposures were of President Lincoln conferring with General McClellan in his tent. Two almost identical likenesses were taken, one being a stereoview and the other a large-plate 8 × 10 photograph. Gardner captioned this view "President Lincoln and General McClellan at Headquarters Army of the Potomac, Antietam, October 4, 1862." His stereoview or album gallery card was assigned as plate 602 and was copyrighted by him on October 11.

Lincoln left Antietam on the morning of October 4 and Gardner wired Brady's Gallery "Got Prest Genls McClellan McClernand Porter Morrell Marcy & Humphrey Will send negatives tomorrow."

A little over a month later, on November 7, 1862, McClellan was relieved of his command by President Lincoln.

August 9, 1863

The first time Lincoln sat for Gardner in his own studio was Sunday, August 9, 1863. Four cartes de visite and three Imperial portraits were taken this date. In his diary entry John Hay, Lincoln's secretary, noted: "I went down with the President to have his picture taken at Gardner's. He was in very good spirits."[15] Nine days later, Hay penned the following letter to Gardner, which was signed by Lincoln:

EXECUTIVE MANSION
Washington, August 18, 1863.

My Dear Sir

Allow me to return my sincere thanks for the cards and pictures which you have kindly sent me. I think they are generally very successful. The Imperial photograph in which the head leans upon the hand I regard as the best that I have yet seen.

I am very truly
Your Obt Sevt
A. Lincoln

November 8, 1863

On November 8 Hay wrote the following in his diary: "Went with Mrs. Ames to Gardner's Gallery and were soon joined by Nico [John G. Nicolay] and the Prest. We had a great many pictures taken . . . some of the Prest. the best I have seen . . . Nico and I immortalized ourselves by having ourselves done in a group with the Prest."[16]

GARDNER, Photographer.

M. B. BRADY, Publisher.

ABOVE: *President Abraham Lincoln with General George B. McClellan at his headquarters at Antietam, October 3, 1862. From left: Colonel Delos B. Sackett, Captain George Monteith, Lt. Colonel Nelson B. Sweitzer, General George W. Morell, Colonel Alexander S. Webb, General McClellan, Scout Adams, Dr. Jonathan Letterman, unidentified officer, President Lincoln, Colonel Henry J. Hunt, General Fitz John Porter, unidentified officer, Colonel Frederick T. Locke, General Andrew A. Humphreys, and Captain George Armstrong Custer. Published as plate no. 23,* Gardner's Photographic Sketch Book of the War. *From an original direct-contact albumen print.*

LEFT: *President Lincoln, Generals McClellan, McClernand, and Marcy, and Messers. Garrett, Hatch, Lamon, Kennedy, and others previous to reviewing the troops on the Battlefield of Antietam. Published as plate no. 605 in Gardner's catalog. From an original stereoview.*

GARDNER, Photographer.

M. B. BRADY, Publisher.

Entered according to act of Congress, in the year 1862, by ALEX. GARDNER, in the Clerk's Office of the District Court of the District of Columbia.

THE PRESIDENT AND GENERAL McCLELLAN

On the Battle-field of Antietam.

President Lincoln and General McClellan at McClellan's headquarters, Army of the Potomac, October 4, 1862. From an original direct-contact albumen print. INSET: *President Lincoln and General McClellan at McClellan's headquarters, October 4, 1862. Published as plate no. 602 in Gardner's catalog. From an original stereoview.*

OPPOSITE PAGE: *Allan Pinkerton, President Lincoln, and General McClernand at McClellan's headquarters, October 4, 1862. From original direct-contact albumen prints.*

GARDNER, Photographer.

M. B. BRADY, Publisher.

THE PRESIDENT, MAJ. GEN. McCLERNAND, AND E. J. ALLEN,

Chief of S. S. U. S.

At Secret Service Department, Headquarters Army of the Potomac, near Antietam.

October 4. 1862.

In one of the photographs taken that day, perspective caused one of Lincoln's feet to appear unusually large. When Lincoln saw this "big foot" photograph, his curiosity was aroused. In conversation with journalist Noah Brooks, Lincoln said: "I can understand why that foot should be so enormous. It's a big foot anyway, and it is near the focus of the instrument. But why is the outline of it so indistinct and blurred? I am confident I did not move it." Brooks suggested to Lincoln that perhaps the throbbing of his arteries might have caused the subtle motion. With this, the president crossed his legs and both he and Brooks watched his foot. "That's it! That's it!" he exclaimed. "Now that's very curious, isn't it?"[17] The next evening, November 9, Lincoln attended a performance at Ford's Theatre of *The Marble Heart*, starring John Wilkes Booth.[18]

February 5, 1865

Gardner's final portraits of Lincoln convey a simple yet tragic sense of loss. For many years, historians have erroneously claimed that this sitting produced *Lincoln's final photograph* and have placed its date as April 10, 1865. The president's half-smile seems to indicate that the burden of the war had been removed from his shoulders. It has been suggested that this was the result of his hearing that Lee had surrendered to Grant at Appomattox the day before. That is a satisfying and pleasant story to associate with these imposing portraits, but it was not the case. The portraits were made several months earlier.

On February 4, 1865, portrait painter Matthew Wilson was introduced to the president by Mrs. Gideon Welles, representing her husband, the Secretary of the Navy. Welles had commissioned Wilson to capture the president on canvas. The next day Wilson entered the following in his diary: "at 2 o'clock met Mr. Lincoln at Gardner's . . ."[19] Gardner took three carte de visite portraits and two Imperial photographs. Wilson wrote that he began his painting, based on these photographs, on February 7 and worked through February 15. Wilson attempted to gain access to the president to finish his painting, but he was put off until February 20. On that date Lincoln allowed Wilson to place the finishing touches on his canvas, thus enabling the artist to complete his commission on February 22.

Another portrait painter, Francis B. Carpenter, made the following observations: "Temporarily upon the wall of the room [Lincoln's office] was a portrait of himself recently painted for Secretary Welles by a Connecticut artist friend. Turning to the picture, Mr. Welles remarked that he thought it a successful likeness. 'Yes,' returned the president, hesitatingly; and then came a story of a western friend whose wife pronounced her husband's portrait, painted secretly for a birthday present, 'horridly like'; 'and that,' said he, 'seems to me a just criticism of this!' "[20]

OPPOSITE PAGE: *Abraham Lincoln, Sunday, August 9, 1863. From an original Imperial portrait.*

ABOVE: *Three views of Abraham Lincoln, Sunday, August 9, 1863. From original cartes de visite.*

BELOW AND LEFT: *Abraham Lincoln, Sunday, August 9, 1863. From copy prints.*

The carte de visite portraits of February were dignified poses, revealing a man at peace with himself. Journalist Noah Brooks declared: "Even when he was pensive or gloomy, his features were lighted up very much as a clouded alabaster vase may be softly illuminated by a light within." These portraits seem to remove the mask protecting Lincoln's intense emotions and bring to mind a description of Lincoln as "a man whose honesty and purpose is transparent."[21]

Truman H. Bartlett, a friend of Gardner's and author of *The Physiognomy of Abraham Lincoln*, presented a copy of Gardner's greatest portrait of Lincoln, an Imperial also taken on February 5, to historian Frederick Hill Meserve some time after Gardner's death. Bartlett relayed to Meserve the story told to him by Gardner: "In the developing process, this negative was broken in two, the fracture cutting through the top of Lincoln's head. By placing two pieces of glass together, Gardner successfully managed to make one print, and only one, before destroying the damaged negative." This likeness of the martyred president has been described as "the most valuable American photograph ever taken."[22]

One of the most commercially popular photographs ever taken of Lincoln was made a year earlier, on February 9, 1864, by Brady operative Anthony Berger and published over Brady's name. This touching portrait of Lincoln with his son Tad has been reproduced in most mediums—from the pages of *Harper's Weekly* to plagiarized copies turned out by other photographers. Gardner was undoubtedly aware of the positive publicity the photograph generated and consciously or subconsciously decided to imitate his old employer and competitor. An indication of the public adulation accorded the picture follows:

> No greater compliment can be paid an artist than so often paid to M. B. Brady, the first of photographists, by the illustrated periodicals of the day, transferring his productions to their volumes, thereby instructing and delighting millions of our happy and free people, and making the name of Brady a household word. What a world of significance is in the picture which will appear in our *Weekly Chronicle* of tomorrow, in which our martyred President is seen in the company of his son, examining an album. Both picture and album are the works of Brady. In fact, the studio of this artist, at 352 Pa. av., near 7th St., is overflowing with gem pictures, and an hour is well spent in viewing them.[23]

Gardner's opportunity to emulate the successful Brady pose came at the February 5 sitting, when he photographed a poignant study of the haggard president and his young son, one of only two sittings taken of them together.

After Lincoln's assassination on April 14, 1865, the lithographic firm of L. Prang & Co., in Boston, Massachusetts, commissioned Matthew Wilson to duplicate the portrait made for Gideon Welles based on Gardner's photographs. Within a short time, Prang had thus memorialized Gardner's final portrait of Lincoln.[24] By April 19, Gardner's publisher, Philp & Solomons, advertised for sale photographs "from life by Gardner—Mr. Lincoln's last sitting." By April 27 they advertised "Photographs of President Lincoln. The Last Picture He Sat For," with a breakdown of sizes and prices.

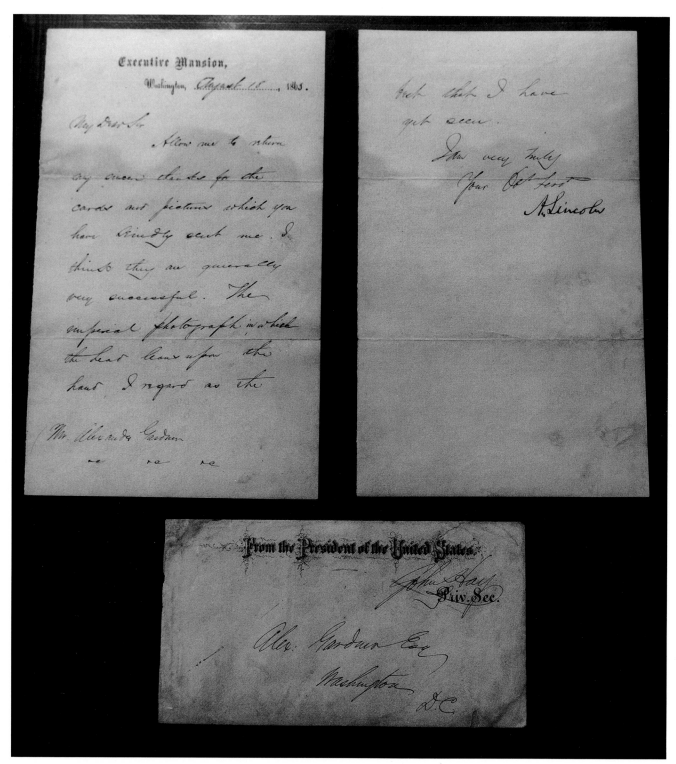

ABOVE: *Letter sent to Gardner by Abraham Lincoln shortly after the August 9 sitting.*

OPPOSITE PAGE
*Abraham Lincoln, Sunday,
August 9, 1863. From a
copy print.*

"Philp & Solomons have just published the following variety of Photographs [by Gardner]." It included "The late President and son Thaddeus."[25]

On May 17, Gardner copyrighted two of the five photographs from the February 5 sitting and captioned them "Abraham Lincoln, President U.S." This description was printed in the lower portion of the photographs he issued.

March 4, 1865

Saturday, March 4, 1865, was cold, rainy, and dreary. Poet Walt Whitman watched Lincoln proceed to the Capitol to give his Second Inaugural Address. "He was in his plain two-horse barouche, and look'd very much worn and tired; the lines . . . of vast responsibilities, intricate questions, and demands of life and death, cut deeper than ever upon his dark brown face; yet all the old goodness, tenderness, sadness, and canny shrewdness, underneath the furrows . . . By his side sat his little boy, of ten years."[26]

Gardner set his Imperial and stereoview cameras along the east front of the Capitol. Seated with Lincoln on the stand were Vice President–elect Andrew Johnson, Vice President Hannibal Hamlin, his cabinet, and members of the Supreme Court. Gardner's first three views show Lincoln seated prior to being introduced. Gardner then took four exposures, capturing Lincoln during his immortal speech: "With malice toward none; with charity for all, with firmness in the right, as God gives us to see the right, let us strive on to finish the work we are in; to bind up the nation's wounds; to care for him who shall have borne the battle, and for his widow, and his orphan— to do all which may achieve and cherish a just, and a lasting peace, among ourselves, and with all nations."[27] During his speech, a soldier described Lincoln's voice as "not very heavy or coarse, but singularly clear and penetrating, with almost a metallic ring."[28]

At least two other cameramen were present on this memorable morning. William Morris Smith, a contract photographer under Gardner, took at least one picture a few hundred yards from the Capitol, and Henry F. Warren, from Waltham, Massachusetts, took at least two photographs prior to the ceremonies, showing spectators off to the side of the Capitol building.

Some historians have suggested that Lincoln's assassin, John Wilkes Booth, and his band of conspirators were on hand at the ceremony and were captured in Gardner's photographs. This assertion has been determined to be in error. While it is clear that Booth did attend the ceremony, it is stretching the truth to allege that his image is identifiable in any of Gardner's photographs.[29]

Finally, on September 22, 1866, Gardner copyrighted "The Last Moments of Lincoln, 15th April, 1865," this being a copy of an original oil painting by E. Hutchinson Miller. The painting depicts Lincoln on his death bed, surrounded by the people present in his final hours. The various cabinet officers and other notables were copied from Gardner photographs.

Abraham Lincoln and his secretaries John Hay and John Nicolay, Sunday, November 8, 1863. From a copy photograph.

Abraham Lincoln, Sunday, November 8, 1863. From a copy print.

OPPOSITE PAGE: *Lincoln and son Tad. From an original Imperial print.*

ABRAHAM LINCOLN, Pres't U S.

Entered according to Act of Congress, by Alex. Gardner, in the year 1865, in the Clerk's Office of the District Court for the District of Columbia.

ABRAHAM LINCOLN, Pres't U S.

Entered according to Act of Congress, by Alex. Gardner, in the year 1865, in the Clerk's Office of the District Court for the District of Columbia.

OPPOSITE PAGE: *Abraham Lincoln, Sunday, February 5, 1865. From an original Imperial print.*

LEFT: *Abraham Lincoln, Sunday, February 5, 1865. Copied by Gardner from the original Imperial print and issued as a carte de visite. The crack in the plate has been masked and retouched. From an original carte de visite.*

Recently discovered photograph of the Capitol before Lincoln was escorted out for his inauguration.

Lincoln's second inauguration. From an original unpublished stereoview.

ABOVE, LEFT TO RIGHT:
An advertisement for his Lincoln photographs, placed by Gardner in the National Intelligencer,
April 19, 1865, and a memorial card issued by Gardner in memory of Lincoln. Memorial card
from an original unpublished carte de visite.

BELOW: *Members of the Supreme Court, 1866. From an original Imperial print.*

Secretary of the Treasury Hugh McCulloch, c. 1865. From an original unpublished carte de visite.

Secretary of the Interior John P. Usher. From an original unpublished carte de visite.

Speaker of the House Schuyler Colfax. From an original unpublished autographed carte de visite.

Vice President Hannibal Hamlin. From an original unpublished carte de visite.

Salmon P. Chase, Secretary of the Treasury, c. 1863. From an original unpublished carte de visite.

Alfred R. Waud, illustrator for Harper's Weekly. From an original unpublished carte de visite.

Ballerina Eliza Florence. From an
original carte de visite.

Unidentified couple photographed
in Gardner's Gallery.

Unidentified women. From an
original carte de visite.

Unidentified soldier. From an
original carte de visite.

Unidentified children. From
original cartes de visite.

Seth Kinman, California trapper
and hunter. From an original
unpublished carte de visite.

Alexander Stephens, Vice President of the Confederacy.
From an original unpublished Imperial print.

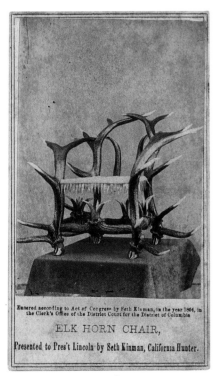

Elk-horn chair made by Seth
Kinman for President Lincoln.
From an original unpublished
carte de visite.

Congressman Benjamin Butler of Massachusetts, one of the Radical Republicans who pursued Andrew Johnson's impeachment. From an original unpublished carte de visite.

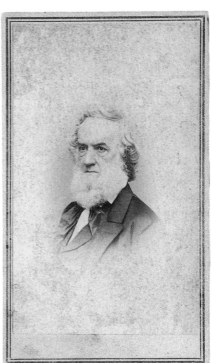

Secretary of the Navy Gideon Welles, September 1868. From an original unpublished carte de visite. The check Welles used to pay Gardner for the portrait appears below.

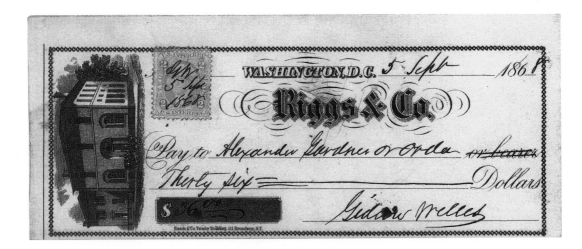

Unidentified man. From an original unpublished Imperial print.

OPPOSITE PAGE: *Three mayors of Washington, D.C.,
a portrait Gardner titled "Mayors of the Olden Time."
From an original unpublished Imperial print.*

5

THE
CONSPIRACY

*I*t has been said that the assassination of Lincoln is a tragedy "which has no parallel in the history of criminal audacity."[1] All of Alexander Gardner's experience was called upon to perform the tasks thrust upon him by this unprecedented assassination.

Abraham Lincoln was fatally attacked by the young zealot John Wilkes Booth during the final performance of *Our American Cousin* on Good Friday evening in 1865. As a military tribunal ultimately confirmed, this act, although carried out by a lone assassin, was the culmination of months of conspiratorial preparation, including a first plan that had called for kidnapping of the president. By holding Lincoln for ransom in Virginia, Booth's band of conspirators, numbering no more than ten, had hoped to win the release of thousands of Confederate soldiers being held in Northern prisons. That was the plan proposed by Booth and supported by the other conspirators. But, after a futile abduction attempt on March 17, 1865, the plot was dropped from consideration.[2] Infuriated and disillusioned, the would-be kidnappers disbanded and scattered in all directions. Booth's insane longing for immortality then led him to the act of murder.

Early that Good Friday morning, April 14, Booth learned that the president and Mrs. Lincoln would attend the theater in the evening accompanied by General and Mrs. Grant. Upon hearing the news, Booth set in motion his plan to kill the president. He summoned his companions, David E. Herold, Lewis Thornton Paine (or Payne, also known as Powell), and George Andrew Atzerodt, to give them their assignments and instructions. Herold was to lead Paine to the home of Secretary of State William H. Seward and later to meet Booth and assist in his escape into Virginia through lower Maryland. Paine's task was to murder Seward. Atzerodt was to kill Vice President Johnson.

At about 10 p.m., Paine appeared at the Seward residence on Lafayette Square. Pretending to have been sent by Seward's physician, Dr. T. S. Verdi, Paine entered the house under the guise of delivering medicine for the secretary. Seward had recently been injured in a carriage accident and was confined to his bed. When Seward's elder son, Frederick, refused to allow Paine access to his father's bedroom, Paine attempted to shoot him, but his pistol jammed. In desperation, Paine struck him over the head with the butt of his gun before savagely attacking the secretary himself, stabbing the old gentleman repeatedly. Seward's other son, Major Augustus Seward, was also stabbed in the arm and forehead. Sergeant George F. Robinson, a convalescing soldier from the 8th Maine Volunteers, who was on duty as a male nurse, wrestled with Paine

Secretary of State William H. Seward. From an original carte de visite.

John Wilkes Booth. This photograph was copied by Gardner for the Secret Service on Monday, April 17, 1865, and used on the government's "Wanted" poster. From an original carte de visite.

OPPOSITE PAGE:
June 17, 1865, Harper's Weekly cover illustration of Secretary of State Seward, based on Gardner's photograph.

HARPER'S WEEKLY.

A JOURNAL OF CIVILIZATION.

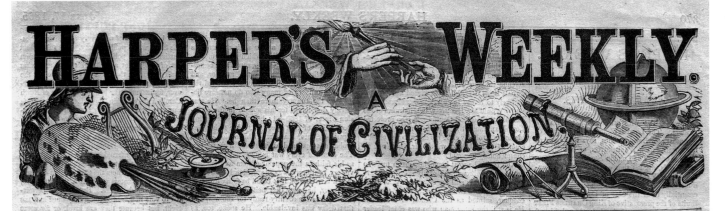

Vol. IX.—No. 442.]   NEW YORK, SATURDAY, JUNE 17, 1865.   [SINGLE COPIES TEN CENTS.
[$4,00 PER YEAR IN ADVANCE.

Entered according to Act of Congress, in the Year 1865, by Harper & Brothers, in the Clerk's Office of the District Court for the Southern District of New York.

HON. WILLIAM H. SEWARD, SECRETARY OF STATE.—[PHOTOGRAPHED BY A. GARDNER, AND PUBLISHED BY PHILP & SOLOMONS, WASHINGTON.]

and is credited with saving Secretary Seward's life. As Paine raced down the stairs toward the front door to make good his escape, he shouted, "I am mad! I am mad!" During the attack, Herold fled from his post in front of the Seward residence, leaving Paine to fend for himself. Fortunately, all the victims survived Paine's attack.

At 10:18 P.M., Booth entered the unprotected box at Ford's Theater, placed his derringer at the back of Lincoln's head, and fired one bullet. In his attempt to escape, Booth stabbed Major Henry R. Rathbone, a guest of the Lincolns', cutting his arm to the bone. As Booth jumped from the president's box onto the stage, the spur on his boot caught on the Treasury flag draped over the railing. Landing off-balance on his left leg, he shattered the bone above the ankle. Ever the instinctive actor with a flair for the dramatic, Booth stood up to the audience and bellowed, *"Sic semper tyrannis"*— "Thus shall it be for tyrants." Brandishing his knife, he hobbled through the rear exit of the theater into an alley and mounted his waiting horse. Edward (Edman) Spangler, a theater scene shifter, had been instructed by Booth to hold the reins of his horse, but Spangler had passed the assignment on to a not-so-bright associate, Joseph Burroughs, a young man nicknamed "Peanuts John."[3] Racing through the darkened city, Booth crossed the Navy Yard Bridge at the Anacostia River and soon was in lower Maryland. Shortly thereafter, Herold also crossed the bridge and caught up with Booth.

George Atzerodt failed in his assignment to assassinate Vice President Johnson. Atzerodt became quite drunk, lost his nerve, and made no attempt to harm Johnson, who was staying at the Kirkwood House, a Washington hotel.

April 15, 1865

The mortally injured Lincoln was carried across the street, opposite the theater, to the home of William Petersen. At 7:22 A.M., on Saturday, April 15, the president died of his wound. Secretary of War Edwin M. Stanton exclaimed at the moment of death, "Now he belongs to the ages."

The ever-efficient and effective Stanton appointed himself to take charge of the confused situation in Washington and immediately began a one-man investigation to apprehend the guilty party or parties. Secretary of the Navy Gideon Welles, another efficient cabinet member, had the U.S.S. *Saugus*, an ironclad monitor anchored in the Anacostia River, manned with a detachment of marines to hold and guard anyone captured as a suspect in the crime.[4]

Immediately after the assassination, detectives from the Provost Marshal General's Office searched Booth's room at the National Hotel. Among the items they found was a photograph of Booth.[5]

On that Saturday morning, Louis J. Weichmann, a boarder in the home of Mary E. Surratt at 541 H Street and a college friend of her son John, was arrested by

OPPOSITE PAGE: *Secretary of War Edwin M. Stanton. At the moment of Lincoln's death, Stanton exclaimed, "Now he belongs to the ages." Stanton took charge of the investigation of the assassination. From an original Imperial photograph.*

The monitor U.S.S. Saugus, which was stationed outside Washington and housed the captured conspirators. From an original photograph.

John Harrison Surratt, Jr., a suspect in the assassination. This photograph was copied on April 17, 1865, by Gardner for the "Wanted" poster. From an original carte de visite.

detectives from the city police force. Caught in a dragnet that brought in anyone remotely suspected in the conspiracy, Weichmann was able to persuade the superintendent of the metropolitan police, Almarin C. Richards, that he was innocent of any crime. Weichmann suggested to Richards that he be allowed to accompany detectives in their search for John Harrison Surratt, Jr., a suspect in the attack on Seward. Richards instructed his detective, Officer James McDevitt, to allow Weichmann to assist in the manhunt. Weichmann took Officer McDevitt to his boarding house, the home of Mrs. Surratt, to procure a photograph of her son from a family album. There was no cause at this time for the police to suspect Mrs. Surratt of any complicity in the crime. From the Surratt house, Weichmann and the detective proceeded to the residence of another suspect David E. Herold, where his mother gave them access to her photograph album. After leafing through the album, Weichmann pointed out a picture he claimed was "a good photograph of the young man." Both the photographs of John Surratt and David Herold were entrusted to Officer McDevitt, who immediately turned them over to the Federal authorities.[6]

On December 27, 1865, Weichmann filed his claim for part of the reward money offered to those who assisted in capturing either Booth, Surratt, or Herold. "He [Louis J. Weichmann] deposes furthermore that on the evening of the 15th of April, he did proceed with James McDevitt to the residence of David E. Herold and that photographs of John Wilkes Booth, John H. Surratt, and David E. Herold procured through his, the said Louis J. Weichmann's exertions . . . were given by James McDevitt to Major General C. C. Augur," the military commander of Washington, D.C. During the subsequent trial of the conspirators, Weichmann testified that on April 15 one of the detectives, "Mr. Holohan, who was in our company, went and procured a photograph of Surratt."[7] In any case, photographs of the three alleged conspirators were secured and in the possession of the United States Government twenty-four hours after Lincoln's death.

Documenting the Tragedy

Shortly after the assassination, Alexander Gardner took it upon himself to document some of the locations that played a key role in the events that were so quickly unfolding. Almost immediately, he photographed the exterior of Ford's Theater, showing the swags of black mourning muslin decorating the facade. Entering the building, he photographed the interior of the theater, including the box where Lincoln was murdered. The detailed photographs even show the tear in the flag caused by the spur of the assassin's boot when he jumped from the box. Gardner then photographed the stables of John C. Howard, where Booth had kept his horse. He also went to the telegraph office from which the world was first informed of Lincoln's death. Finally, Gardner traveled to the site of Booth's escape across the Navy Yard Bridge and photographed it.

Ford's Theater shortly after the assassination. Copied from an original photograph.

OPPOSITE PAGE: *The President's box inside Ford's Theater. Booth caught his spur in the draped flag on the right as he leaped to the stage. From an original direct-contact albumen print.*

Colonel Lafayette C. Baker, chief of the Secret Service, having been summoned from New York City, took charge of the investigation on Sunday, April 16.

> I could learn but little more than that John Wilkes Booth was the supposed assassin and Harrold [sic] was his accomplice. I asked if any photographs of the supposed assassins, or descriptions of their persons, had been secured or published. To my surprise, I learned that nothing of the kind had been done; during the afternoon of Sunday, rumors were freely circulated throughout the city, connecting the name of John Surratt with the other assassins. I immediately secured pictures of those mentioned above, and on Monday the 17th, had them copied with a full and accurate description of each assassin printed in a circular, in which I offered a reward of Ten Thousand Dollars. . . . These photographs and descriptions were the first ever published or circulated.[8]

Because Gardner had already demonstrated his value to the Secret Service, it was only natural for Baker to approach him and request his services in duplicating the portraits of John Surratt, Booth, and Herold.

On April 22, Brevet Brigadier General Charles H. Crane, assistant surgeon general, wrote to Lt. Colonel Thomas A. McParlin, head of the Medical Department, Army of the Potomac. In that letter Crane describes a "cast of gloom" over the city of Washington following Lincoln's assassination. He enclosed a photograph of Booth: "I enclose a photograph of J. Wilkes Booth, the alleged assassin, . . . we had a number struck off at our 'gallery.' "[9] Additional evidence of Gardner's work is the fact that two of the three photographs featured on the original April 20 "Wanted" poster—those of Booth and Surratt—are on original Gardner Gallery card mounts. Thus, at Colonel Baker's order, on Monday, April 17, Gardner had produced copies of original photographs of the suspects involved in the assassination.

In his much-heralded book on the Lincoln assassination, *The Web of Conspiracy,* Theodore Roscoe makes an attempt to discredit the accuracy of Baker's description of the suspects and of the photographs used on the wanted poster, suggesting the poster was little more than "hollow sham." He bases his case on the premise that the photograph of John Surratt was suspect, and that Baker's descriptions of the suspects were vague and misleading. Roscoe is wrong on both points. First, the photograph used on the wanted circular originally issued on April 20 is in fact a documented portrait of John H. Surratt, Jr.[10] Second, Roscoe leads one to believe that the descriptions in the wanted circular were "deliberately contrived." This assertion is absolutely false. The descriptions on the wanted posters match the information in the official records issued by Secretary of War Stanton on April 20 except for two minor details: (1) a suggestion that Booth might have shaved off his mustache; (2) the name of Herold is spelled incorrectly as "Harold."[11] Colonel Baker made no attempt to mislead anyone relevant to these issues. His source of information for the wanted circular was correspondence included in the official records.

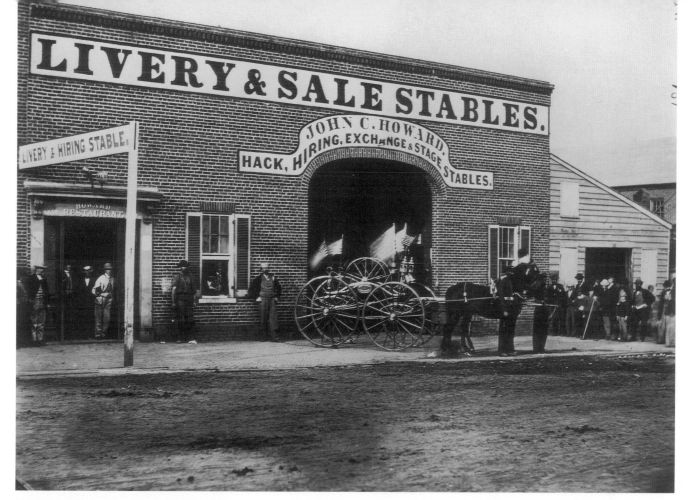

Howard's Livery Stable, where Booth kept his getaway horse prior to the assassination. Copied from an original photograph.

Telegraph office in Washington where word of Lincoln's assassination was dispatched. From an original unpublished carte de visite.

TELEGRAPH OFFICE WHERE THEY FLASHED THE NEWS OF LINCOLN'S DEATH, APRIL 15, 1865.

Navy Yard Bridge, which Booth crossed into Maryland. Copied from an original photograph.

OPPOSITE PAGE:
*"Wanted" poster, issued by
Colonel Lafayette C. Baker on
April 20, 1865, using
photographs copied
by Gardner. From an
original poster.*

| SURRAT. | BOOTH. | HAROLD. |

War Department, Washington, April 20, 1865,

 # $100,000 REWARD!

THE MURDERER

Of our late beloved President, Abraham Lincoln,

IS STILL AT LARGE.

$50,000 REWARD

Will be paid by this Department for his apprehension, in addition to any reward offered by Municipal Authorities or State Executives.

$25,000 REWARD

Will be paid for the apprehension of JOHN H. SURRATT, one of Booth's Accomplices.

$25,000 REWARD

Will be paid for the apprehension of David C. Harold, another of Booth's accomplices.

LIBERAL REWARDS will be paid for any information that shall conduce to the arrest of either of the above-named criminals, or their accomplices.

All persons harboring or secreting the said persons, or either of them, or aiding or assisting their concealment or escape, will be treated as accomplices in the murder of the President and the attempted assassination of the Secretary of State, and shall be subject to trial before a Military Commission and the punishment of DEATH.

Let the stain of innocent blood be removed from the land by the arrest and punishment of the murderers.

All good citizens are exhorted to aid public justice on this occasion. Every man should consider his own conscience charged with this solemn duty, and rest neither night nor day until it be accomplished.

EDWIN M. STANTON, Secretary of War.

DESCRIPTIONS.—BOOTH is Five Feet 7 or 8 inches high, slender build, high forehead, black hair, black eyes, and wears a heavy black moustache.

JOHN H. SURRAT is about 5 feet, 9 inches. Hair rather thin and dark; eyes rather light; no beard. Would weigh 145 or 150 pounds. Complexion rather pale and clear, with color in his cheeks. Wore light clothes of fine quality. Shoulders square; cheek bones rather prominent; chin narrow; ears projecting at the top; forehead rather low and square, but broad. Parts his hair on the right side; neck rather long. His lips are firmly set. A slim man.

DAVID C. HAROLD is five feet six inches high, hair dark, eyes dark, eyebrows rather heavy, full face, nose short, hand short and fleshy, feet small, instep high, round bodied, naturally quick and active, slightly closes his eyes when looking at a person.

NOTICE.—In addition to the above, State and other authorities have offered rewards amounting to almost one hundred thousand dollars, making an aggregate of about TWO HUNDRED THOUSAND DOLLARS.

The Conspirators

On Monday, April 17, 1865, Edward Spangler, who'd been assigned to hold Booth's horse behind Ford's Theater, was arrested by Colonel H. S. Olcott and placed in Old Capitol Prison. The first of the captured conspirators was booked as an accomplice.[12] Samuel Arnold, a boyhood friend of Booth's was arrested in Fortress Monroe, Virginia, by officers Voltaire Randall and Eaton G. Horner. Another boyhood friend of Booth's, Michael O'Laughlin, was arrested at the home of a family friend in Baltimore.[13] Evidence was mounting against Mary Surratt to indicate that she had assisted in the plot to assassinate Lincoln. Her son was identified as a member of the conspiracy, and testimony provided by Louis J. Weichmann indicated that Booth had met with the others at her home. At 11 P.M. on April 17, General Christopher C. Augur ordered Colonel Olcott to raid her home and obtain whatever evidence could be found. At 11:20 P.M., Lewis Paine entered the home of Mrs. Surratt. Holding a pickaxe, Paine claimed to be a day laborer employed by Mrs. Surratt to dig a gutter the next morning. Mrs. Surratt denied ever having seen or known him. (This statement proved extremely damaging to her credibility during her trial.)

Everyone taken into custody was delivered to the headquarters of General Augur. Shortly thereafter Paine was positively identified as Seward's assailant by the secretary's houseboy, William Bell. The next day, April 18, Paine was taken to the monitor U.S.S. *Saugus* and placed in double shackles.[14]

George Atzerodt was arrested at the residence of his cousin, Hartman Richter, in the early morning of April 20. Richter was also arrested for attempting to protect his cousin from the inquiring detectives. Both men were confined and chained on the *Saugus*.[15]

Booth and Herold were still at large. On the morning of April 15, they traveled to Mrs. Surratt's tavern in Surrattsville (Mrs. Surratt's late husband had been postmaster of the town, which he named) and picked up a package she had left them. (This fact, coupled with her lie about not knowing Paine, sealed her fate and led to her execution.) In the package were a carbine, binoculars, cartridges, and some whiskey. From there they made their way to the residence of Dr. Samuel A. Mudd, arriving at around 4 A.M. Dr. Mudd treated Booth's broken leg and allowed him to rest in his guest room until 4 o'clock the next afternoon. The pair then traveled deep into lower Maryland, finally crossing the Rappahannock River into Virginia on April 24.

The Assassin

Early in the morning of April 26, a detachment from the 16th New York Cavalry, commanded by Lt. Edward P. Doherty, surrounded Booth and Herold in a barn belonging to Richard Garrett, near Port Royal, Virginia. Accompanying the cavalrymen were two detectives, Luther B. Baker, a cousin of Colonel Lafayette C. Baker, and Everton J. Conger. The soldiers encircled the barn, demanding the surrender of the

Old Capitol Prison, which temporarily housed some of the suspects in the conspiracy and assassination of Lincoln. From an original photograph.

two fugitives. After some time Herold surrendered, but Booth refused. Conger finally set fire to the barn. At 3:15 A.M., Booth was shot once in the neck by Sergeant Boston Corbett, a member of the 16th New York Cavalry. He was immediately removed from the barn and placed on the porch of the Garrett house, where he died three hours later. His final words, spoken while staring at his hands, were "Useless, useless."[16]

As the assassin lay dying, Everton Conger took charge of Booth's personal effects and quickly set off on horseback for Washington.[17] Booth's body was sewn into an old army blanket. At 8:30 A.M. the body was placed on a wagon and the return trip to Washington began. The procession crossed the Rappahannock River into Port Conway and went from there to Belle Plain on the Potomac River. Some time after 6 P.M., Booth's body, along with the prisoner Herold, was placed on board the steamer *John S. Ide.*[18]

COL. L. C. BAKER PLANNING THE CAPTURE OF BOOTH.

LT. L. B. BAKER.   COL. L. C. BAKER.   LT. COL. E. J. CONGOR.

" There, you may rest assured, you will find him within five miles of Port Con-
w. . . you will have a detail of cavalry, who will be strictly subordinate to your
order. There must be no shooting, the villian must be captured alive at every
hazard."—*Col. Baker's instructions to his Assistants.*
Booth was found within three miles of the place designated.

Published by Philp & Solomons, Washington, D. C.

War Department
Washington City,
April 27th 1865.
10 o'clock A.M.

To the Commandant
of the Washington Navy Yard.

You will permit Surgeon
General Barnes and his assistant, accompanied
by Judge Advocate Gen. Holt, Hon. John A. Bing-
ham, Special Judge Advocate, *Major Eckert,* Wm. G. Moore, clerk
of War Department, Col. L. C. Baker, Lieut. Baker,
Lieut. Col. Conger, *Chas Dawson* J. L. Smith, Gardner (photographer) & assistant
board the Montauk, and see the body of John
Wilkes Booth

Immediately after the Surgeon
General has made his autopsy, you will have the body placed in a
strong box, and deliver it to the charge of Col. Baker—the box being carefully sealed.

Gideon Welles
Secy Navy
Edwin M Stanton
Sec of War

Rec'd Apr. 27

Mr. Gideon Wells. Sec. of Navy.

ABOVE: *Secretary of the Navy
Gideon Welles, 1865. From an
original unpublished carte
de visite.*

LEFT: *Order issued jointly by
Secretary of the Navy Gideon
Welles and Secretary of War Edwin
M. Stanton, allowing the autopsy
of Booth. One of the few civilians
allowed to attend was Alexander
Gardner, who was instructed to
take one photograph of the event.
Previously unpublished document.*

OPPOSITE PAGE: *Colonel
Lafayette C. Baker, chief of the
Secret Service; Lieutenant
Luther B. Baker; and Lt. Colonel
Everton J. Conger, planning the
capture of Booth. From an
original photograph.*

Conger had also arrived in Washington by steamer, at about 5 P.M., and reported directly to Colonel Baker at his headquarters. Baker and Conger immediately went to the home of Secretary Stanton, where they turned over Booth's personal effects, including his diary, to Stanton. Baker was directed to requisition a tugboat and proceed to Alexandria, Virginia. He was to transfer the assassin's corpse from the *Ide* to the tug. From there, Baker was to deliver it on board the monitor, U.S.S. *Montauk*, docked adjacent to the *Saugus*. At 10:40 P.M., Booth's corpse and Herold were transferred to the tug. At 1:45 A.M. on April 27 aboard the *Montauk:* "A tug came alongside, on board of which was Colonel Baker, the detective, with a dead body, said to be that of J. Wilkes Booth. . . . Said body was placed on board for safekeeping. Herold was put in double irons and placed in the hold of the vessel. The body of Booth was taken out of the blanket and placed on deck in charge of a guard." Shortly after the arrival of the corpse in Washington, Commodore J. S. Montgomery, commandant of the Washington Navy Yard, sent a message to Secretary of the Navy Gideon Welles: "David E. Herold, prisoner, and the remains of Wilkes Booth were delivered here at 1:45 this morning. The body of Booth is changing rapidly. What disposition shall be made of it? It is now on board the iron-clad *Montauk*."[19]

Booth's Autopsy and the Missing Photograph

An autopsy was performed on the corpse of the assassin. Gideon Welles directed that the following persons present themselves for this autopsy: Surgeon General Barnes and his assistant; Judge Advocate General Holt; Honorable John A. Bingham; Major Eckert; William G. Moore, clerk of the War Department; Colonel Lafayette C. Baker; Lieutenant Luther B. Baker; Lt. Colonel Everton Conger; Charles L. Dawson; J. L. Smith; and Alexander Gardner, photographer, and his assistant (Timothy H. O'Sullivan). Welles further directed that "Immediately after the Surgeon-General has made his autopsy, you will have the body placed in a strong box and deliver it to the charge of Colonel Baker, the box being carefully sealed."[20]

Also present at the autopsy were Dr. J. F. May, a Washington physician who had once removed a tumor from the back of Booth's neck, and Dr. Merrill, Booth's dentist. All present made a positive identification of the body.[21] Dr. May readily found the scar. Charles L. Dawson, a clerk at the National Hotel, who had been acquainted with Booth for many years, was able to identify the body from a small tattoo, "J. W. B.," at the juncture of the thumb and forefinger.[22]

On April 28, the *New York Tribune* published this report under the credit "Associated Press Dispatch":

> Yesterday, a photographic view of the body was taken before it was removed from the Monitor.

For many years historians have speculated about the existence of this photograph, which has never been publicly displayed. Historian Theodore Roscoe speculates

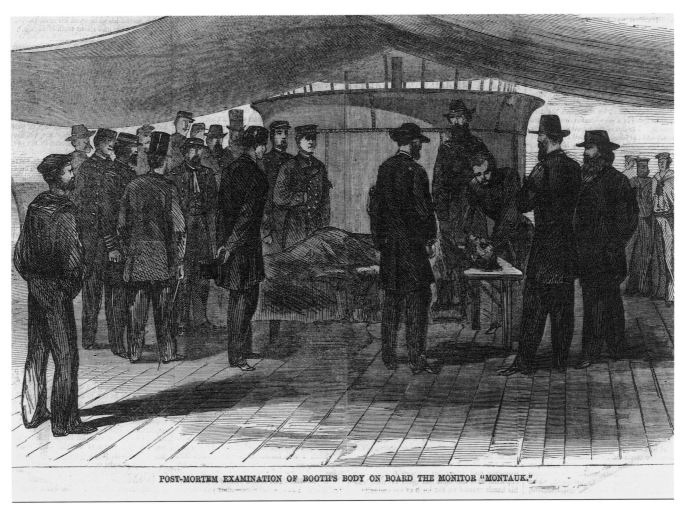

POST-MORTEM EXAMINATION OF BOOTH'S BODY ON BOARD THE MONITOR "MONTAUK."

May 13, 1865, Harper's Weekly *illustration based on the lost Booth postmortem photograph. Alexander Gardner is standing to the extreme right.*

that the negative may "lie undeveloped in the muds at the bottom of the Potomac."[23] On May 13 *Harper's Weekly* illustrated an engraving possibly based on this missing photograph. However, a recently discovered and hitherto unpublished letter might very well solve this century-old mystery.

On August 5, 1896, historian Osborn H. Oldroyd, who was interested in locating the Booth photograph, interviewed James A. Wardell, a resident of Alexandria, Virginia. According to Oldroyd, Wardell was a government detective with the War Department from 1862 through 1869. Later he became a policeman in Virginia. Oldroyd was convinced that the following statement by Wardell was accurate:

> When I came on duty at 6:00 o'clock on the morning of April 27, 1865, at the National Detective Bureau, I reported to the adjutant for any instructions which might be there for me. I was at that time unassigned, having spent day and night since the assassination of the president in the saddle until the previous evening at 7:00 when I returned from southern Maryland. I was told to get some rest and report in at the next morning.

The adjutant told me that there were instructions for me to remain at headquarters until patrolman Camp had returned. He had been sent to get the photographer Gardner so that pictures might be taken of Booth's body when it arrived. Patrolman Camp came in in a few minutes and with him was a man with a darky. I was told that the man was Gardner, the photographer who I did not know. I was then instructed to go with him to the Navy Yard and to stay with him and to get further instructions at the yard. Under no circumstances was I to allow him or his assistant out of my sight until they had taken a picture and made the print, and then I was to bring the print and the glass back to the War Department and give it only to Col. Baker or Secretary of War Stanton. I went with Gardiner [sic] and the darky and saw that they had a wagon with them and on the seat was another man [O'Sullivan]. I climbed up onto the seat and the darky hung on the side and we went to the Navy Yard. When we got there there was no pass for us and we had to wait at the gate for someone to come and get us in. The marine would not let us in even after I showed my badge.

At about 10:30 a carriage rolled up and I saw Col. Baker lean out and talk to the guard. I approached the Col. and told him that I had the photographer with me. He then said to follow his coach and we did. We drove to the pier and then got out. We went aboard the boat and the darky and the assistant carried the camera and the chest of apparatuses. We went forward and were told to wait until General Barnes arrived. He came in a few minutes from back toward the back of the boat. He had a man with him and the man said to Gardner that he could set his camera up and take a picture. He was told that only one plate was to be made and it was to have only one print made and both were to be given to me when finished. I was told that the plate and print was to be brought to the War Department and given to either Col. Baker or Secretary Stanton. Col. Baker was present when this conversation went on.

Gardner took the plate and then gave it to the assistant and told him to take it and develop it and to make one print. I went with him and even went into the dark room. About 4:00 in the afternoon I got the plate and the print from the assistant and took it to the War Department. I went in to the outer office and Col. Baker was just coming out of the War Office. I gave him the plate and print and he stepped to one side and pulled it from the envelope. He looked at it and then dismissed me.

When I appeared before the commission I told them about this but they seemed to doubt me. They had seen no picture and the Secretary of War denied that one had been taken but I know that it had been. It looked just like the pictures of Booth that had been attached to the posters except that the hair was longer on the sides, the moustache was shaggy and dirty and there was a growth on his chin.

I did not actually go forward to see the body but I did look at the picture after I left Gardner's studio and I think it was Booth.

I hope that you are able to find the plate but I doubt that you will. The War Department was very determined to make sure that Booth was not made a hero and some rebel would give a good price for one of those pictures or the plate. If I can tell you anything else or help in any way just let me know.

Your Obedient Servant
I am
James A. Wardell[24]

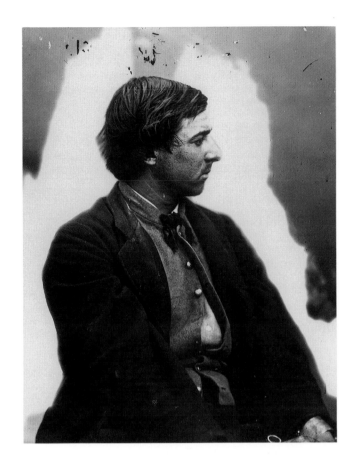

Conspirator David E. Herold. Taken on the monitor U.S.S. Montauk, *April 27, 1865. From the original collodion negatives.*

It is extremely doubtful that the original plate or print will ever turn up. The suppressed photograph was taken only for the benefit of the Secret Service, who undoubtedly destroyed it to keep it from falling into the hands of those who might have wanted Booth to be revered as a martyr.

Mug Shots on the *Montauk* and the *Saugus*

After the Booth autopsy Gardner's associate, O'Sullivan, returned to the gallery along with Wardell. Gardner was now free to take photographs of the other conspirators, an obvious concession made to Gardner by Colonel Baker and the Secret Service. David Herold, who was captured the night before, was brought up to the deck of the *Montauk*. With the canvas awning as a backdrop, Gardner took three photographs of Herold, who still appeared to be in shock from his recent capture.

A Portuguese sea captain, Joao M. Celestino, was one of the many persons dragged into this "web of conspiracy." Celestino was also brought out on the deck, where three portraits were taken of him. It seems that he had made the unfortunate mistake of independently threatening the life of William H. Seward. Because of his passing remark, he was arrested in Philadelphia on April 18. Celestino was transferred from Old Capitol Prison to the hull of the monitor on April 25. The charges against him of complicity in the assassination were dropped on June 17, but he was held until July 8.[25] Interestingly enough, of all the conspirators photographed by Gardner, only three were not handcuffed: Paine, Celestino, and Samuel Arnold.

Like almost everyone, Gardner was apparently fascinated with Lewis Paine. Not only did Gardner take at least ten photographs of him on possibly two occasions, but he also took the trouble of copyrighting six of these ten on May 17, 1865. Of all the photographs of the conspirators and their execution, these were the only ones he copyrighted. On the *Montauk* Gardner took at least six views of Paine in front of the canvas awning. When Paine was first brought out, he was wearing his hat and was handcuffed. The cuffs were removed, and five photographs were taken with a guard standing next to him.

The exact dates of the other photographs of the conspirators are uncertain. They were probably taken on board the monitor U.S.S. *Saugus* the same day, April 27. All the conspirators were seated in identical locations behind the turret of the monitor. There are four photographs of Paine and two each of George Atzerodt, Edward Spangler, Michael O'Laughlin, Samuel Arnold, and Hartman Richter, Atzerodt's cousin. The photographs are of interest because they are perhaps the earliest known of a criminal lineup. Of further significance is the fact that when one of the conspirators wore a hat, at least one was also taken with the hat off. Gardner also set a precedent by taking one frontal photograph of each conspirator and another in profile, which eventually became standard law-enforcement practice. This series also seems to foreshadow the "rogues' gallery," which Gardner established in 1873 for the Washington, D.C., Metropolitan Police Department.[26]

Portuguese sea captain and suspect Joao
M. Celestino, photographed on the Montauk,
April 27, 1865. From the original collodion
negatives.

PAYNE, *alias* **WOOD,** *alias* **HALL,**
Arrested as one of the Associates of Booth in the Conspiracy.

Entered according to Act of Congress, by Alex. Gardner, in the year 1865, in the Clerk's Office of the District Court for the District of Columbia

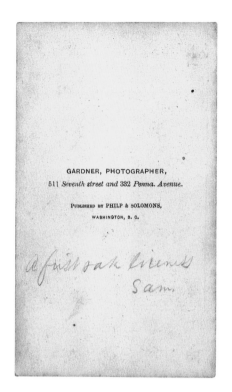

GARDNER, PHOTOGRAPHER,
511 *Seventh street and 332 Penna. Avenue.*

PUBLISHED BY PHILP & SOLOMONS,
WASHINGTON, D. C.

A first rate likeness
Sam.

PAYNE, *alias* **WOOD,** *alias* **HALL,**
Arrested as an Associate of Booth in the Conspiracy.

Entered according to Act of Congress, by Alex. Gardner, in the year 1865, in the Clerk's Office of the District Court for the District of Columbia

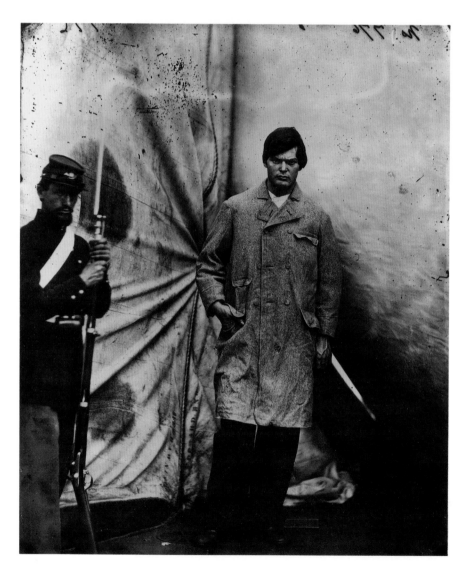

OPPOSITE PAGE AND ABOVE: *Lewis Paine,*
another conspirator, on the Montauk, *April 27, 1865.*
A note on the back of the second Paine portrait, in the
hand of fellow conspirator Samuel Arnold, reads,
"A first-rate likeness." From the original cartes de
visite (opposite page, top row) and the original
collodion negatives.

Paine on the Saugus, *April 27, 1865. From the original collodion negatives.*

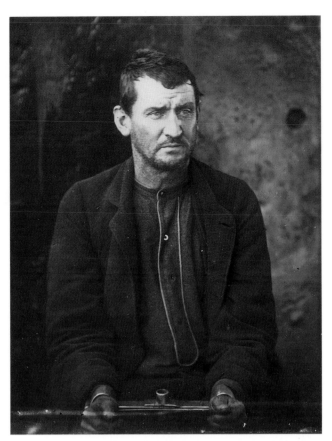

Edman Spangler, another suspect, on the Saugus, *April 27, 1865. From the original collodion negatives.*

GEORGE A. ATZERODT.

Entered according to Act of Congress, in the year 1865, by A. Gardner, in the Clerk's Office of the District Court for the District of Columbia.

George Atzerodt, also a conspirator, on the Saugus, *April 27, 1865. Left, from an original carte de visite. Right, from the original collodion negative.*

Conspirator Michael O'Laughlin on the Saugus, *April 27, 1865. From the original collodion negatives.*

Samuel Arnold, another conspirator, on the Saugus, *April 27, 1865. From the original collodion negatives.*

Suspect Hartman Richter on board the Saugus, *April 27, 1865. From the original collodion negatives.*

Suppressing Photographs of Booth

On May 2, 1865, General Lew Wallace issued his General Order no. 95 from his Headquarters, Middle Department, VIII Corps, Baltimore, Maryland:

> The sale of portraits of any rebel officer or soldier, or of J. Wilkes Booth, the murderer of President Lincoln, is forbidden hereafter in this department. All commanding officers and provost-marshals are hereby ordered to take possession of such pictures wherever found exposed for sale, and report the names of the parties so offending, who will be liable to arrest and imprisonment if again guilty of a violation of this order.
>   By Command of Major General Wallace:
>
>   Samuel B. Lawrence,
>   Assistant Adjutant-General

On May 27, this order banning the sale of photographs of Booth was rescinded by Assistant Adjutant-General E. D. Townsend.

Why would the government of the United States attempt to forbid the sale of photographs of John Wilkes Booth? Theodore Roscoe maintains that the reason was that the corpse returned to the *Montauk* did not resemble Booth. He suggests that the photograph was therefore suppressed "until such time, at least, as those who viewed the remains on the monitor forgot the grisly features of the corpse."[27] This assumption is also false. What Roscoe seems to overlook is the fact that the initial order forbidding the sale of photographs of Booth was not issued on April 27, the day of the autopsy, but on May 2, five days *after* the autopsy was performed. James Wardell's contention in his testimony is much more plausible: The government authorities were concerned about Booth's being made into a martyr. The last thing they wanted was for him to become a heroic symbol to Lincoln's foes.

C H A P T E R

6

SIC SEMPER SICARIIS

''T H U S   I T   I S   F O R   A S S A S S I N S''

On May 1, 1865, President Andrew Johnson was informed by Attorney General James Speed that inasmuch as Lincoln and Seward were officers of the Federal Government, all persons accused of the assassination of President Lincoln were triable by military commission, rather than in a civil court. Such an arrangement would allow Secretary of War Stanton to retain jurisdiction in the case. Johnson ordered a commission. The opinion was bitterly contested, with the defense claiming that since the alleged acts occurred in the city of Washington, D.C., the case belonged in the local courts. At the time the Supreme Court was considering a similar jurisdictional dispute. Although it ultimately ruled that a military commission could not legally hear a case against a private citizen when the civil courts were functioning, the ruling did not come soon enough. A military commission tried the Lincoln assassination case.

According to the presidential order of May 1, the assistant adjutant-general was to detail nine officers to serve on the commission. The judge advocate general was ordered to prefer charges against the accused and was allowed to obtain an assistant and special judge advocate. The following officers were chosen to serve on the commission: Major General David O. Hunter, Major General Lew Wallace, Brevet Major General August V. Kautz, Brigadier General Albion P. Howe, Brigadier General Robert S. Foster, Brevet Brigadier General James H. Ekin, Brigadier General Thomas M. Harris, Colonel Charles H. Tompkins, Lieutenant Colonel David R. Clendenin, Brigadier General Joseph Holt, judge advocate and recorder. Ohio Congressman John A. Bingham and General Henry L. Burnett were selected as special judge advocates. General John F. Hartranft was appointed marshal of the court and had immediate responsibility over the prisoners.

The reporters for the court were Benn Pitman, R. Sutton, D. F. Murphy, R. R. Hitt, J. J. Murphy, and Edward V. Murphy. The charges leveled against the accused were for being "maliciously, unlawfully and traitorously in aid of the existing rebellion . . . combining, confederating, and conspiring to kill and murder Abraham Lincoln, the late president; Andrew Johnson, vice-president; William H. Seward, secretary of state; Ulysses S. Grant, commander of the army of the United States." Dr. Samuel A. Mudd was represented by Frederick Stone and General Thomas Ewing. Mary Surratt was represented by Reverdy Johnson, Frederick Aiken, and John Clampitt. Lewis Paine and George A. Atzerodt were counseled by William E. Doster. David E. Herold was represented by Frederick Stone. Samuel Arnold, Michael O'Laughlin, and Edward Spangler were defended by General Ewing and Walter Cox.[1]

President Andrew Johnson. From an original unpublished carte de visite.

ANDREW JOHNSON, Pres't U. S.

Entered according to Act of Congress, by Alex Gardner, in the year 1865, in the Clerk's Office of the District Court for the District of Columbia

The military commission that tried and convicted the Lincoln conspirators. From left: Lt. Colonel David R. Clendenin, Colonel Charles H. Tomkins, Brigadier General Thomas M. Harris, Brigadier General Albion P. Howe, Major General Lew Wallace, Brigadier General James A. Eakin, Major General David Hunter, Major General August V. Kautz, Brigadier General Robert S. Foster, Congressman John A. Bingham of Ohio, General Henry L. Burnett, and Brigadier General Joseph Holt. From an original photograph.

The trial opened on May 10. By May 23 the prosecution had presented 131 witnesses. The defense called 128 witnesses between then and June 29, when final deliberations began. On July 5 the commission reached its verdict, which was approved by the president. Mary Surratt, Lewis Paine, David Herold, and George Atzerodt were sentenced to be executed "by proper military authority under the direction of the secretary of war on 7th of July between 10 o'clock A.M. and 2 o'clock P.M. of that day." Dr. Samuel Mudd, Samuel Arnold, Michael O'Laughlin, and Edward Spangler were each sentenced to prison at the Federal penitentiary in Albany, New York.[2]

The Execution

On July 5 General Hartranft informed the "executioner," Captain Christian Rath, of the court's findings and instructed him to prepare the scaffold for the execution in the courtyard of Old Arsenal Prison. Rath earlier in his career, while provost marshal and ordnance officer on the staff of General Orlando B. Wilcox, had been required to construct a gallows. He "borrowed" the plans for that gallows from the sheriff of Level Plains, Virginia, and used them to design the new one. Construction began immediately.[3]

Once the orders were signed, passes were issued to those authorized to attend the execution. On July 5 Gardner was issued his pass, signed by General Hunter, president of the commission. Though he had little more than a day to prepare for the event, Gardner understood the importance of his participation. He was the *only* photographer permitted to document the proceeding. He knew that what he was about to undertake was unprecedented. This historically important commission was the sum of his ten years of work, his photographic experience, and his accomplishments in the war. He would be fully prepared for the day's events, which would enable him to further expand the horizons of the new art of photojournalism.

Christian Rath was obsessed with the quality of rope to be used for the hanging. "I was determined to get rope that would not break, for you know when a rope breaks at a hanging there is a time-worn maxim that the person intended to be hanged was innocent." Rath located some three-quarter-inch, 32-strand Boston hemp for the job. He tested the ropes with bags containing "300 pounds of artillery shells, to be sure they would not break."

> The night before the execution I took the rope to my room and there made the nooses. I preserved the piece of rope intended for Mrs. Surratt for the last. By the time I got at this I was tired, and I will admit that I rather slighted the job. Instead of putting seven turns to the knot, as a regulation hangman's knot was seven turns, I put only five in this one. I really did not think Mrs. Surratt would be swung from the end of it, but she was, and it was demonstrated to my satisfaction, at least, that a five-turn knot will perform as successful a job as a seven-turn knot.

I had the graves for the four persons dug just beyond the scaffolding. I found some difficulty in having the work done, as the arsenal attachés were superstitious. I finally succeeded in getting soldiers to dig the holes but they were only three feet deep.

The hanging gave me a lot of trouble. I had read somewhere that when a person was hanged his tongue would protrude from his mouth. I did not want to see four tongues sticking out before me, so I went to the storehouse, got a new white shelter tent and made four hoods out of it. I tore strips of the tent to bind the legs of the victims.[4]

Gardner and Timothy O'Sullivan arrived at the arsenal on the prison grounds at approximately 11 A.M. and immediately set up their cameras. Facing the scaffold and gallows were two windows, each allowing an excellent view of the proceedings. Gardner's large 8 × 10 view camera, which O'Sullivan was to operate, was placed inside the window closest to the corner of the building. The stereoview camera was placed in the next window, to be operated by Gardner. As the arsenal grounds were beginning to fill, Gardner instructed O'Sullivan to photograph the inside of the courtyard. It was the first photograph in the series. By the time the image was made, from a vantage point above the courtyard, the gallows drops were being tested. As O'Sullivan was making his way back to his position in the building, he came face to face with the officers responsible for the execution. He persuaded them to pose for a group portrait, with General Hartranft seated at the center in a folding camp chair. Captain Richard Watt, Lieutenant Colonel William H. McCall, Colonel Levi A. Dodd, and Captain Christian Rath were each seated in the chairs that would be placed on the scaffold for the convicted conspirators.

William Coxshall, D. F. Shoupe, G. F. Taylor, and F. B. Haslett, all members of the Veteran Reserve Corps, were assigned the task of carrying out the execution. Coxshall and Shoupe were to knock the post out from beneath the drop of Mrs. Surratt and Paine. Taylor and Haslett had the same responsibility for the drop under Herold and Atzerodt.

The morning of July 7 was unbearably hot. At 9 A.M. the detail led by Coxshall was informed that the execution would take place around 2 P.M. The arsenal grounds were already beginning to fill up with officers and other spectators. The outside walls were patrolled by members of the 6th Regiment, Veteran Volunteers. At 11 A.M. the arsenal yard opened to persons holding a special pass. A half hour later Captain Rath approached the waiting detail, instructing them to test the drops once again. The drop to be used by Coxshall had malfunctioned, and the arsenal carpenters had been called in to make some minor adjustments, planing the side post down a bit. On the second try, the drop worked perfectly. All was in readiness.

At 12:40 P.M. the four armchairs were placed on the scaffold. General Winfield Scott Hancock arrived at the prison and requested the presence of General Hartranft. Hancock entered a room inside the arsenal and took Hartranft aside. A few words passed between them in low voices, with Hartranft nodding in agreement. In a some-

Reverdy Johnson, legal counsel for
Mrs. Mary E. Surratt. From an
original unpublished carte de visite.

Captain Christian Rath, executioner
of the Lincoln conspirators. From an
original carte de visite.

Major General Orlando B. Wilcox.
From an original unpublished
carte de visite.

what louder voice, General Hancock stated: "Get ready, General; I want to have everything put in readiness as soon as possible."[5] With this, a signal was given for the interviews of the clergymen, relatives, and friends of the prisoners to cease so that preparations for the execution could begin. Frederick Aiken, legal counsel for Mrs. Surratt, immediately approached General Hancock, pleading for his client, but to no avail.

Earlier that morning Mrs. Surratt's counsel had applied to the Supreme Court of the District of Columbia for a writ of habeas corpus, citing the unconstitutionality of the trial. Justice Andrew Wylie endorsed the motion, directing General Hancock as commander of the Middle Department and having jurisdiction over the arsenal and the prisoners to appear in his presence with Mrs. Surratt. At 11:15 A.M. Hancock and Attorney General Speed appeared before Justice Wylie. Committed to following through with his order, President Johnson issued his own edict to General Hancock.

Executive Office, July 7, 1865, 10 A. M.

To Major General W. S. Hancock,
Commander (etc.):

I Andrew Johnson, President of the United States, do hereby declare that the writ of habeas corpus has been heretofore suspended in such cases as this, and I do hereby especially suspend this writ, and direct that you proceed to execute the order heretofore given upon the judgment of the Military Commission, and you will give this order in return to the writ.

Andrew Johnson, President

Courtyard at the Old Arsenal Prison, Washington (since renamed Fort Lesley J. McNair).   This picture was taken shortly before the execution of the Lincoln conspirators. The windows facing the gallows from the building to the left housed the two cameras used by Gardner and Timothy H. O'Sullivan. From an original photograph. From The Washington Star, *July 7, 1865: "At twelve o'clock the click of a hammer was heard in the upper story of the old workshop of Penitentiary Days, in the center of the prison yard, and the eyes of all were turned in that direction. Presently a window was raised, and forthwith was seen protruding the familiar snout of the camera, showing that the inevitable photographer was on hand. Gardner's good-humored face presently was seen over the camera, as he took 'a sight' at the gallows, to see that it was focused properly."*

MILITARY COMMISSION,
Washington, *July 5 th* 1865.

ADMIT *Alexander Gardner*

D. Hunter
President of the Commission.

Pass that allowed Gardner to photograph the execution, dated July 5, 1865, and signed by David Hunter, president of the military commission. Previously unpublished.

The men who hanged the Lincoln conspirators, shortly before the execution. From left: Captain Richard A. Watt, Lt. Colonel George W. Frederick, Lt. Colonel William H. McCall, Lieutenant D. G. Geissinger, Major General John F. Hartranft, Assistant Surgeon George L. Porter, Colonel Levi A. Dodd, and Captain Christian Rath. From an original photograph.

Major General Winfield Scott Hancock, commander of the Veteran Reserve Corps, who was directed by President Johnson to perform the execution. From an original carte de visite.

The court ruled that it would yield to the suspension of the writ by the president of the United States. The suspension of habeas corpus terminated all possible legal proceedings in Mrs. Surratt's defense.[6]

Just prior to 1 P.M., General Hancock came into the courtyard calling General Hartranft to his side. After a brief discussion, Hartranft was heard to exclaim in a shocked voice, "My God, not the woman too?"

General Hancock answered emphatically, "Yes, the woman too!"

At 1:10 P.M., the heavy door to the prison swung open, and a few reporters along with Hancock passed into the yard. The door slammed behind them. For the final time, Hancock made a survey of the preparations. Satisfied, he reentered the prison.

Inside the conspirators were leaving their cells and lining up for the solemn procession to the gallows. Just before she left her cell, as the soldiers were preparing to take her away, Mrs. Surratt turned to Father Jacob A. Walter and said: "Father, I wish to say something." He answered, "Well what is it my child?" She stated, "That I am innocent."[7]

At 1:15 P.M. the procession made its way out the back door of the prison and down the steps into the yard. The proceedings were described by William Coxshall, a member of the Veteran Reserve Corps assigned the task of dropping the trapdoor on the left side of the gallows.[8]

> The prison door opened and the condemned came in. Mrs. Surratt was first, near fainting after a look at the gallows. She would have fallen had they not supported her. Herold was next. The young man was frightened to death. He trembled and shook and seemed on the verge of fainting. Atzerodt shuffled along in carpet slippers, a long white nightcap on his head. Under different circumstances, he would have been ridiculous. With the exception of Payne [Paine], all were on the verge of collapse. They had to pass the open graves to reach the gallows steps and could gaze down into the shallow holes and even touch the crude pine boxes that were to receive them. Payne was as stolid as if he were a spectator instead of a principal. Herold wore a black hat until he reached the gallows. Payne was bareheaded, but he reached out and took a straw sailor hat off the head of an officer. He wore it until they put the black [sic] bag on him. The condemned were led to the chairs and Captain Rath seated them. Mrs. Surratt and Payne were on our drop, Herold and Atzerodt on the other.

Mrs. Surratt ascended the steps of the scaffold and was led to an armchair, where she was seated. To protect her from the sun, her two attending priests, Father Walter and Father Bernardin F. Wiget, held an umbrella above her head. She wore a black veiled alpaca bonnet with a black bombazine dress. During General Hartranft's reading of the order for execution, her priests held a small crucifix before her, which she fervently kissed. At the completion of prayers by the other clergy, and while her eyes were closed in private prayer, she was approached by Colonel McCall. Assisted by other officers, he removed her bonnet, tied strips of cotton below her knees, and then tied her arms together. At one point she cried out in pain, "It hurts." Someone on the scaffold remarked, "Well, it won't hurt for long." The noose was placed around her neck and her face was covered with a white hood that reached her shoulders.

Paine crossed the steps with his head upright and erect, supported by his spiritual advisor, the Reverend Daniel G. Gillette, on one side and a soldier on the other. He was dressed in a blue flannel shirt and pants. "He ascended the steps leading to the scaffold with the greatest of ease and took his seat on the drop with as much 'sang froid' as though he was sitting down to dinner." He occasionally glared down at the soldiers and civilians in the courtyard and on one occasion glanced upward toward the top of the gallows as if he were inspecting its construction. Paine passively accepted being bound while watching with great interest this final act. At one point a gust of wind blew off his straw hat. He turned around to see where it went and upon its recovery gestured that it was no longer required. Captain Rath adjusted the noose around his neck. Paine lifted his neck as if to be helpful. Rath said in a low voice, "I want you to die quick." Paine replied, "You know best, Captain." Reverend Gillette advanced and made some remarks on Paine's behalf. "He thanked the different officials for the attention and kindness bestowed on Paine, and exhorted the criminal in a few impassioned words to give his entire thoughts to his future state."

Herold was dressed in a black coat, light pants, and a white collarless shirt. He also wore a black slouch hat until the white hood was placed over his head. "At times he looked wildly around, and his face had a haggard, anxious, inquiring expression. He seemed to desire to engage in conversation with those around him. While sitting in his chair awaiting the end, his spiritual advisor, Reverend Mr. Olds, was assiduous in his attentions to the wretched man.

"Atzerodt ascended the steps of the scaffold without difficulty, and took his seat at the south end of the drop without exhibiting any particular emotion." He was dressed in a dark gray coat and pants, black vest with a white linen shirt and no collar. On his feet he wore a pair of wool slippers but no socks. Atzerodt wore no hat; however, he did wear a white handkerchief over his head. During the reading of the death warrant, Atzerodt kept perfectly quiet and listened attentively to the statements read by General Hartranft. On one occasion Atzerodt looked around and muttered some incoherent sentences not directed to anyone on the scaffold. His spiritual advisor, the Reverend J. George Butler, came forward and stated that Atzerodt "desired to return his sincere thanks to General Hartranft and the other officials for their many acts of kindness extended toward him." He then called on God "to forgive George A. Atzerodt for his many sins." Butler then turned to Atzerodt, reminding him that "While the wages of sin were death, whomsoever placed their hope in the Lord Jesus Christ were not forgotten." Butler continued by stating that he "hoped that God would grant him a full and free forgiveness," and ended by saying: "May the Lord God have mercy on you, and grant you his peace."

Atzerodt stood up and faced the assembled audience. His knees trembled slightly and his legs were bent forward. Atzerodt directed a few words to General Hartranft, after which he shook hands with Reverend Butler and a few others standing near him. While his arms were being bound, he muttered to himself as if he were engaged in silent prayer. Suddenly, he loudly exclaimed, "Gentlemen, beware who you . . ." and then stopped as if overcome with emotion. As the white hood was being placed over his head, he said, "Good-bye, gentlemen; may we meet in the other world. God take me now!"

> Umbrellas were raised above the woman and Hartranft, who read the warrants and findings. Then the clergy took over talking what seemed to me interminably. The strain was getting worse. I became nauseated, what with the heat and the waiting, and taking hold of the supporting post, I hung on and vomited. I felt a little better after that, but not too good.
> Payne stood forward at the very front of the drop. Mrs. Surratt was barely past the break, as were the other two. Rath came down the steps and gave the signal.

General Hancock was standing outside the prison gate hoping for a last-minute reprieve for Mrs. Surratt. The spectators in the courtyard continued to look to the rear, fully expecting to see a messenger bringing an order for a stay of execution for her. General Hancock had stationed couriers with swift horses to act as relays between the White House and the arsenal, anticipating President Johnson's reprieve. None was forthcoming. Mrs. Surratt would be the first woman in the history of the United States to be executed. Gardner and O'Sullivan continued to photograph the events.

General Hancock reentered the arsenal courtyard and yelled, "All is ready, Captain. Proceed!" Rath asked, "Her too?" Hancock replied in the affirmative.

General Hancock clapped his hands twice. On the third clap, the "executioner," Captain Christian Rath, signaled Coxshall and the others to perform their duty. The time was 1:26 P.M.

> Shoupe and I swung with all our might. Mrs. Surratt shot down and I believe died instantly. Payne was a strong brute and died hard. It was enough to see these two without looking at the others, but they told us both died quickly.

At the signal, Mrs. Surratt was leaning forward and fell with a jerk, giving a swinging motion to her body. Her death was instantaneous; she died without a struggle.

Paine stood immobile as a statue until the drop fell. While suspended, he exhibited bodily contortions, an "involuntary vibration of the muscles of his legs."

Herold died the hardest, exhibiting "more tenacity of life than any of the others, and he endeavored several times to draw himself up as if for the purpose of relieving himself from the rope by which he was suspended."

At the moment his fall began, Atzerodt was muttering something loud enough for those close enough to hear. After hanging a few seconds, his stomach heaved considerably and his legs quivered slightly.

The bodies swung freely in the afternoon breeze. They remained suspended for approximately thirty minutes. Gardner and O'Sullivan continued to take their photographs.

ABOVE: *The gallows, constructed under the direction of Christian Rath. From an original photograph.* BELOW: *The conspirators have just mounted the scaffold and are seated. Paine's spiritual advisor is on his knees praying for Paine. This is the only view that clearly shows Paine's face. From an original unpublished carte de visite.*

Execution of the Conspirators, 7 July, 1865. No. 1.
Entered according to Act of Congress in the year 1865, by A. Gardner in the Clerk's Office of the District Court of the District of Columbia.

Incidents of the War

ABOVE: *The conspirators have stepped forward. An umbrella is immediately placed over Mary E. Surratt—it is well over 100 degrees. From an original albumen print.* BELOW: *From an original carte de visite.*

Execution of the Conspirators, 7th July, 1865. No. 2.

TOP: *General John F. Hartranft reads the decision of the military commission and the order signed by President Johnson.*
ABOVE: *White canvas hoods are placed over Mrs. Surratt and Paine. Christian Rath (in white coat) is placing noose around the neck of Herold, as Atzerodt speaks wildly. William Coxshall, stationed at the post holding up the trap door on the left, was vomiting at this point due to the heat and tension. Both from an original photograph.*

The conspirators plummet to their deaths. From an original stereoview.

Coxshall continued his narrative:

Ten minutes later we cut them down, put them in pine boxes, and buried them. When the signal was given, a soldier dashed forward and slashed the rope of Atzerodt. The body crashed to the ground as the man snipped off a piece of rope as a souvenir. In each grave we placed a bottle with the name of the occupant.

All the bodies, starting with Atzerodt's, were taken down, and, as they lay on their individual coffins were examined by surgeons Otis, Woodward, and Porter. They were later buried in the arsenal grounds, a few feet from the gallows. Captain Rath supervised the division of the ropes and gallows into one-foot lengths for relics.[9] Outside the prison gates the departing spectators were served lemonade and cakes.

Incidents of the War

SIC SEMPER SICARIIS.

(Thus be it ever with Assassins.)

No. 4.

July 7, 1865.

Execution of the Conspirators, 7th July, 1865. No. 4.

*The bodies hang motionless
in the afternoon heat as the
spectators prepare to leave.*
ABOVE: *From an original
albumen print.* LEFT: *From
an original carte de visite.*

Moments later, momentum or a breeze has altered the positions of the bodies. Within 15 minutes, they were cut down, beginning with Atzerodt's. Copied from a photograph.

This view to the right of the gallows shows the coffins and graves where the conspirators were buried. Bottles containing identifying documentation were placed in the coffins. From an original photograph.

Gardner's Execution Series

The photographs of the Lincoln conspirators and of their execution remain the most vivid images from the assassination of Lincoln. It was the longest photographic picture-story recording of an event to date, capturing a complex, significant sequence of events. Gardner and O'Sullivan's execution series was a nineteenth-century precursor of the kind of photojournalism that subsequently became so important in reporting the news.[10]

The documentation of the conspiracy and of the execution was not commercially motivated. It seems clear that the photographs were made for the Secret Service and the government. Nonetheless, Gardner kept both the photographs and all rights to publish them. After providing the government with prints from his negatives, Gardner offered cartes de visite for sale, some copied from the large-format prints. Sales were not impressive, for these or his Civil War photographs. The public seemed to want to forget the pain and suffering that had dominated their lives for the past four years, and were not clamoring to purchase either Gardner's morbid graphic series depicting the execution or his portraits of the conspirators. Public interest in these images was apparently satisfied by *Harper's Weekly*. The July 1, 1865, issue contained illustrations of all the suspected conspirators, based on Gardner's photographs; the July 22 issue reproduced the portraits of those condemned to death and also featured illustrations of Gardner's photographs of the execution itself.

"Remember Andersonville!"

On June 17, 1865, *Harper's Weekly* published wartime illustrations based on photographs taken by Chaplain J. J. Geer of the 148th Ohio Volunteers. Those photographs revealed the "living dead," prisoners recently released from the infamous Andersonville Prison in Georgia. They, more than any other recollection, brought to the forefront the horror and reality of the savagery experienced by some returning Union prisoners. (Eighty years later, the world would similarly be shocked by the sight of the surviving victims of the Holocaust at Dachau, Buchenwald, and Auschwitz.)

Public outrage led to the demand for vengeance on the commandant of Andersonville Prison, Captain Henry Wirz. From the halls of Congress to the streets of Washington the cry was "Hang Wirz." Sufficient pressure was brought to bear upon the government to set the wheels in motion. Witnesses were rounded up, including rebel guards and former inmates—Boston Corbett, the man who killed John Wilkes Booth, was one. Already in jail, Wirz was charged, on August 21, 1865, with inflicting wanton cruelty upon Union soldiers at Andersonville and conspiring to injure the health and destroy the lives of United States prisoners held by the Confederate states. Also included were thirteen counts of murder "in violation of the laws and customs of war."[11]

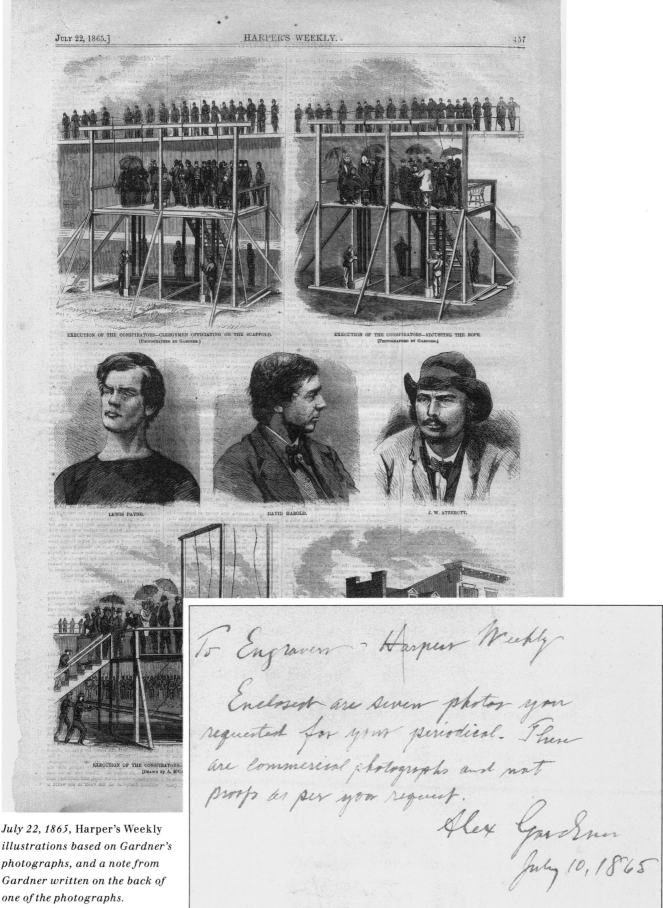

July 22, 1865, Harper's Weekly illustrations based on Gardner's photographs, and a note from Gardner written on the back of one of the photographs.

Henry Wirz was a Swiss physician who, at the outbreak of the war, was practicing medicine in Louisiana. He served for a short time as a clerk at Libby Prison in Richmond. Wounded at Seven Pines, he was subsequently promoted to the rank of captain. In the summer of 1863, he was sent by President Jefferson Davis to Europe as a Confederate agent and dispatch carrier. He became commandant of Andersonville Prison, Georgia, in January 1864 and served the remainder of the war there.[12]

At Andersonville, Wirz was in constant terror of a violent uprising by the hunger-maddened prisoners. Wirz's rule was firm and brutal; Andersonville had the highest death rate of any Confederate prison due to disease, insufficient food and clothing, improper medical care, and the wholesale shooting of those who crossed the "dead line." The dead line was a wood railing encircling the interior prison yard. No prisoner could stretch his hand beyond it without fear of being shot. An average of one hundred twenty-seven men died every day—one man every eleven minutes.[13]

Wirz's trial was held by a military commission, headed by General Lew Wallace (who later wrote *Ben Hur*). According to reporters, Wirz was of "medium height, slender, stoopshouldered, with grey and restless eyes." The indictment originally named General Robert E. Lee; General John H. Winder, the provost marshal of Richmond (who was already dead); Confederate Secretary of War James Seddon; and other Confederate generals and officials. On August 22 General Wallace informed the commission that it had been dissolved by President Johnson. A new indictment had been drawn up charging Wirz alone in the crimes. His legal counsel immediately resigned. Wirz rose and in a high, shrill voice shouted that "without counsel I would surely die on the gallows."[14]

The new trial began the following day, with new counsel for the defendant. One of the most damaging witnesses for the prosecution was Dr. A. W. Burrows, physician for the 27th Massachusetts Volunteer Regiment. His testimony reflected the wanton cruelty of Wirz to the prisoners at Andersonville. Burrows described how seven hundred men, nearly all naked, died in the winter of 1864 "as they huddled in old coats under strips of canvas, or burrowed like rats in their holes." In the stockade, he stated, "they were like ants and bees." Burrows asserted that he had seen Wirz on horseback, followed by a pack of vicious dogs, inspect the camp, warning the prisoners that if anyone escaped, "I'll starve every damn Yankee for it."[15]

There were horrible stories of inhumanity and torture, of living "human skeletons" strung up until their toes barely touched the ground, and of naked men spread-eagled on the frozen ground. Fifteen- or sixteen-year-old boys were lying in filthy mud holes while their limbs rotted away from gangrene. And of course there was the dead line.

Wirz was found guilty on November 6 and sentenced to hang on the morning of the 10th. Only two hundred fifty cards were issued for spectators to witness the execution. The gallows were constructed on the grounds of Old Capitol Prison. Soldiers

BENJAMIN T. DAUGHERTY (Fig. 1), Co. K, Thirty-first Illinois.

BENJAMIN T. DAUGHERTY (Fig. 2).

JOHN H. MATTHEWS,
Corporal Company F, Fourth Pennsylvania.

JOHN W. JANUARY, Corporal, Co. B, Fourth Illinois.   CALVIN BATES (Fig. 1), Corporal, Co. E, Twentieth Maine.   CALVIN BATES (Fig. 2).

"The Living Dead." These views of Northern prisoners freed from Andersonville were published in Harper's Weekly *on July 17, 1865. They so outraged the public that calls for retribution arose.* **INSET:** *Captain Henry Wirz, commander of Andersonville Prison, possibly photographed during his trial. Photographer unknown. From an original unpublished carte de visite.*

Correspondents covering the execution of Captain Wirz, November 10, 1865. From an original direct-contact albumen print. From The Washington Star, *November 10, 1865: "Gardner was early on hand with his camera taking views of the prison yard, scaffold, and scene of execution for Harper's Weekly.*

"The press-gang present, seated on some dilapidated steps were taken in characteristic outfit of shocking bad hats, pencils and notebooks, and the rush of the group to see the negative was immediately followed by a scatteration and rush in the direction of the scaffold as the prisoner was brought out somewhat sooner than had been anticipated by the crowd."

and spectators not fortunate enough to secure a place in the courtyard climbed elm trees outside the prison yard. At 9 A.M., four companies of soldiers marched into the prison yard and formed a human square around the gallows.

The Execution of Captain Henry Wirz

The photographic commission for this event was again awarded to Alexander Gardner, who was accompanied by a large contingent of newspaper correspondents. Gardner and his group were ushered into the courtyard at 9 A.M., shortly after he had photographed the newspapermen.

At 10:15 A.M., Wirz, "his face flushed from the copious draughts of whiskey"[16] he had downed in his cell, was accompanied by two Catholic priests, fathers Francis E. Boyle and Bernardin F. Wiget.

> Spectators in the trees shouted curses and jeered, others in the yard hooted and whistled while the soldiers, standing at attention, began to chant: "Wirz, remember Andersonville . . . Wirz, remember Andersonville."
>
> Wirz, his face impassive, walked slowly up the thirteen steps, to face a Major Russell, who would read the death warrant. The officer had to shout the official words above the tumult, then held out his hand and said that he "deplored this duty." Wirz smiled and said dryly, "I know what orders are, major."
>
> As Russell turned away, Wirz called out: "And I am being hanged for obeying them."
>
> As they tied his hands the priest asked if he wished to make a confession. Wirz shook his head.
>
> "No, I am not guilty, father."
>
> When they tied his legs he again called out, "I go before my God—Almighty God—who will judge between us. I am innocent and I will die like a man."
>
> He then thanked his jailers, the black hood was slipped over his head, and the noose was adjusted. The priests and the others stepped back. A spring was touched, the trap opened and Wirz plunged down.[17]

The fall failed to break his neck. He writhed and shook at the end of the rope and slowly strangled to death. His final agonizing moments were filled with the shouting and hooting of the spectators, who chanted, "Wirz, remember Andersonville . . . Wirz, remember Andersonville."[18]

Gardner captured this event in five moving photographs. One view shows Major Russell reading the death warrant; the next shows the noose being adjusted over Wirz's head. One of his priests is inquiring about his desire to confess. The soldiers at the base of the gallows are chanting, while the crowd hoots and jeers. The fourth photograph was taken at the moment the trap was sprung. This view, more than any other, captures the mood of the morning. The dome of the Capitol is in the background and the soldiers are leaning over from their positions, straining to get a better look. One can almost feel the tension. The final photograph displays Wirz writhing in agony while the soldiers continue their taunt. His head is clearly visible between the upper horizontal planks of the scaffold.

ABOVE: *Reading of the execution warrant against Wirz.* BELOW: *Noose being placed around Wirz's neck. Photos from original direct-contact albumen prints.*

Wirz's body hangs while soldiers in the trees chant, "Wirz, remember Andersonville!" From original direct-contact albumen prints.

After a short time, Wirz's body was cut down from the gallows and buried in the courtyard of the old arsenal prison, near the bodies of the hanged conspirators.

Harper's Weekly ran illustrations based on Gardner's photographs of the execution in the November 25 issue.

The Wirz Autopsy Photograph

After Wirz's body was removed from the scaffold, it was not immediately buried, as has generally been presumed. Instead, the corpse was brought into one of the prison buildings where an autopsy was performed. This event was documented and photographed by Alexander Gardner, a fact hitherto unnoted. This brings to three the number of suppressed photographs taken during the period—two of them by Gardner. The first was the photograph taken of Lincoln by Jeremiah Gurney while the president's body was lying in state in New York City on April 24, 1865. After Stanton read in the newspaper that the picture had been taken, he angrily demanded that the plate be

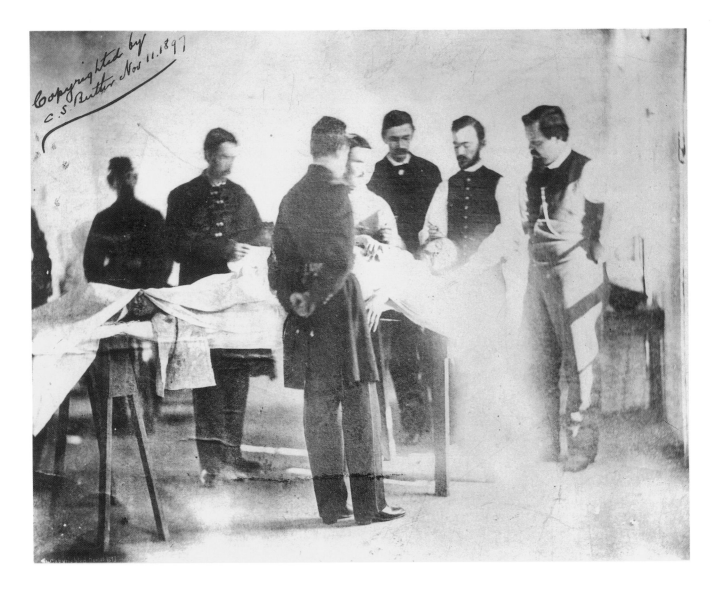

destroyed. The plate was seized and destroyed, but not before one print was made. That print was sent to Stanton, who retained possession of it throughout his life. Years later, Stanton's son sent the print to Lincoln's secretaries John Hay and John Nicolay, who by then were compiling a biography of Lincoln. The photograph was deposited in the Hay-Nicolay papers of the Illinois State Historical Society, where it rested in obscurity until it was rediscovered in 1952.

Then, of course, there was the mystery-shrouded photograph of the Booth autopsy. The recovery of this third important historical photograph, aside from its intrinsic interest, lends credence to the supposition that Gardner continued to act as an agent for the United States Government—namely, the Secret Service. The photograph was found along with a letter, "Reporting the Execution and Burial of Henry Wirz," written by General Christopher C. Augur. Augur had jurisdiction over the Provost Marshal General's Office, the military arm of the police, detectives, and intelligence for the War Department. He was the immediate superior of Colonel Lafayette C. Baker and reported only to Secretary of War Stanton.

> Headquarters Department of Washington,
> Washington D.C., November 11, 1865
>
> Sir: I have the honor to report that the sentence and orders of the President in the case of Henry Wirz, as promulgated in General Court-martial Orders No. 607, dated War Department, Adjutant General's Office, Washington, November 6, 1865, have been duly executed (between the hours of 10 and 11 A.M.) yesterday, November 10, and his body has been interred by the side of Atzerodt, in the arsenal grounds.
>
> I am, General, very respectfully, your obedient servant,
>
> C. C. Auger,
> Major General Vols., Commanding Department
> The Adjutant General of the Army

"This picture of the body of Henry Wirz, was taken in the Old Capitol Prison, Washington, D.C. immediately after the execution, Nov. 10th 1865."[19]

OPPOSITE PAGE:
The previously unpublished photograph of the Wirz autopsy, taken by Gardner for the government. From a contemporary copy of the lost direct-contact albumen print.

C H A P T E R

7

THE UNION PACIFIC RAILROAD EXPEDITION OF 1867

*T*he postwar years saw Gardner's gallery thriving, despite some setbacks and complications. For the most part Gardner kept busy with a variety of projects in the years leading up to his involvement in the Union Pacific Railway Expedition of 1867. His photographic coverage of the war had firmly established his reputation. *Harper's Weekly* had made the following announcement in July 1865: "The present perfection of the art of photography enables an illustrated paper like ours to depict persons and events with the utmost precision. During the War now happily ended we have been in the daily receipt of the greatest variety of views and portraits from all the armies and from every part of the country so that we have been enabled from these to construct a truly exact and living history of the time. . . . Among our photographic friends and allies, none have been more constant and serviceable than Mr. Alexander Gardner of Washington."

Gardner returned to Gettysburg on July 4, 1865, to document the laying of the cornerstone for the Soldier's National Monument.

At about the same time, Gardner undertook a rather formidable project, acting as printer and publisher for Henry DeWitt Moulton's *Rays of Sunlight from South America.* In 1859 Moulton had traveled in Peru, where he photographed cities and cathedrals. When he returned to the United States, in 1863 or 1864, he approached Gardner with the idea of publishing a photographically illustrated book from his negatives. Gardner agreed and printed from Moulton's negatives. Philp & Solomons published the book, in which seventy original gold-toned albumen prints were tipped in. The book resembled Gardner's own forthcoming *Sketch Book.* Each plate was captioned "Negative by H. D. Moulton, and printed by A. Gardner." According to Douglas Keith McElroy, in his unpublished dissertation "The History of Photography in Peru in the Nineteenth Century, 1839–1876," only two complete sets are known to exist: one in the New York Public Library and the other in the Library of Congress.[1]

On January 24, 1865, a devastating fire engulfed the Smithsonian Building in Washington. According to the *Washington Daily National Intelligencer:* "The appearance of the fire at the Smithsonian yesterday was at once grand and saddening. We are glad to learn that Mr. Gardner was on the ground, and took photographs from two or three standpoints." Unfortunately, only one of these photographs has survived, and that one had been altered to dramatize the flames. *Harper's Weekly* illustrated Gardner's photograph in the February 1865 issue.

Ironically, nine months to the day following this fire, Gardner's own studio was seriously damaged by flames. On September 25 the *Washington Daily National In-*

ABOVE: *Baltimore Street, looking north toward the center of the town of Gettysburg, Pennsylvania, July 4, 1865. Gardner was there for the laying of the cornerstone of the Soldier's Monument. From an original photograph.*

telligencer reported: "Serious Fire—Last night, shortly after twelve o'clock, a serious fire broke out in the establishment of Mr. Gardner, photographer, in the Intelligencer Building. Owing to the promptness of Officer Maxwell and other officers the spread of the flames was materially checked. The store of Messrs. Stewart & Foster and of the other merchants in the same block were considerably damaged by water. We learn that the loss of Mr. Gardner is fully covered by Insurance. The lateness of the hour precludes further details, which will be duly furnished in our next edition."

The next day the *Washington Daily National Intelligencer* elaborated: "The Fire Sunday Night—The loss of Mr. Alexander Gardner, photographer, from the fire in the Intelligencer Building on Sunday night will amount to $4,000 or $5,000; which is

John Burns with officers of the 50th Pennsylvania Regiment, July 4, 1865. Copied from an original photograph.

OPPOSITE PAGE: *View from the Soldier's National Cemetery, Gettysburg, July 4, 1865. From an original photograph.*

not fully covered by insurance. The fire originated in the washing and toning room, in the third story; and how it originated is a mystery, for it first burst forth in a corner where there was nothing else than silver [illegible] and paper, and no one had been in the room subsequent to two o'clock in the afternoon. The room where the fire originated was badly damaged, the ceiling being burned a large aperture being burned to the wall. The fire was confined to this room and was extinguished yesterday by the firemen, who deserve all praise for the miracle which they worked. While all around seemed excited they did not seem to lose their presence of mind at the moment and let the fire rage within the room it originated until the water was ready to be put on. This plan worked well, and the result was a speedy extinguishing of the flames. . . .

"The ceiling of Mr. Gardner's fine gallery of pictures was injured by the water, but his pictures were all saved; and in removing them only one glass was broken. The police deserve all praise for their efforts in this behalf. All of the negatives of Mr. Gardner's splendid collection of photographs of the war and battle scenes were also saved; although a few were slightly injured; but it is gratifying to know that he has lost nothing of his splendid collection that he cannot replace. Most of the damage was caused by water. His chemicals and some other stock are, however all destroyed; but he has sent to New York for a new supply and will be in full operation again in a few days. Gardner's enterprise is so well known that it is needless to say any more than that before a week elapses his popular gallery will be as attractive and instructive as ever in all particulars, despite the late accident."

Gardner formally reopened his gallery a little more than a week later, on Wednesday, October 4. In his announcement he advertised: "*Once More in Running Order;* The damage caused by the late fire has been so far repaired that business will be resumed. . . . Mr. G takes this opportunity to thank his numerous friends and customers for past kindness, and to say it shall be his constant aim to continue to merit the rare liberal encouragement heretofore extended to him." Variations of this advertisement ran constantly in the *Washington Daily National Intelligencer* from October 1, 1865, through October 1, 1868.

General Robert E. Lee was summoned to appear before a congressional committee on reconstruction and the conduct of the war on February 7, 1866. The following day he made his rounds to two of Washington's premier photographers, Matthew B. Brady and Alexander Gardner. Gardner took at least four exposures of Lee: three cartes de visite and one large-format view. He copyrighted his photographs on March 7, along with one of General Grant. Lee's views were titled "R. E. Lee No. 1–4," and Grant's was captioned "U.S. Grant, Lt. Gen. U.S.A."

During this same period, Gardner was the first in a succession of three Washington operatives to act as "official" photographer for the Mount Vernon Preservation Association.[2] In this capacity he took numerous views of the famous estate, which were sold as a numbered series to tourists.

In 1867 and early 1868 Gardner devoted a small amount of attention to a court

A retouched photograph of the burning of the Smithsonian Building, January 24, 1865. Copied from an original photograph.

fight with photographer James Gibson. The two had formed a partnership on July 18, 1862, and copyrighted images made prior to the Antietam campaign. Gardner terminated the arrangement less than a month later, on August 14. Gibson sued Gardner, Franklin Philp, and Adolphus Solomons on January 4, 1867, apparently disputing the termination. The records are not clear on how the conflict was resolved.

Gardner's next major preoccupation came as a consequence of the building of the railroads, a project which had been underway in the West throughout the war years, and which in 1867 offered him a subject worthy of his talent and experience.

GENERAL ROBERT E. LEE.

Entered according to act of Congress in the year 1866, by A. Gardner, in the Clerk's Office of the District Court of the District of Columbia.

GENERAL ROBERT E. LEE.

Entered according to act of Congress, in the year 18__, by A. Gardner, in the Clerk's Office of the District Court of the District of Columbia.

GENERAL ROBERT E. LEE.

Entered according to act of Congress in the year 1866, by A. Gardner, in the Clerk's Office of the District Court of the District of Columbia.

THIS PAGE: *General Robert E. Lee, February 18, 1866. From original cartes de visite.*

OPPOSITE PAGE: *From an original cabinet card.*

General Ulysses S. Grant, c. 1865.
From an original Imperial photograph.

In 1862 Congress had authorized construction of the first transcontinental railway, from Omaha, Nebraska, through Wyoming and Utah to California, terminating at San Francisco. In 1864 tracks were simultaneously being laid eastbound from California by the Central Pacific Railroad and westbound from Nebraska by the Union Pacific Railroad. The two were destined to meet at Promontory Point, near Ogden, Utah, on May 10, 1869.

As early as 1864, a California photographer, Alfred A. Hart, had photographed and published stereoviews of the Central Pacific Railroad. In October 1866 Chicago photographer John Carbutt published his *Union Pacific Rail Road Excursion to the 100th Meridian*. Although Carbutt's photographic series was financed by the Union Pacific Railroad, its promoters hoped it would help raise capital from eastern bankers and investors. Through the publication of these photographs, the public anxiously followed the western progression of the various rail lines.[3] Not since the morbid views of the battlefield had such public interest been shown in photographs of a news event.

Dr. William A. Bell, a British physician, had come to the United States seeking adventure. Bell sought and obtained a position on the Kansas-Pacific Survey being mounted by the Union Pacific.[4] Though he had no skills, he signed on as photographer, since all the other jobs were taken. "A photographer alone was wanted; and as no idle man could be allowed among the party . . . I accepted the office with, I must confess, considerable diffidence, as only a fortnight remained before starting to learn an art with which I was then quite unaquainted."[5] The object of the survey was "to ascertain the best general route for the extension of the company's road from the end of the track near Fort Wallace, in western Kansas, by a southern parallel, through New Mexico and Arizona, to the Pacific Coast," according to General William Jackson Palmer, who commanded a troop of cavalry to protect the expedition.[6]

An official of the Kansas Pacific Railroad, Charles B. Lamborn, wrote to General Palmer in July 1867, advising him: "you must not forget to establish the status of Mr. Gardner as Chief Photographer before you leave—in case your stay should be short—and make him the responsible party and have *all* photographs, etc., retained for the use of the Company—Wright [General William W. Wright, superintendent of railroads] intimated that Dr. B. was desirous of using them for the purpose of private speculation."[7]

Alexander Gardner was appointed chief photographer of the Union Pacific Rail Way, Eastern Division. In September 1867 he closed his gallery and, with his son Lawrence and old friend William Pywell, headed for St. Louis. Dr. Bell accompanied the portion of the expedition that steered a course along the thirty-second parallel. Gardner was with the group that traveled along the thirty-fifth parallel. Gardner arrived at the offices of the Union Pacific Rail Way in Wyandotte, Kansas—the end of the line—sometime in the middle of September. He carried three cameras: a stereoscopic camera, a large-plate camera, and an Imperial camera.[8]

On September 21, 1867, the *Lawrence Daily Tribune* carried this notice:

Colonel Charles B. Lamborn and friends, St. Louis, Missouri, September 1867. Published as plate no. 6½ in Gardner's series Across the Continent on the Union Pacific Railway, Eastern Division. *From an original unpublished stereoview.*

Mr. Gardner, a photographic artist from Washington City, is in Lawrence, having come to Kansas for the purpose of taking photographic views of remarkable and noted places in our state. He comes here, we believe, under the auspices of the Union Pacific Railway to make draughts of points on the road. He will take a view of Massachusetts Street this forenoon. These views will be a fine advertisement for our state and we hope the artist may have all the assistance and courtesy which our citizens can render him.[9]

Gardner's perception of the landscape was obviously that of an easterner. The open prairies held a fascination for his camera and he took numerous views of the wide and barren land. Gardner's camera also captured the newly developed towns of

ABOVE: *Railroad yard, Wyandotte, Kansas, 286 miles west of St. Louis. Published as plate no. 15 in* Across the Continent on the Union Pacific Railway, Eastern Division. *From an original stereoview.*

BELOW: *Steamer* Mary McDonald, *Wyandotte, Kansas. Published as plate no. 19 in* Across the Continent on the Union Pacific Railway, Eastern Division. *From an original stereoview.*

NO RIDING OR DRIVING, FASTER THAN A WALK

Gardner seated in his photographic wagon at the Turnpike Bridge, Lawrence, Kansas, 323 miles west of St. Louis. Published as plate no. 29 in Across the Continent on the Union Pacific Railway, Eastern Division. *From an original stereoview.*

Ellsworth (only three months old) and Hays (less than six months old). He photographed Joseph G. McCoy's stockyards in Abilene, which was then a small village.[10] Gardner completed his Kansas series on or about October 19, in Hays, and returned to Washington.

Robert Sobieszek has eloquently placed Gardner's Kansas photographic series as follows: "Historically, they provide a view of the prairies never before seen in such detail and veracity. The building of the first railroads in a drive to join the two coasts, the early settlements and the new founded towns, in addition to a resulting view and sense of the plains' vast emptiness and spatial distances are pictured in this portfolio with more immediacy and 'naturalism' than any of the early lithographs provided. . . . Gardner's vision is basically topographic; in every sense he is far closer to the scientific renderings of A. Schott than he is to the playful images of early Kodak snapshots. And it is because of this vision, with all of its subsequent unpretentiousness, naivete, and simplicity toward the making of pictures, that these images garner their strength and conviction. It is also the clarity of vision joined with the veracity of the photograph that helped to crystalize the East's formulation of a more reasonable idea of the West. The mirror of nature brought the West east to the civilized world. Gardner's pictures bring a no longer existent land as well as a visual freshness to the modern voyager. The Gardner pictures were the first large-scale photographic presentation of the generally uncharted terrain beyond the frontier. . . . The photographs of Alexander Gardner from the portfolio *Across the Continent on the Kansas Pacific Railroad* are therefore the beginning of a long and considerably fruitful tradition of Western landscape photography."[11]

Massachusetts Street, Lawrence, Kansas, September 21, 1867. Published as plate no. 34 in Across the Continent on the Union Pacific Railway, Eastern Division. *From an original stereoview.*

At the completion of the expedition, Bell's photographs were critically assessed. "The pictures taken by Dr. Bell are not of much account. Most of them are too dim or not well finished and the photographer here complains much of the negative and says the result is caused by carelessness."[12] After Bell submitted his negatives to Gardner, he requested photographic copies; Gardner replied that he "forgot to take them with him to Washington." After failing to secure prints from Gardner, Bell obtained them from General Palmer. On October 23, 1868, Bell wrote to Palmer: "I never want [them] into Gardiners [sic] hands."[13] Mistrust and animosity are distinctly present in their final correspondence.

Gardner's stereoviews are titled *Across the Continent on the Union Pacific Railway, Eastern Division,* and his large-plate images were captioned *Across the Continent on the Kansas Pacific Railroad.* (From 1863 until 1867 the railroad was called the Union Pacific Rail Way, Eastern Division. In 1868 it was changed to the Kansas Pacific Railroad. In 1880 it became The Union Pacific.)[14]

Although the portfolio contained views of New Mexico, Arizona, and California, which were taken along the thirty-second parallel and carried the caption of a Gardner photograph, they were undoubtedly taken by Dr. Bell. Gardner had stopped photographing in Hays, Kansas, in October 1867. The expedition arrived in San Francisco in September 1868.[15] As official photographer for the expedition, Gardner was allowed to publish all the expedition photographs under his name. In 1867 he stated in a deposition that although a photograph was identified on the mount as a "Photograph by A. Gardner," it simply meant that it was printed or copied in his gallery; he was not necessarily the photographer.[16] The other photographers on the expedition were Dr. William A. Bell, William R. Pywell, and Gardner's son, Lawrence, who apprenticed on the expedition.

In the April 1868 issue of the *Philadelphia Photographer,* the readership of this leading photographic publication was advised that "a very interesting collection was shown [to the Philadelphia Photographic Society] taken on the line of Union Pacific Railway, Eastern Division, by Mr. A. Gardner of Washington, D.C., and were loaned by Mr. Josiah C. Reiff of Philadelphia. The sizes range from 8 × 10 to 11 × 14, and include Fort Harker, Fort Riley, Abilene, Junction City, Salina, and other towns in Kansas. Many of them are views of the Plains. Thanks were tendered Mr. Josiah C. Reiff of U.P.R.W.,E.D."

OPPOSITE PAGE, TOP: *Fifth Street, Leavenworth, Kansas, 309 miles west of St. Louis. Published as plate no. 52 in* Across the Continent on the Union Pacific Railway, Eastern Division. *From an original stereoview.*

OPPOSITE PAGE, BOTTOM: *Delaware Avenue, Leavenworth, Kansas. Published as plate no. 53 in* Across the Continent on the Union Pacific Railway, Eastern Division. *From an original stereoview.*

On top of Pilot Knob, Leavenworth, Kansas. Believed to be Gardner, left, and William Pywell. Published as plate no. 56 in Across the Continent on the Union Pacific Railway, Eastern Division. *From an original unpublished stereoview.*

Photographic outfit outside Leavenworth, Kansas. Pywell is in front of the wagon, Gardner is in back. Published as plate no. 59½ in Across the Continent on the Union Pacific Railway, Eastern Division. *From an original stereoview.*

"A Rare Specimen Found on Hill above Fort Riley, Kansas." Gardner, seated, is holding the lens of his camera. Published as plate no. 104½ in Across the Continent on the Union Pacific Railway, Eastern Division. *From an original stereoview.*

OPPOSITE PAGE, BOTTOM: *Alexander Gardner seated on his camera in the railroad depot, Manhattan, Kansas, 402 miles west of St. Louis. Published as plate no. 95 in* Across the Continent on the Union Pacific Railway, Eastern Division. *From an original stereoview.*

Pottawatomie Indians at St. Mary's Mission, 375 miles west of St. Louis. Published as plate no. 92 in Across the Continent on the Union Pacific Railway, Eastern Division. *From an original stereoview.*

Railroad section men at Salina, Kansas, 470 miles west of St. Louis. Published as plate no. 124 in Across the Continent on the Union Pacific Railway, Eastern Division. *From an original stereoview.*

ACROSS THE CONTINENT ON THE UNION PACIFIC RAILWAY, E. D.

Earliest known photograph of the 7th U.S. Cavalry, Fort Harker, Kansas, October 1867. Lt. Colonel George Armstrong Custer, commander of the regiment, was on trial at Fort Leavenworth at the time. Front row, seated third from left: Major Alfred Gibbs; second row, standing fifth from left: Dr. Henry Lippincott; standing second from right: 1st Lieutenant Myles Moylan, awarded the Medal of Honor for his gallantry against the Nez Percé at Bear Paw Mountain, September 30, 1877; among those standing on the porch: Captain Louis McLane Hamilton, killed at the Battle of the Washita, November 17, 1868, and Lieutenant Samuel Marshall Robbins; on the far right, Lieutenant John Mitchell Johnson. From an original unpublished direct-contact albumen print.

Fort Harker, Kansas, 503 miles west of St. Louis. Published as plate no. 124 in Across the Continent on the Union Pacific Railway, Eastern Division. *From an original stereoview.*

Pioneer ranchers with tame elk, Clear Lake, Kansas, 498 miles west of St. Louis. Published as plate no. 127½ in Across the Continent on the Union Pacific Railway, Eastern Division. *From an original stereoview.*

"The Escort at Indian Cave" in Kansas, 494 miles west of St. Louis. Published as plate no. 137 in Across the Continent on the Union Pacific Railway, Eastern Division. *From an original stereoview.*

Bull train crossing the Smoky Hill River at Ellsworth, Kansas. Published as plate no. 145 in Across the
Continent on the Union Pacific Railway, Eastern Division. *From an original stereoview.*

*Walnut Street, Ellsworth,
Kansas, 508 miles west of St.
Louis. Published as plate no.
143 in* Across the Continent
on the Union Pacific Railway,
Eastern Division. *From an
original stereoview.*

ABOVE: *U.S. Express Overland Stage, starting for Denver from Hays City, Kansas, 580 miles west of St. Louis. Published as plate no. 148 in* Across the Continent on the Union Pacific Railway, Eastern Division. *From an original stereoview.*

Incidents of the War.

*Pontoon bridge from Georgetown to Analostan
Island (later renamed Theodore Roosevelt Island)
on the day of the Grand Review, May 24, 1865.
Photographed by W. Morris Smith. From an original
direct-contact albumen print.*

OPPOSITE PAGE, BOTTOM:
*"Westward, the Course of Empire Takes Its Way."
Laying track 600 miles west of St. Louis, outside
Hays City, Kansas: the end of the line. Published as
plate no. 152 in* Across the Continent on the Union
Pacific Railway, Eastern Division. *From an original
stereoview.*

*Gardner's advertisement for his
Civil War photographs. From
the original (1865).*

GARDNER'S
PHOTOGRAPHIC INCIDENTS
AND
MEMORIES OF THE WAR,
THE ONLY COMPLETE
Pictorial History of the Rebellion
CONSISTING OF
VIEWS OF
AND
SCENES ON THE BATTLE-FIELDS
OF THE
FIRST BULL RUN, FAIR OAKS, SAVAGE STATION,
MECHANICSVILLE, GAINES' MILL, CHICKAHOMINY,
MALVERN, HILTON HEAD, PULASKI, CHANTILLY,
SECOND BULL RUN, SOUTH MOUNTAIN, ANTIETAM,
SHARPSBURG, HARPER'S FERRY, FREDERICKSBURG,
CHANCELLORSVILLE, GETTYSBURG, VICKSBURG,
BRANDY STATION, CULPEPER, MINE RUN, CEDAR RUN,
WILDERNESS, SPOTTSYLVANIA COURT-HOUSE,
NORTH AND SOUTH ANNA, COLD HARBOR,
PETERSBURG, FORT FISHER, RICHMOND,
TOGETHER WITH
PORTRAITS OF ALL THE DISTINGUISHED GENERALS
OF THE ARMY.
PHILP & SOLOMONS, Publishers and Sole Wholesale Agents, Washington.

ABOVE: *Corcoran's Art Building (now known as the Renwick Gallery, Smithsonian Institution), at the corner of 17th Street and Pennsylvania Avenue in Washington.* BELOW: *The U.S. Capitol, April 1865. Mourning cloth hangs from the marble pillars. Photos from original unpublished Imperial prints.*

Officers of the St. Andrews Society, November 1865.
From left: Joseph P. Wilson, Alexander Gardner,
William R. Smith, Fred B. McGuire, T. W. Spence,
and photographers David Knox and John Reekie.
From an original unpublished Imperial print.

Railroad industrialists, 1872.
From left: James Fisk, Thomas
Rosser, unidentified. From
an original unpublished
Imperial print.

THE
INDIANS

*T*he fire in the Smithsonian Building on January 24, 1865, destroyed many priceless American Indian paintings. In the aftermath of that loss, it was suggested by Smithsonian Secretary Joseph Henry that photographic portraits of Indian delegations visiting Washington be taken. The idea was vigorously supported by Commissioner of Indian Affairs Lewis V. Bogy, who wrote that it was time "to begin anew . . . a far more authentic and trustworthy collection of likenesses of the principal tribes of the United States. The negatives of these might be preserved and copies supplied at cost to any who might desire them. . . . The Indians are passing away so rapidly that but few years remain within which this can be done and the loss will be irretrievable and so felt when they are gone. The photographs . . . should be single and of what is known as Imperial size, the half length being sufficient, and the head divested of any covering so as to show its conformation. In short the pictures should be portraits of the men and not of their garments or ornaments."[1]

Unfortunately, Congress did not agree and failed to provide the necessary funding. However, a wealthy English collector and speculator, William Henry Blackmore, was willing to finance the endeavor. Alexander Gardner and Antonio Z. Shindler agreed to begin photographing the Indian delegations, who were arriving in Washington with increasing frequency. One of Gardner's first commissions was to photograph the Sauk and Fox delegation at the White House in February 1867.[2] Over the next few years he took many pictures of Indians from a variety of tribes, and in 1872 Gardner became the official photographer for the Office of Indian Affairs, charged with photographing all the incoming Indian delegations. Gardner's portraits were eventually installed in the William Blackmore Museum, Salisbury, England.[3]

The Fort Laramie Treaty

Lieutenant William J. Fetterman fought with distinction in the 18th Infantry Regiment during the Civil War. By 1867, the 18th Infantry was serving in the Mountain District of the Department of the Platte. Fort Phil Kearny was situated along the Bozeman Trail, which cut through Sioux land in the Wyoming Territory. The Sioux chief, Red Cloud, swore to destroy the trail. Fetterman was a presumptuous braggart who felt the Sioux, "enemies who struck and ran, who never faced up to battle," were unworthy opponents of a well-disciplined army unit. Openly contemptuous of the Sioux, Fetterman once boasted that with eighty men he could "cut through the entire Sioux Nation." On December 21, 1866, Fetterman's overconfidence allowed him and

Sauk and Fox delegation. From an original unpublished carte de visite.

his eighty men to be lured into a well-planned trap on Lodge Trail Ridge along the
Bozeman Trail. Within forty minutes, more than two thousand Indians completed their
massacre. Evidence indicated that Fetterman had committed suicide.[4]

Fetterman was declared a national hero, and the public demanded retribution.
But the powers that be in Washington had come to question whether the Bozeman
Trail was worth defending. The railroad to be built to its south would soon render it
obsolete. If the hostile tribes would allow the construction of the railroad, then perhaps
a treaty could end the hostilities and the Bozeman Trail could be abandoned.

A treaty conference was scheduled for spring 1868 at Fort Laramie, Wyoming.
The Brule, Oglala and Minneconjou Sioux, Crow, and northern Cheyenne and Ara-
pahoe were invited to attend. Red Cloud of the Oglala Sioux stipulated that he would
not attend until the military abandoned the Powder River forts and the Bozeman Trail.

President Andrew Johnson appointed Nathaniel G. Taylor, commissioner of
Indian affairs, as president of the peace commission. Taylor, a noted humanitarian,
deeply cared for the Indians' welfare, as did the commission's other members, Samuel

OPPOSITE PAGE:
*Sauk and Fox delegation. From
an original direct-contact
albumen print.*

Sauk and Fox delegation with Commissioner of Indian Affairs Lewis V. Bogy, standing.

F. Tappen and Missouri Senator John B. Sanborn. The military was represented by General William T. Sherman, commander of the Department of the Missouri, General Alfred H. Terry, General Christopher C. Augur, and General William S. Harney. The military contingent, especially Sherman, would have preferred to take punitive action against the Indians, but the president insisted they implement a policy of good will. The primary goal of the treaty was to "establish peace, define tribunal boundaries, and provide mechanisms for civilizing the Indians." Another goal was to stop treating tribes as "domestic dependent" nations and hold them accountable to American laws.

The United States Government intended to completely transform the Indians' life. In a public statement General Sherman stated: "Indians on their reservations should be subjected to such influences of a civil nature as will induce them to become self-supporting and which will lead to their ultimate civilization."[5]

On April 4, 1868, Brule chief Spotted Tail met the commission at North Platte and cast himself as intermediary between the hostile factions and the commissioners. Spotted Tail told the commissioners: "We want to live with the whites. We are all one." Members of the commission were skeptical but proceeded to Fort Laramie, arriving on April 10. Two hundred lodges of Oglalas and Brules were waiting at Fort Laramie, but there was no sign of Red Cloud. Present at this time were Sanborn, Terry, Harney, and Augur.

It was no surprise that Alexander Gardner was invited to be the "official photographer" for the Fort Laramie Treaty. Just three years before, General Augur, now on the peace commission, had, as commander of the Department of Washington, with direct jurisdictional charge of the Lincoln conspirators, been instrumental in giving Gardner access to the conspirators and the investigation. Augur had also obtained the commission for Gardner to photograph the execution of the Lincoln conspirators and Henry Wirz. Gardner had also photographed General Sherman on at least one occasion.

Gardner left Washington on April 14, 1868, on the Kansas Pacific Railroad. Commission Secretary A. S. H. White wired ahead to the Kansas Pacific agent in Omaha: "Gardner left Washington last night. Send him along right and one gallon whiskey." Gardner arrived in Cheyenne on April 23, and at Fort Laramie on the 29th. On the final leg of his trip he traveled in the company of General Sherman and Samuel F. Tappan.

The first treaty conference was held on April 28 with the Brules. Prior to signing the agreement, they were warned: "If you continue at war your country will soon be overrun by white people; military posts will be located on all the rivers; your game and yourselves will be destroyed. This is the last effort of the President to make peace with you and save for you a country and home." Iron Shell, spokesman for the Brules, responded: "Our country is filling up with whites. . . . Our great father is shutting up on us and making us a very small country. . . . You come over here and get all our gold, minerals, and skins. I pass over it all and do not get mad. I have always given the whites more than they have given me." The treaty was signed the next day.[6]

The Crows signed their treaty on May 6 and 7, whereupon the commissioners distributed presents to them. Gardner photographed the Crow camp, the disbursement of the gifts, and numerous individuals.

The Cheyennes and Arapahoes signed their treaty on May 10. Gardner photographed the signing, and the campsites, and made more portraits. While awaiting the Oglalas, Gardner photographed Fort Laramie and the nearby plains.

The earliest known portrait of Spotted Tail, c. 1860, who served as mediator at the Fort Laramie Treaty Council and later fought beside Crazy Horse at the Little Big Horn. Photographer unknown. From an original unpublished carte de visite.

William Blackmore with Red Cloud, the Oglala Sioux leader who fought to close the Bozeman Trail and was the last to sign the Fort Laramie Treaty.

OPPOSITE PAGE, BOTTOM: *Commissioners and Indian leaders at Fort Laramie. From left: unidentified, Packs His Drum (sitting), John Finn, Amos Bettleyoun (standing), W. G. Bullock (sitting), Old Man Afraid of His Horses, Benjamin Mills (sitting), Red Bear, James Bordeau.*

PREVIOUS PAGES:
Studio portrait of Luis Morago (Pima) with turban (left), and with his hair down (right).

Dakota Sioux encampment near Fort Laramie, Wyoming, 1868.

On May 21 the northern Oglala Sioux chief, Old Man Afraid of His Horses, arrived with seventy lodges. He brought word that Red Cloud would refuse to sign the treaty until after the military had abandoned the Powder River forts. Of all the councils, that with Old Man Afraid of His Horses created the greatest show. On May 24 Gardner took many pictures of the council lodge, with soldiers on all sides observing the proceedings. At one point the chief was photographed looking pensive, and on another lighting his ceremonial catlinite pipe. On May 25 he was informed by the commissioners that the government would indeed abandon its Powder River forts. With great pleasure, he signed the treaty, stating: "From this time out, we want to depend on the Government that our people will be taken pity on."

Although they knew the Oglalas did not understand the boundaries of their reservation as described in the treaty, the commissioners nevertheless accepted their signatures. Four Bears was justifiably skeptical in stating prior to his signing: "You say that you will protect us for thirty years, but I do not believe it."

The commissioners met with the Minneconjous on May 28. Their chief, Lone Horn, stated: "This is our land and yet you blame us for fighting for it." Gardner photographed a group portrait of the leading Sioux chiefs: Spotted Tail, Roman Nose, Lone Horn, Old Man Afraid of His Horses, and others. Leaving a copy of the treaty for Red Cloud to sign, the commissioners and Alexander Gardner departed shortly thereafter.[7]

In October the commission filed its final report on the Fort Laramie Treaty. Their recommendations "signaled the end of the old way of life for the Indians on the plains":

> Resolved: That it be recommended that henceforth, the Government shall cease to recognize the Indian tribes as domestic dependent nations, except so far as it may be absolutely required to so recognize them by existing treaties, and that hereafter the Indians individually shall be considered and held to be personally subject to the laws of the United States, like other persons owing allegiance to the Government.[8]

Thus began a new stage in the methodical assault on the Indian nations.

In November Red Cloud, with a large contingent of Oglalas and Brule, finally signed the treaty. The government did in fact abandon the Powder River forts around the end of the following July. But conflict continued and escalated, as the government allowed civilians to violate the sacred Black Hills despite the protection of those lands guaranteed in the Laramie agreements. On November 27, 1868, General George Armstrong Custer and members of the 7th Cavalry attacked Black Kettle's village on the Washita River. Fighting continued for years, until the June 1876 defeat of General George Crook and the massacre of General Custer and the 7th Cavalry at the Little Big Horn. An irony in all these years of conflict was that some Indians, who began with every intention of abiding by their treaties, ended up active participants in the fighting. Among these was Spotted Tail, mediator at Fort Laramie, who fought alongside Crazy Horse at the Little Big Horn.[9]

Council meeting at Fort Laramie. Indians present include Spotted Bear, Old Man Afraid of His Horses, Big Mouth, and Pawnee Killer. Commissioners include General William S. Harney, General William T. Sherman, General Alfred H. Terry, Senator John B. Sanborn, General C. C. Augur, J. B. Henderson, Nathaniel G. Taylor, and Samuel F. Tappan.

Gardner returned to Washington with some two hundred negatives; half were approximately 8 × 10 and the rest were stereoviews. The large-format views, published as "Scenes in the Indian Country," were given to the members of the commission in a bound portfolio.[10]

Journalist Raymond J. DeMallie has written that "Gardner's photographs are the only ones known to have been taken of any of the activities of the 1860s commissions. They are valuable because they document the commissions, but even more so, they are valuable because they are the earliest surviving photographic record of the Indians of the Northern Plains taken in their own territory."[11]

ABOVE: *Old Man Afraid of His Horses smoking the pipe at the 1868 Fort Laramie Treaty Council.*

OPPOSITE PAGE, TOP: *Commissioners at the Fort Laramie Council distributing presents.*

OPPOSITE PAGE, BOTTOM: *Fort Laramie portrait. Left to right, standing: White Horse, Black Foot, Yellow Bull; sitting: Gray Blanket, White Fawn, Little Face, unidentified.*

Members of the Dakota tribe at the Fort Laramie Council butchering a cow.

OPPOSITE PAGE, TOP:
*Dakota women and children
at Fort Laramie.*

OPPOSITE PAGE, BOTTOM: *Portrait from the
Fort Laramie Treaty Council. From left: Spotted Tail
(Brule), Roman Nose (Minneconjou), Old Man Afraid
of His Horses (Oglala), Lone Horn (Minneconjou),
Whistling Elk (Minneconjou), Pipe (Oglala), and
Slow Bull (Oglala).*

Fort Laramie Council portrait of members of the Crow tribe. From left: Fox Tail, unidentified, Yellow Bull, Yellow Top, Bull That Goes Hunting, Yellow Coat, and Squaw Who Walks on Ice.

Oglala burial platform near Fort Laramie, 1868.

OPPOSITE PAGE, BOTTOM:

Grey Eyes' Camp at Fort Laramie.

President Grant, c. 1870. From an original unpublished cabinet card.

Little Wolf and Morning Star, Cheyenne leaders, photographed in Washington, D.C., in November 1873. A Cheyenne delegation met with President Ulysses S. Grant in a futile attempt to resolve differences in interpreting terms of the 1868 Fort Laramie Treaty.

Stone Calf and his wife (Cheyenne) in
Washington, D.C., 1872.

Little Boy, aka George Washington (Caddo), in
Washington, D.C., 1872. Washington was a
captain in the Confederate Army, and led a
company of Indian scouts.

Wicai we, Bloody Mouth (Hunkpapa Dakota),
in Washington, D.C., 1872.

Che tań ska, White Hawk (Oglala Dakota),
in Washington, D.C., 1872.

Richard Komas (Ute) in Washington, D.C., 1872.

Ístasapa, Black Eye (Upper Yanktonai Dakota), in Washington, D.C., 1872.

Sleeping Wolf and his wife (Kiowa) in Washington, D.C., 1872. Sleeping Wolf was a prominent leader during the Kiowa outbreak of 1874–75.

Kan gi i yo tan ka, Sitting Crow (Blackfoot Dakota), in Washington, D.C., 1872.

SMENT NUMBER
58.

Sir and Brother:

are hereby notified that brother WIL...

M. Morris, late of St. Columba Lodge...

...bacco, Md., and of this Association, die...

...October, 187... from the effects of lith...

...o reimburse the Treasury, you wi...

...to the undersigned immediately; faili...

...date—forfeits membership and all clai...

...ICE OF THE ASSOCIATION, 616 Eleventh stree...

...M. The Secretary *pro tem.* will transact b...

...P. M., at Photographic Gallery, 921 Penns...

...have been credited with payment on all asse...

9

THE PHILANTHROPIST

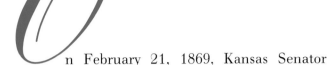n February 21, 1869, Kansas Senator
Samuel C. Pomeroy submitted a petition to Congress on behalf of Alexander Gardner,
urging it to purchase and preserve Gardner's negatives. Pomeroy submitted it, but
Gardner had written the petition in his own hand.

The undersigned respectfully represents that he is a photographer at 511 Seventh
Street, Washington. That he has followed the profession of photographing in the
city of Washington and in the vicinity of the same for the past ten years. That at
the outbreak of the Rebellion he conceived the idea of furnishing of it a consecutive
Photographic History.

That he was most of his time with the Army of the Potomac and held the
position of Photographer to said army, and his services were in constant requisition
in the furnishing of copies of maps and plans, etc.

That during that period he photographed all the important scenes and incidents
which in the aggregate compose the only history of the Rebellion in that form
and are known as *Gardner's Photographic Incidents and Memories of the War for
the Union.*

They embrace among others, views of and scenes on the battlefields of the First
Bull Run, Fair Oaks, Savage Station, Mechanicsville, Gaines Mill [*sic*], Chickahominy, Malvern, Hilton Head, Pulaski, Second Bull Run, Chantilly, South
Mountain, Antietam, Sharpsburg, Harpers Ferry, Fredericksburg, Chancellorsville, Gettysburg, Vicksburg, Brandy Station, Culpeper, Mine Run, Cold Harbor,
Petersburg, Fort Fisher, Chatanooga [*sic*], Lookout Mountain, Richmond, together with portraits of the distinguished Generals of the Army. The collection
contains *all* and the *only* photographs taken representing the Battlefields of Antietam, Gettysburg, and Spotsylvania Court House during and immediately after
the engagements.

In procuring the above views the undersigned devoted much time, great labor,
and considerable expense. He has always regarded them as having a National
character and has long indulged the hope that they would someday belong to the
Nation. They are beyond the reach of private enterprise in both their value and
importance. As a specimen of what they represent, he submits for inspection two
volumes already published [the *Sketch Book*], which form a small portion of the
collection. Without wishing to disparage the labors of others, he believes and is
so advised that there is no such collection extant, as indeed might be inferred
from the fact that he is the *only* artist who had free access to the Army and its
Headquarters at all times as well when in active movement as in camp.

Regarding the results of his labor as of priceless value, preserving as they do
imperishably, pictures of scenes, the memory of which the country will not readily
let die, he is prepared to dispose of them on terms that may seem reasonable and
just to the Representatives of the People.

[Signed] Alex Gardner

Four days earlier, on February 17, Massachusetts Senator Henry Wilson had submitted a petition on behalf of Matthew B. Brady. Wilson urged congressional expediency in considering the purchase and preservation of Brady's negatives.

That at the very commencement of the Rebellion, with a view to the collection and preservation of valuable historical material, he organized, at great expense, an efficient corps of Artists for the production of photographic views illustrating prominent incidents of the War. The result of these labors is an extensive and attractive collection of pictures showing Battle Fields, Military Camps, Fortifications, Bridges, Processions, Reviews, Siege Trains, Valleys, Rivers, Villages, Farmhouses, Plantations, Famous Buildings of the South, etc., etc., etc.; also groups and likenesses of the principal actors in the Rebellion in the performance of their duty; around bivouac fires; in the trenches; and on the decks of ironclads; the whole forming a magnificent Pictorial History of our great National Struggle. . . . These War Views and Portraits are illustrative of the most interesting and important periods of our national history and are reliable authority for Art. They are absolutely faithful and the Portraits, according to an eminent authority, are superior in real instruction to half a dozen written biographies. For the most part they can be reproduced from the material in the possession of your memorialist. Many of the prominent personages are dead. The fortifications are in ruins; the bridges over which armies have marched have been destroyed; the picturesque military camps have been broken up; and the battlefields wear a changed appearance.

The preservation of all this rich historical material becomes, therefore, a matter of National importance.

It is too precious to remain in the hands of any private citizen and your memorialist hereby respectfully proposes to dispose of the entire Collection of Views and Portraits, properly mounted, together with the Negatives to Congress; that the same may be placed on permanent exhibition at the National Capitol, where the pictures and negatives may be secure from injury or loss by fire; and at the same time, accessible to the historical student, the artist, and the public.

And your memorialist respectfully asks to be heard in person on this subject.

[Signed] M. B. Brady[1]

Unfortunately, Congress showed little if any interest, and the Joint Committee on Library asked to be discharged from further consideration of either petition.[2]

What is interesting in Gardner's petition is his failure to deprecate Brady and his competing petition. The facts are quite clear: that Brady "organized an efficient corps of Artists" for the production of war views, though it was Gardner alone who "conceived the idea of furnishing of it, a consecutive Photographic History." And he was the "*only* artist who had free access to the army and its headquarters."

Copyright Law and Photography

In his late 40s Gardner became active again in the kind of work that reflected the ideals that had informed his life as a young man.

After the war Gardner was active in lobbying for issues that were important to the profession of photography. In 1866, with Brady, Jeremiah Gurney, and Charles

Alexander Gardner, c. 1868. From an original carte de visite.

ABOVE, LEFT AND RIGHT: *Senator Henry Wilson of Massachusetts, who sponsored Brady's petition asking Congress to acquire his photographs. From an original unpublished carte de visite. Senator Samuel C. Pomeroy of Missouri, who sponsored Gardner's petition to Congress for the same purpose. From an original unpublished autographed carte de visite.*

D. Fredericks, he exerted pressure on Congress to repeal the revenue tax on photographs. Gardner and the others personally called upon members of Congress and circulated a petition from the National Photographic Association urging repeal of the tax. The two-cent tax had been imposed as a revenue-raising measure during the war, in August 1864. The petitioners were successful, and, exactly two years after it was created, the revenue tax on photographs was repealed.[3]

Most nineteenth-century American photographers were concerned over their lack of copyright protection, what the *Philadelphia Photographer* termed "piratical stealing." The National Photographic Association appointed Gardner to lobby Congress to protect photographers' interests, and he is credited for the "interpolations" made in the law.[4]

In 1870, bill H.R. 1714 was introduced to the 41st Congress to amend the existing patent and copyright law. Although Gardner did not testify at the formal committee hearings, his influence led to its passage that year.

"Tam o' Shanter"

The year 1868 marked the 110th anniversary of the publication of "Tam o' Shanter," by the Scottish poet Robert Burns, presenting Gardner with another publishing project. He conceived the idea of republishing the landmark poem with illustrations by the Washington artist E. Hutchinson Miller. Gardner photographically reproduced seven of Miller's illustrations for a leather-bound limited edition that was published in New York by W. J. Widdleton. No more than ten copies of the book are known to exist today.

Rogues' Gallery

In 1873 the civic-minded Gardner worked once again with the Washington, D.C., Metropolitan Police Department. He copied nearly one thousand daguerreotypes in the metropolitan police files and made them uniform in size and style.[5] Gardner's "mug shots" of the Lincoln conspirators had led to the revolutionary development in law enforcement—a "rogues' gallery" of local criminals.

The Masonic Mutual Relief Association

"He was deeply interested in all plans to encourage self-reliance among the poor and lowly and to recognize the common brotherhood of man."[6] In 1866 eight members of a masonic organization met in Washington to form a relief association to benefit widows and orphans of Master Masons—the Masonic Mutual Relief Association.[7] In 1868 twenty-two members of that organization motioned to petition Congress for a charter for the group. Later that year Congressman Fernando Wood of New York submitted a bill for it that Congress approved early in 1869. Senator Benjamin F. Rice of Arkansas informed the Senate about the association: "It is with a view of concentrating certain funds, so that there shall always be a sufficiency to supply not only temporarily but permanently the widows and orphans of deceased Masons. The association is to be made up of members of all the lodges, and this is to be a perpetual fund that is not to be used or diverted for any other purpose, or ever to be distributed among the members, but is to remain to the corporation to be devoted to that exclusive purpose." The bill passed the Congress and President Johnson signed it on March 3, 1869.

The new organization was to be operated on an assessment system, in contrast to life insurance companies which, like today, required regular premium payments. Each member would pay $3.10 to become insured. Whenever an existing member died, all remaining members would pay an additional $1.10. Of this, the dollar would go to the beneficiary and ten cents would be used to defray expenses. It was the secretary's responsibility to issue the collection cards and collect the assessment. If a member failed to pay the $1.10 assessment, he was dropped from the rolls of the association.

Appointed secretary pro tempore of the Masonic Mutual Relief Association on April 13, 1874, Gardner was formally elected to the position on November 18. On November 22, 1882, he was elected president of the association.[8]

His interest in life insurance led Gardner to collect information about the working of other organizations. He issued a letter to Masonic associations nationwide, inquiring about their plans to meet the present and prospective needs of the brethren and their families. Gardner was amazed to discover that, by and large, other plans were based on the expectation of charity. He responded thusly: "When Relief or Mutual Benefit Associations began to take definite form in this country, their founders had

Alexander Gardner, c. 1872, as
secretary of the Masonic Mutual
Relief Association.

Card assessing members of the Masonic Mutual Relief
Association a fee upon the death of a fellow member, signed by
Gardner November 18, 1874.

but one idea with regard to them, and that was that they were charities in the broadest
and fullest sense of the term."[9] Although charity was an integral part of the formulation
of the associations, Gardner knew that in order to ensure permanency the entire
Masonic Mutual Relief Association had to be built on a sound business foundation.
Gardner also felt that a national convention, meeting annually, was imperative for the
membership to express opinions and share information.

Gardner was also concerned about the continuous decline in membership,
caused by the inability of members to meet the small assessment required upon the
death of another member. He suggested to the association's directors a class grading
of members, but the idea failed to gather support. Gardner believed that "by prudent,
intelligent and honest management, it [the association] would secure the confidence
of the public and give to the policy holders insurance at about one-half the cost of
ordinary life insurance."[10]

Gardner refused to attack the efforts made by other life insurance companies to
secure business. "We are all engaged in the same beneficent work, we make no attack
on life insurance companies, but we have often been forced to reply to many misre-
presentations which they keep so industriously circulating."[11]

When the assessment plan was attacked, his anger was evident: "It is not to
be supposed that an institution which holds out so many advantages, will escape the
keen and observant eye of the rapacious vulture who is ever ready to pounce upon
whatever may tend to his own self aggrandizement."[12] To the end Gardner staunchly
supported his plan of assessment over the conventional life insurance plan. "May God
speed the day which will inaugurate the adoption by the ordinary life insurance com-

panies of the assessment plan—our plan, simple, reliable, economical, the plan of common sense, the only true plan."[13]

While he continued to work with the Masonic Mutual Relief Association, Gardner also formed the Washington Beneficial Endowment Association of the District of Columbia, receiving his charter from Congress in April 1877.[14] He was continually interested in any plan to improve the condition of working people. He rejected anything that would stimulate the greed of a few, and steadfastly opposed any alliance with an association he felt was even remotely speculative. "He believed and lived as he believed, that a good name was more to be desired than great riches."[15]

The Philanthropist

Gardner also examined the variety of plans upon which building associations were based. Selecting one that promised the best results for those who sought aid in securing a home, he became one of the earliest members of the Equitable Co-operative Building Association. In November 1882 he was elected its president.

Gardner's concern for the well-being of Washington's poor led him to found with other like-minded Masons the Saint John's Mite Association, a local charity. The organization was of great importance to him and he cheerfully did his work "faithfully and unostentatiously."[16]

While still in Scotland, in 1854, Gardner had reached the third degree of Master Mason. Fourteen years later he transferred his affiliation to Lebanon Lodge No. 7 in Washington where, in 1881, he received first the Order of the Red Cross in the Washington Commandery Knights Templar and then the Order of the Temple.[17] Gardner participated in the St. Andrew's Society, which had been established in Glasgow in 1854, to bring together brother Scotsmen worldwide to honor Saint Andrew, patron saint of Scotland. The Washington chapter of the society was founded in 1855. Gardner's exact date of membership is uncertain; however, in 1865 he was its secretary and in 1872 was listed as treasurer. The 1872 directory also indicates that "St. Andrew's Society, City of Washington, D.C., meets 2nd monday evening of each month at Gardner's Gallery, Pennsylvania Avenue between 9th and 10th N.W."

Gardner's Gallery continued to operate for some years. In 1870 he was no longer listed in the business directory, but a home address of 412 7th Street was provided. In 1871 the gallery was listed at a new location, at 921 Pennsylvania Avenue, an address shared with the Masonic Mutual Relief Association. Alexander Gardner formally retired from photography in 1879, devoting the rest of his life to the Washington Beneficial Endowment Association and the Masonic Mutual Relief Association.

The Death of Alexander Gardner

Alexander Gardner became ill in December 1882; over a two-week period his condition deteriorated rapidly. On December 5 the *Washington Post* reported:

MR. ALEXANDER GARDNER VERY ILL

Mr. Alexander Gardner, president of the Masonic Relief Association and secretary of the Mutual Beneficial Endowment Association, is lying at his residence on Virginia Avenue, Southwest, very low with diabetes and other complications. But little hope is entertained of his recovery. Mr. Gardner is a well-known and much-respected citizen, and his illness will be sincerely regretted by a large circle of friends.

A few days later, on December 9, Joseph M. Wilson, a fellow Mason, joined with Gardner and his family: "though the sweep of the wings of Azreal could almost be felt in the grief-haunted chamber, and though the very air seemed to be conscious of the impending sorrow, he often hopefully said 'I hold the fort.' His vitality was marvelous, and gave promise if not of possible recovery, of at least a delay of the final summons. As the wants of the patient sufferer were supplied, he met every act of kindness with looks of gratefulness, and with a faint smile and comforting words tried to soothe the saddening hearts of those he loved; but the work of disintegration went on, and the restlessness of approaching dissolution increased, as one by one 'the pins were taken out of the tabernacle,' and to this restlessness was added sensations of special distress, causing at times half audible indications of intense pain. These conditions and the attendant nervousness failed to respond to the medical remedies provided.

"And so the sad vigils of the night went by, but ere the longed for morning light appeared a sudden cry of agony, a violent convulsion of the limbs, a pressing of his hands across the heart and a tremor of the whole frame proved that man's last enemy had conquered, and the soul of our friend passed over the river of death. . . ."[18]

Gardner died on December 10, 1882, at about 6 A.M. He was 61 years old. Burial occurred two days later. His many mourners noted that in death "his high forehead, his finely cut features, his flowing beard of almost patriarchal fullness" seemed to be in repose, as though he were only asleep. His long, melancholy funeral train had as its destination the Glenwood cemetery, where the rites of the Presbyterian Church and the services of the Knights Templar were performed.[19] The *Washington Post* reported on his funeral the following day.

The issue of the *Philadelphia Photographer* published soon after Gardner's death asked: *"Who, in Photography, Has Not Heard of Alexander Gardner?* He was one of our veterans—one of photography's staunchest friends. We knew much of him personally, and years ago, when photography was more hampered than it is now, Alexander Gardner was always one of the first and readiest to give help and sympathy. He was an early member of the National Photographic Association, and by his works was known throughout the fraternity. Happy we are in having one who knew him and wrought with him, to give us so much information concerning the useful light which has gone out of our art.

"We feel his loss, and regret that we shall never see his genial face or grasp his hand. . . ."[20]

Photographs

There has been placed in my hands for sale a "Photographic Sketch Book of the War."

Mr. Gardner was employed as photographe and during the intervals of his official work he paigns of that army. Soon after the war he sele published them.

What now remains of that publication is hundred sets were originally published and that

The photographs are 8 x 10 inches, mounted printed descriptions of the views, and well bour

The original price of the set was $150. I b one set with two prints missing, which will be which will be sold for $50. There are also a few $1 each. The following is a complete list of the a * have one or more duplicate prints that will

Volume I.

* 1 Marshall House, Alexandria.
* 2 Slave Pen, Alexandria.
* 3 Fairfax Court House.
* 4 Stone Church, Centreville.
* 5 Fortifications on Centreville Heights.
* 6 Quaker Guns, Centreville.
* 7 Ruins of Stone Bridge, Bull Run.
* 8 Matthews House, battle-field of Bull Run.
* 9 Ruins at Manassas.
*10 Ruins at Manassas Junction.
 11 Fortifications at Manassas Junction.
*12 Battery No. 1, in front of Yorktown.
 13 Battery No. 1, in front of Yorktown.
 14 Battery No. 4, in front of Yorktown.
*15 Moore House, Yorktown.

C H A P T E R

10

EPILOGUE

*A*lexander Gardner executed his last will and testament on April 19, 1882, designating his "beloved wife and partner" Margaret Sinclair Gardner as sole heir and executor. A year after Gardner's death, in December 1883, his widow petitioned the court to enter his will into probate. Gardner's estate was quite small: "consisting of books, household furniture, pictures, etc., of the probable value of $250 and $1,000 possible value in stock of the Washington Beneficial Endowment Association." The petition also indicated that the only debt known was: "balance due on the purchase money for the homestead in which he resided." On January 26, 1884, the court formally admitted the will into probate.

Why would Alexander Gardner die with little, if any, property? The answer is that he probably gave his family his personal and real property as gifts. In the 1860 census Gardner valued his personal property at $1,000.

Gardner's wife died on April 14, 1897. She left two parcels of real estate to her son, Lawrence, one at 609 10th Street, Northeast, and one at 305 9th Street, Southeast. The rest of her worldly goods were left to her daughter, Eliza.

Eliza Gardner never married and was always known by her family and friends as "Miss Eliza." Like her parents she was active in the Church of New Jerusalem, donating to them some of her father's most cherished possessions: an original oil painting of him by Charles Armor of Washington; the congressional chair from Gardner's gallery that Abraham Lincoln and many other prominent personages had sat and posed in; a desk; and a personal letter from President Lincoln to her father. All but the oil painting are still owned by the church. Eliza Gardner died on February 28, 1932. Although she owned no real property, she left a large amount of money. One of her bequests was to "The Masonic Eastern Star Home of Washington, D.C. In memory of my father the late Alexander Gardner." She also placed in trust $300 to Glenwood Cemetery "to invest and apply the income thus arising to the care of my lot the monument, grass, and anything pertaining to Lot N.E. ½ lot 38, Sec. C." This lot houses the monument to Alexander Gardner. Buried there alongside him are his mother, his wife, his daughter, his son, Lawrence, and his son's wife, Elizabeth K. Gardner.

Alexander Gardner's niece, Margaret "Robbie" Sinclair, had been adopted after her father's death by a prominent attorney in McGregor's Landing in Iowa, John T. Stoneman. In 1877 she married Stoneman's law partner, Asahel Chapin. They had two daughters, Florence and Esther. "Robbie" Chapin died on November 5, 1936.

Lawrence Gardner's wife, Elizabeth, died on April 13, 1940. Her estate consisted entirely of personal property and was valued at $6,441. Lawrence Gardner and his wife had no natural children, but they had adopted two girls, Carrie Lee Keating and Mary Regina McLaughlin. Mary Regina married David Moore and they had a son, Gardner Moore, who died in 1985. Gardner Moore's second wife, Helen, talked with this writer in 1985. During the conversation she revealed that after the death of Carrie Lee Keating (Lawrence Gardner's last surviving daughter) her husband, Gardner Moore, burned boxes of papers, documents, and photographs believed to have belonged to Alexander Gardner.

The following are brief biographical sketches of employees and associates of Alexander Gardner.

James Gardner accompanied his older brother Alexander to Washington in 1858 and worked with him as a photographer. James also worked for his brother during the Civil War, producing many classic photographs. The 1865 Washington directory states that James Gardner was an "operator at A. Gardner's, 511 7th St." However, after 1865 James Gardner's whereabouts become a mystery. A James Gardner was purportedly with geologist and mountaineer Clarence King in California in 1866. A James Gardner was also with the western photographer William Henry Jackson during the Hayden Expedition of 1871, but that Gardner was identified as James T. Gardner and was definitely not a photographer.

The mount of a recently uncovered photograph of James Gardner suggests that around 1870 he was a partner in the photographic firm of Gilman & Gardner at 123 Washington Street in Boston. Unfortunately, there is no information in the directories or other sources for the firm.

Lawrence Gardner, Alexander's son, was born in Glasgow, Scotland, on December 11, 1847. He attended Mount Saint Mary's in Emmitsburg, Maryland, from 1862 to 1864. He accompanied his father in 1867 during the Kansas Expedition as an apprentice photographer. Between 1869 and 1878 Lawrence is listed in the directories as a photographer for his father, in 1879 as an insurance agent, and from 1883 to 1884 as secretary of the Washington Beneficial Endowment Association. The assessment system developed by his father did not stand the test of time. Lawrence became very active in the Democratic party in Washington. He was a member of the Democratic National Committee for the District of Columbia, secretary of the National Association of Democratic Clubs, secretary of the Democratic Congressional Committee, and chairman of the Inaugural Ball Committee for President Grover Cleveland. He was chairman of the Executive Committee whose responsibility was to take charge of laying the cornerstone of the United States Capitol during the centennial celebration. At the time of his death, on September 18, 1899, Lawrence Gardner was treasurer and a director of the St. Joseph's Orphan Asylum in Washington.

James Gardner, c. 1870. From an original stereoview (published by the firm Gilman and Gardner, 123 Washington Street, Boston).

Gardner's daughter, Eliza. From an original unpublished carte de visite.

Photographer William Pywell with his two sisters in 1868. Laura is seated to the left; the other's name is unknown. From an original unpublished carte de visite.

William Reddish Pywell was born on June 9, 1843, in Baltimore, Maryland. During the Civil War, he worked closely with Gardner and his corps of photographers. The 1865 Washington directory states that Pywell was an "Operator at Gardner's." Pywell's father, Robert, was the co-owner of the livery stable of Keleher & Pywell. On the night of the Lincoln assassination, conspirator George Atzerodt rented a horse from Robert Pywell. In 1867 Pywell accompanied Gardner on the Kansas Expedition and from there went to Texas, where he worked as a photographer at the Houston City Photographic Gallery. In late 1868 Pywell returned to Washington and married Margaret Schoefield. From 1869 to 1877 Pywell worked as a photographer in and around Washington. His sister, Laura, married his friend and former Gardner associate Timothy H. O'Sullivan. In 1873 Pywell was the official photographer for the Yellowstone Expedition commanded by Lt. Colonel George Armstrong Custer. He went to Louisiana as a photographer in 1878 and was proprietor of the Excelsior Photographic Studio in Rustin at his death in 1887.

William James Oliphant was a Confederate soldier in the Civil War, serving his home state of Texas. When he returned home, this nineteen-year-old decided to become a photographer and gave the following account: "I took up the study of photography in an art studio opened by two northern men in Austin, Texas. At this time, tintypes were giving way to the regular photographs, and in 1868 I went to Washington to study photography in Alexander Gardner's studio on Seventh Street, not far from where the Post Office Department was situated at that time. I met George Robertson, who was also with Gardner. He became interested in Texas and talked much about life there. After returning to Austin I opened a studio on Pecan Street, now Sixth Street, over my father's store. I corresponded with Robertson and arranged to have him come to Texas, which he did about 1872. At that time the stereoscope was much in vogue, and a new thing. I bought a stereoscope camera and started building up different series of views. The most popular series was entitled 'Life on the Frontier.' While Robertson was with me, he made two trips, one with the buffalo hunting expedition, and the other with a geographical survey of Texas. All his views were put into the 'Life on the Frontier' series."[1] Oliphant and Robertson were good friends with William Pywell, and Oliphant was photographed with Pywell by Alexander Gardner.

William Frank Browne was a private in Company C, 15th Vermont Volunteer Infantry, which he served until his discharge on August 5, 1863. Shortly thereafter, Browne attached himself to General Judson Kilpatrick's 3rd Cavalry Division, Headquarters, 5th Michigan Cavalry, as a camp photographer. In April 1865 Browne was employed as a contract photographer under Alexander Gardner. He took 120 stereoviews in and around Richmond, Virginia, along the James River. This series, titled *View of Confederate Water Batteries on James River*, was published by Gardner with

Photographer George Robertson, by Gardner operative David Knox. From an original unpublished carte de visite.

Photographers William James Oliphant and William Pywell, 1868. From an original unpublished autographed carte de visite.

Joseph F. Gedney, Gardner's friend and associate. From an original unpublished carte de visite.

Photographer George N. Barnard. Copied from an original unpublished autographed carte de visite.

William Frank Browne, an operative for Gardner, in 1865. From an original ⅙ plate tintype.

photographic credit given to Browne. (The numerical sequence runs from 1032 to 1151.) Browne returned home to Northfield, Vermont, where he died of consumption in 1867.[2]

Joseph Francis Gedney was born in LaHavre, France, in 1826, and arrived in Philadelphia in 1851. Three years later, he and his wife, Sara E. Greene, moved to Washington where he established a printing and engraving business, working almost exclusively for the government. Upon the outbreak of the war in 1861, Gedney enlisted in Company A, Washington Light Infantry. He was discharged on July 10, having served his ninety-day enlistment. Throughout the war Gedney worked in several capacities for the Secret Service. After the war he continued in his profession as a printer, engraver, and lithographer.

Joseph Gedney and Alexander Gardner were close friends, brother Masons, members of Lebanon Lodge No. 7, Washington Commandery Knights Templar, and of the Masonic Mutual Relief Association. One can speculate that Gedney may have helped Gardner in his various printing productions. Gedney died in Washington in October 1906.

George N. Barnard was born in Coventry, Connecticut, in 1819, but spent his early childhood in Nashville, Tennessee. By 1847 Barnard was operating his first studio in Oswego, New York. He moved to Syracuse in 1854. In 1860 Barnard was in Cuba under the tutelage of E. & H. T. Anthony. Upon his return to New York, he became a cameraman for Brady. At the outbreak of the war, Barnard joined Gardner in the field. When Gardner broke with Brady, Barnard followed. In 1864 he became a photographer for the Military Department of the Mississippi under General Sherman. In 1866 Barnard published his photographic portfolio titled *Photographic Views with Sherman's Campaigns*, incorporating sixty-one original photographs.

The Chicago fire of 1871 destroyed the gallery Barnard had established there after the war. He returned to Charleston, to 263 King Street, where another fire and an earthquake drove him from that city. In 1884 Barnard was employed by George Eastman and was inducted with him into the Rochester Photographic Association. On February 4, 1902, Barnard died at his daughter's home in Onondaga, New York.[3]

OPPOSITE PAGE:

Gardner portrait of Lincoln copyrighted and claimed to have been taken by M. P. Rice.

Copyright '91, by M.P. Rice

ABRAHAM LINCOLN.

From the only original unretouched negative, made in 1864, at the time he commissioned General U. S. Grant Lieut. General of all the Armies of the Republic. It was suggested that this negative (with that of Gen'l U. S. Grant) be made in commemoration of that event.

Gardner's Negatives: A Tragedy

What became of the extensive collection of negatives Gardner had once offered for purchase to the U.S. Congress? The answer lies with a portrait photographer, Moses Preston Rice, a contemporary of Gardner. Rice arrived in Washington from Nova Scotia in 1861. He is said to have opened a photographic studio, but directories from the period do not show him until 1865. He is then listed as a photographer at 520 Pennsylvania Avenue, which is the photographic establishment of J. Orville Johnson. For the rest of his life, Rice operated a photographic studio in Washington.

In 1953 Charles Bender, a scrap-glass dealer in Washington, relayed his story of buying old glass negatives: "About forty-five years ago I was in business with my father buying up old negative glass at Pennsylvania Avenue near the Capitol in Washington, D.C. There was a photographer there whose name was Orville Johnson, and I bought some old negatives from him. During my conversation with him, he referred me to a photographer by the name of Rice on F Street. . . . A famous photographer

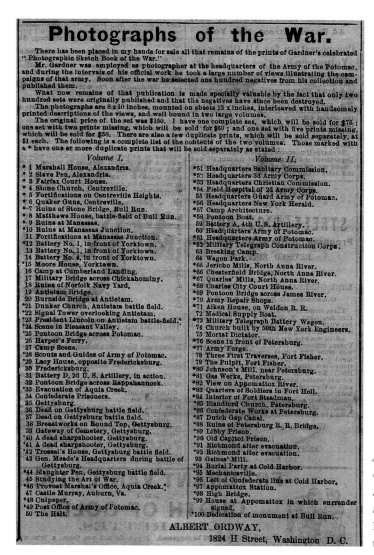

Advertisement placed by Albert Ordway in the Army and Navy Journal, *July 12, 1884, offering to sell prints from* Gardner's Photographic Sketch Book of the War.

whose name was Brady worked with Rice as assistant photographer and left all his negatives of the Civil War [1861–1865]. Mr. Rice took me over to Ford's Theatre, where Lincoln was shot, and there I purchased all the original wet-plate negatives made by Brady. There were about ninety thousand of these negatives stored there. There were a lot of original negatives made by Brady of Abraham Lincoln, General Grant, and all the officials and celebrities, the entire collection gathered by Brady. I offered to sell the original negatives of Lincoln and other celebrities of the time to the *Philadelphia Inquirer* and the *Philadelphia Public Ledger* and *The Bulletin*, but they told me they already had negatives of Lincoln and although their negatives were not originals, they were not interested. So my dad said to me that if the negatives had any value, Brady and Mr. Rice would not have sold the collection to us, and so we went to work and salvaged the negatives by removing the emulsion and retaining the silver, and we sold the glass to photographers, and gas meter manufacturers. . . ."[4]

Bender must have meant that Rice worked as an assistant to Brady, not Brady for Rice. On October 29, 1891, Rice copyrighted the classic full-face portrait of Lincoln and the Imperial portrait of General Grant. In 1892 he copyrighted General Philip H. Sheridan and his staff, the board that tried the conspirators, and Secretary of War Stanton. In 1901 Rice copyrighted another portrait of Lincoln.

In numerous documents Rice claimed that the photograph of Lincoln was "made in Washington by Moses P. Rice in 1864, at the time [Lincoln] commissioned General U. S. Grant, Lieutenant General of all the armies of the Republic." This of course is not true. The Lincoln portrait was taken in November 1863 and the Grant portrait in 1865. All the photographs published by M. P. Rice were originally taken by Gardner.

There is, of course, the possibility that Rice was an employee of Gardner's during the Civil War and might have been present when Lincoln sat for a photograph. However, under no circumstances could Moses Preston Rice have been the original photographer of those portraits!

E. & H. T. Anthony, the firm Gardner was associated with during the war years, obtained a set of Brady's negatives for nonpayment of bills. About 1882 two photograph collectors, General Albert Ordway and Colonel Arnold Rand, began compiling for future publication "a complete portrait record of the war." They purchased Anthony's collection, then housed in storage, "and they added two thousand negatives made by or under the direction of Gardner after he had left Brady's staff." In 1884 Ordway and Rand attempted to sell all their negatives to the government but were unsuccessful. Finally, about 1885, they sold the collection to John C. Taylor of Huntington, Connecticut, who offered prints from the negatives to the general public. In 1905 Taylor & Huntington sold the negative collection to Edward B. Eaton of Hartford, Connecticut, who was the president of *Connecticut Magazine*. In 1916 Eaton stored the negatives in the vault of the Phelps Publishing Co., where they remained, forgotten, until 1942. In that year the Library of Congress paid the storage fee and obtained possession of and title to the entire collection.[5]

APPENDIXES

A. CATALOG OF GARDNER'S PHOTOGRAPHIC SKETCH BOOK OF THE WAR

This appendix is a listing of all the photographs published in *Gardner's Photographic Sketch Book of the War* in 1865 and 1866. In this and the following appendixes, important factual and spelling errors have been corrected, although Gardner's idiosyncratic captions and spelling have for the most part been preserved.

PLATE NO.	PHOTOGRAPHER	DESCRIPTION
1.	William R. Pywell	Marshall House, Alexandria, Va., August 1862
2.	William R. Pywell	Slave Pen, Alexandria, Va., August 1862
3.	T. H. O'Sullivan	Fairfax Court House, Va., June 1863
4.	Barnard & Gibson	Stone Church, Centerville, Va., March 1863
5.	Barnard & Gibson	Fortifications on Heights of Centerville, Va., March 1862
6.	Barnard & Gibson	Quaker Guns, Centerville, Va., March 1862
7.	Barnard & Gibson	Ruins of Stone Bridge, Bull Run, March 1862
8.	Barnard & Gibson	Matthews' House, Battlefield of Bull Run, Va., March 1862
9.	Barnard & Gibson	Ruins at Manassas, March 1862
10.	Barnard & Gibson	Ruins at Manassas Junction, March 1862
11.	Barnard & Gibson	Fortifications at Manassas, March 1862
12.	Wood & Gibson	Battery no. 1, Near Yorktown, Va., May 1862
13.	Wood & Gibson	Battery no. 1, Near Yorktown, Va., May 1862
14.	Wood & Gibson	Battery no. 4, Near Yorktown, Va., May 1862
15.	Wood & Gibson	Moore House, Yorktown, Va., May 1862
16.	Wood & Gibson	Inspection of Troops at Cumberland Landing, Pamunkey, Va., May 1862
17.	David B. Woodbury	Military Bridge across the Chickahominy, Va.
18.	James Gardner	Ruins of Norfolk Navy Yard, Va., December 1864
19.	Alexander Gardner	Antietam Bridge, Md., September 1862
20.	Alexander Gardner	Burnside Bridge, across Antietam Creek, Md., September 1862
21.	James Gardner	Dunker Church, Battlefield of Antietam, Md.
22.	T. H. O'Sullivan	Signal Tower, Elk Mountain, Overlooking Battlefield of Antietam, September 1862
23.	Alexander Gardner	President Lincoln on Battlefield of Antietam, October 1862
24.	Alexander Gardner	Scene in Pleasant Valley, Md.
25.	Alexander Gardner	Pontoon Bridge, across the Potomac, at Berlin, Md., November 1862
26.	James Gardner	Meeting of the Shenandoah and Potomac, at Harpers Ferry, July 1865
27.	Alexander Gardner	What Do I Want, John Henry? Warrenton, Va., November 1862
28.	Alexander Gardner	Scouts and Guides to the Army of the Potomac, Berlin, Md., October 1862
29.	Alexander Gardner	Lacy House, Falmouth, Va., December 1862
30.	T. H. O'Sullivan	Fredericksburg, Va.
31.	T. H. O'Sullivan	Battery D, 5th U.S. Artillery, in action, Fredericksburg, 1863
32.	T. H. O'Sullivan	Pontoon Bridge, across the Rappahannock, May 1863
33.	T. H. O'Sullivan	Evacuation of Aquia Creek, Va., June 1863
34.	T. H. O'Sullivan	Group of Confederate Prisoners at Fairfax Court-House, June 1863
35.	T. H. O'Sullivan	Gettysburg, July 1863
36.	T. H. O'Sullivan	A Harvest of Death, Gettysburg, July 1863
37.	T. H. O'Sullivan	Field Where General Reynolds Fell, Gettysburg, July 1863
38.	T. H. O'Sullivan	Interior of Breastworks on Round Top, Gettysburg, July 1863
39.	T. H. O'Sullivan	Gateway of Cemetery, Gettysburg, July 1863
40.	Alexander Gardner	A Sharpshooter's Last Sleep, Gettysburg, July 1863
41.	Alexander Gardner	Home of a Rebel Sharpshooter, Gettysburg, July 1863
42.	T. H. O'Sullivan	Trossel's House, Battlefield of Gettysburg, July 1863
43.	T. H. O'Sullivan	Headquarters Maj. Gen. George G. Meade, During the Battle of Gettysburg, July 1863
44.	T. H. O'Sullivan	Slaughter Pen, Foot of Round Top, Gettysburg, July 1863
45.	Alexander Gardner	Studying the Art of War, Fairfax Court House, June 1863
46.	T. H. O'Sullivan	Provost Marshal's Office, Aquia Creek, Va., February 1863
47.	T. H. O'Sullivan	Castle Murray, Near Auburn, Va., November 1863
48.	T. H. O'Sullivan	Culpeper, Va., November 1863

49.	T. H. O'Sullivan	General Post Office, Army of the Potomac, Brandy Station, Va., December 1863
50.	T. H. O'Sullivan	The Halt, May 1864
51.	James Gardner	The Shebang, or Quarters, U.S. Sanitary Commission, Brandy Station, November 1863
52.	James Gardner	Residence, Quartermaster Third Army Corps, Brandy Station, December 1863
53.	James Gardner	Headquarters Christian Commission, in field, Germantown, September 1863
54.	James Gardner	Field Hospital, Second Army Corps, Brandy Station, February 1864
55.	T. H. O'Sullivan	Guard Mount Headquarters, Army of the Potomac
56.	T. H. O'Sullivan	Headquarters New York Herald, Army of Potomac, Bealton, September 1863
57.	T. H. O'Sullivan	Camp Architecture, January 1864
58.	T. H. O'Sullivan	Pontoon Boat, February 1864
59.	James Gardner	Battery A, Fourth U.S. Artillery, Robertson's Brigade
60.	T. H. O'Sullivan	Headquarters Army of the Potomac, February 1864
61.	T. H. O'Sullivan	Commissary Department, Headquarters Army of the Potomac, February 1864
62.	T. H. O'Sullivan	U.S. Military Telegraph Construction Corps, April 1864
63.	James Gardner	Breaking Camp, Brandy Station, May 1864
64.	T. H. O'Sullivan	Wagon Park, Brandy Station, May 1863
65.	Alexander Gardner	Jericho Mills, North Anna, Va., May 1864
66.	T. H. O'Sullivan	Chesterfield Bridge, North Anna, Va., May 1864
67.	Alexander Gardner	Quarles' Mill, North Anna, Va., May 1865
68.	T. H. O'Sullivan	Charles City Court-House, Va., June 1864
69.	James Gardner	Pontoon Bridge, across the James, June 1864
70.	T. H. O'Sullivan	Army Repair Shop, February 1864
71.	John Reekie	Aiken House, on Weldon Railroad, Va., February 1865
72.	John Reekie	Medical Supply Boat, Appomattox Landing, Va., January 1865
73.	David Knox	Battery Wagon, Front of Petersburg, September 1864
74.	T. H. O'Sullivan	Poplar Grove Church, February 1865
75.	David Knox	Mortar Dictator, Front of Petersburg, October 1864
76.	David Knox	A Fancy Group, Front of Petersburg, August 1864
77.	David Knox	Forge Scene, Front of Petersburg, August 1864
78.	T. H. O'Sullivan	Three First Traverses on Land End, Fort Fisher, N.C., January 1865
79.	T. H. O'Sullivan	The Pulpit, Fort Fisher, N.C., January 1865
80.	T. H. O'Sullivan	Johnson's Mill, Petersburg, Va., May 1865
81.	T. H. O'Sullivan	View of the Petersburg Gas Works, May 1865
82.	T. H. O'Sullivan	View on the Appomattox, Near Campbell's Bridge, Petersburg, Va., May 1865
83.	T. H. O'Sullivan	Quarters of Men in Fort Sedgwick, Generally Known as Fort Hell, May 1865
84.	T. H. O'Sullivan	View of the Interior of Fort Stedman, May 1865
85.	T. H. O'Sullivan	Blandford Church, Petersburg, Va., April 1865
86.	T. H. O'Sullivan	Interior View of Confederate Line at Gracie's Salient, May 1865
87.	John Reekie	Dutch Gap, James River, Va., March 1865
88.	Alexander Gardner	Ruins of Richmond and Petersburg Railroad Bridge, Across the James
89.	Alexander Gardner	Libby Prison, Richmond, Va., April 1865
90.	William R. Pywell	Old Capitol Prison, Washington, D.C.
91.	Alexander Gardner	Ruins of Arsenal, Richmond, Va., April 1865
92.	Alexander Gardner	View on Canal, Near Crenshaw's Mill, Richmond, Va., April 1865
93.	John Reekie	Ruins of Gaines' Mill, Va., April 1865
94.	John Reekie	A Burial Party, Cold Harbor, Va., April 1865
95.	John Reekie	Mechanicsville, Va., April 1865
96.	John Reekie	Extreme Line of Confederate Works, Cold Harbor, Va., April 1865
97.	T. H. O'Sullivan	Appomattox Station, Va., April 1865
98.	T. H. O'Sullivan	High Bridge, Crossing the Appomattox
99.	T. H. O'Sullivan	McLean's House, Appomattox Court-House, Va. Where the Capitulation was Signed Between Generals Grant & Lee, April 1865
100.	W. Morris Smith	Dedication of Monument on Bull Run Battlefield, June 1865

B. CATALOG OF GARDNER'S CIVIL WAR PHOTOGRAPHS AND INCIDENTS OF THE WAR

This appendix combines Gardner's own 1863 catalog entries with information collected from original Gardner prints and stereo-views, including images taken prior to 1863 that were not included in the published catalog and images taken subsequently. Photographs marked with an asterisk (*) were printed and published in folio size (8 × 10) with no identifying numbers. Numbered photographs were printed and published in stereoview or album gallery card format (half a stereoview mounted on a card). I consider this appendix a work in progress, as there are undoubtedly other Gardner photographs of which I am not yet aware.

NO.		NEGATIVE BY:
1.	Capitol, Washington	G. N. Barnard
100.	Long Bridge across the Potomac.	"
103.	Pensacola Steam Frigate off Alexandria.	"
*	Harpers Ferry, June, 1861.	"

ILLUSTRATIONS OF SHERMAN'S EXPEDITION TO SOUTH CAROLINA.—Mounted as stereographs and album cards.

150. Negro Family on Rhett's Plantation, Beaufort, South Carolina.	T. H. O'Sullivan
151. Group on J. J. Smith's Plantation, Beaufort, S.C.	"
152. Negro Family representing five generations all born on the Plantation of J. J. Smith, Beaufort.	"
153. Headquarters, General Stevens, Beaufort, S.C.	"
154. Scouting Party on J. J. Smith's Plantation, Beaufort.	"
155. Rhett's House, Beaufort, South Carolina.	"
156. Fiftieth Pennsylvania Volunteers (Colonel Christ) at Beaufort, South Carolina.	"
157. Building a Pontoon Bridge at Beaufort, S.C.	"
158. Moss Covered Tomb, over 150 years old on Rhett's Plantation, Port Royal Island, South Carolina.	"
159. Preparing Cotton for the Gin.	"
160. Negro Quarters on Smith's Plantation, Port Royal Island, South Carolina.	"
161. Mock Battery erected by the Seventy-ninth New York.	"
162. View in Beaufort, South Carolina.	"
163. General Stevens and Staff at Beaufort, S.C.	"
164. General Stevens at Beaufort, South Carolina.	"
166. Siege Train, Hilton Head, South Carolina.	"
167. Mary Stuart's House, Beaufort, South Carolina.	"
168. Fuller's House, Beaufort, South Carolina.	"
169. View on Mills' Plantation, Port Royal Island, S.C.	"
170. Dock built by Federal troops, Hilton Head, S.C.	"
171. Boat Landing at Beaufort, South Carolina.	"
172. Signal Station, Beaufort, South Carolina.	"
187. Graves of Sailors killed at Bombardment, Hilton Head, South Carolina.	"
188. Fort Pulaski, Georgia; front view.	"
189. Fort Pulaski, Georgia; rear view.	"
190. Fort Pulaski, Georgia; distant view, showing the effect of the fire from the assaulting batteries.	"
191. Ruins of Fort Pulaski, Georgia; inside casemate, wall 14 feet thick.	"
192. The Breach, Fort Pulaski, Georgia.	"
194. Fort Pulaski, Georgia; rear parapet, entrance.	"
195. Ruins on channel side of Fort Pulaski, Georgia.	"
197. Beauregard Gun, Fort Pulaski.	"
198. Fort Pulaski, Georgia; view on front parapet.	"
199. Dismounted Mortar, Fort Pulaski.	"
200. View of Guns, Jeff Davis, Beauregard and Stephens Fort Pulaski, Georgia.	"
201. Coosaw Ferry, Port Royal Island, S.C. Battle-field of 1st January, 1862, in the distance.	"
202. Natural Arch at Seabrook Point, South Carolina.	"
203. Fort Beauregard, Bay Point, S.C.; linework in the distance.	"
204. Fort Beauregard, Bay Point, South Carolina.	"
206. Fort Walker, Hilton Head, South Carolina.	"
207. Fort Walker, Hilton Head, South Carolina, rear view.	"
208. Our Mess at Beaufort, South Carolina.	"
209. Headquarters General Hunter, Hilton Head, S.C.	"
210. Army Bake-house, Hilton Head, South Carolina.	"

ILLUSTRATIONS OF THE WAR IN VIRGINIA, from the Battle of Bull Run until the evacuation of Manassas by General Johnston:

* Harpers Ferry, June, 1861.	G. N. Barnard
224. Castle Murray, near Auburn, Va, Headquarters.	T. H. O'Sullivan
288. Georgetown Aqueduct.	"
289. Georgetown Aqueduct and College.	"
290. Examining Pass at Georgetown Ferry. "All Right!"	"
291. Georgetown Ferry.	"
300. Forts on Heights of Centerville.	"
* Fortifications at Centerville, March, 1862, No. 1.	Barnard & Gibson
* Fortifications at Centerville, March, 1862, No. 2.	"
* Fortifications at Centerville, March, 1862, No. 3.	"
* Fortifications at Centerville, March, 1862, No. 4.	"
* Quaker Guns, Centerville, March, 1862.	"
* Confederate Encampment, Centerville, March, 1862.	"
* Grigsby House, Headquarters, Gen. Johnston, Centerville, March, 1862.	"
* Stone Church, Centerville, used as a hospital after the battle of 18th July, 1861.	"
* Ruins of Stone Bridge, Bull Run, March, 1862, No. 1.	"
* Ruins of Stone Bridge, Bull Run, March, 1862, No. 2.	"
* Manassas Junction, March, 1862.	"
* Fortifications at Manassas, March, 1862, No. 1.	"
* Fortifications at Manassas, March, 1862, No. 2.	"

*	Fortifications at Manassas, March, 1862, No. 3.	Barnard & Gibson
*	Encampment at Manassas, March, 1862.	"
302.	Stone Church, Centerville, used as a hospital after the battle of 18th July, 1861.	G. N. Barnard
303.	Grigsby House, Centerville, Headquarters of Gen. Johnston.	"
304.	Confederate Graves. Centerville.	"
306.	Departure from the Old Homestead.	"
307.	Cub Run.	"
308.	Mrs. Stevens' House, near Centerville.	"
309.	Mrs. Spinner's House, near Centerville.	"
310.	Ruins of Stone Bridge, Bull Run, looking upstream.	"
311.	Ruins of Stone Bridge, Bull Run, looking across.	"
312.	Ruins of Stone Bridge, Bull Run.	"
313.	Sudley's Ford, Bull Run.	"
314.	Sudley's Ford and Church, Bull Run.	"
315.	Sudley's Church, Bull Run.	"
316.	Hecatomb at Sudley's Church.	"
317.	Thorburn's House, Bull Run.	"
318.	Matthew's House, Bull Run.	"
319.	Robinson's House, Bull Run.	"
320.	Ruins of Mrs. Henry's House, Bull Run.	"
321.	Soldiers' Graves, Bull Run.	"
322.	Battle-field, Bull Run.	"
323.	Fortifications at Manassas.	"
327.	Beauregard's Headquarters, Manassas.	"
330.	Confederate Encampment, Centerville.	"
331.	Winter Quarters, Confederate Army, Centerville.	"
332.	Winter Quarters, Confederate Army, Centerville, south view, March, 1862.	"
333.	Principal Fort at Centerville.	"
334.	Fort on Heights of Centerville, mounting Quaker Guns, March, 1862.	"
336.	Fortifications at Manassas.	"
337.	Ruins at Manassas.	"
338.	Ruins at Manassas.	"

ILLUSTRATIONS OF GENERAL MCCLELLAN'S CAMPAIGN OF THE PENINSULA—Mounted as stereographs and album cards.

*	Battery No. 1 at Farnhold's House, York River, Mounting one 200-pound and five 100-pound rifled guns, May, 1862, No. 1.	Wood & Gibson
*	Battery No. 1 at Farnhold's House, York River, mounting one 200-pound and five 100-pound rifled guns, May, 1862, No. 2.	"
*	Battery No. 1 at Farnhold's House, York River, mounting one 200-pound and five 100-pound rifled guns, May, 1862, No. 3.	"
*	Battery No. 1 at Farnhold's House, York River, mounting one 200-pound and five 100-pound rifled guns, May, 1862, No. 4.	"
*	Battery No. 4, near Yorktown, mounting ten 13-inch mortars, each weighing 20,000 pounds, May, 1862, No. 1.	"
*	Battery No. 4, near Yorktown, mounting ten 13-inch mortars, each weighing 20,000 pounds, May, 1862, No. 2.	"
*	Battery No. 4, near Yorktown, mounting ten 13-inch mortars, each weighing 20,000 pounds, May, 1862, No. 3.	"
*	Moore House, Yorktown, where Cornwallis signed the capitulation.	"
350.	General McClellan's Tent, Camp Winfield Scott, near Yorktown, May, 1862.	James F. Gibson
351.	Group—T. Anderson, Esq, Lieutenant Colonels Fletcher and Neville, Major Pearson, Prince de Joinville, Compte de Paris, General Van Vliet, G. Sheffield, S. L. Arny, Duc de Chartes, at Camp Winfield Scott, near Yorktown, May, 1862.	"
352.	Group—Prince de Joinville and friends at Camp Winfield Scott, near Yorktown, May 1, 1862.	"
353.	Group—Gen. Van Vliet and friends at Camp Winfield Scott, near Yorktown, May 1, 1862.	"
354.	Group—Gen. Van Vliet, Compte de Paris, Duc de Chartes, and friends at Camp Winfield Scott, near Yorktown, May 1, 1862.	"
355.	Group—Gen. Marcy and friends at Camp Winfield Scott, near Yorktown, May 3, 1862.	"
356.	Group—Duc de Chartes and friends, Camp Winfield Scott, near Yorktown, May 3, 1862.	"
357.	Group—Compte de Paris, Duc de Chartes, Prince de Joinville, and friends, at Camp Winfield Scott, near Yorktown, May 1, 1862.	"
358.	Camp Life at Camp Winfield Scott, near Yorktown, May 3, 1862.	"
359.	Group—Servants of Officers of Staff, Camp Winfield Scott, near Yorktown, May 3, 1862.	"
360.	Farnhold's House with part of Federal Battery No. 1 in the distance.	"
361.	View of Gloucester and Yorktown.	"
362.	View of Yorktown and Fleet from Farnhold's House, with Battery No. 1 in foreground.	"
363.	Northeast view of Battery No. 1, at Farnhold's House, York River, mounting one 200-pound and five 100-pound rifled guns.	"

364. View of Battery No. 1, at Farnhold's House, York River, mounting one 200-pound and five 100-pound rifled guns.   James F. Gibson
365. Southwest view of Battery No. 1, at Farnhold's House, York River, mounting one 200-pound and five 100-pound rifled guns.   "
366. Group—Topographical Engineers, at Camp Winfield Scott, near Yorktown, May 2, 1862.   "
367. Headquarters, Camp Winfield Scott, near Yorktown, May 3, 1862.   "
368. Headquarters, Gen. McClellan, Camp Winfield Scott, near Yorktown, May 7, 1862.   "
369. Headquarters, Gen. Lafayette, before the Battle of Yorktown.   "
370. Headquarters, General Porter, Farnhold's House, and York River in the distance.   "
371. Clark's House, Regular Hospital for the Reserve.   "
372. Group of Contrabands at Headquarters of General Lafayette.   "
373. Battery No. 4, near Yorktown, mounting ten 13-inch mortars, each weighing 20,000 pounds.   "
374. Battery No. 4, near Yorktown, mounting ten 13-inch mortars, each weighing 20,000 pounds; south.   "
375. Battery No. 4, near Yorktown, mounting ten 13-inch mortars, each weighing 20,000 pounds; south end.   "
376. Battery No. 4, near Yorktown, mounting ten 13-inch mortars, each weighing 20,000 pounds; south end.   "
377. Battery No. 4, near Yorktown, mounting ten 13-inch mortars, each weighing 20,000 pounds; east south end.   "
378. Battery No. 4, near Yorktown, mounting ten 13-inch mortars, each weighing 20,000 pounds; east south end.   "
379. Battery No. 4, near Yorktown, mounting ten 13-inch mortars, each weighing 20,000 pounds; east north end.   "
380. Battery No. 4, near Yorktown, mounting ten 13-inch mortars, each weighing 20,000 pounds; east south end.   "
381. Group—Generals Franklin, Slocum, Barry, Newton and friends, May 14, 1862.   "
382. Group—Generals Barry, Slocum, Newton, Franklin &c, May 14, 1862.   "
383. Contrabands on Mr. Toller's Farm, Cumberland, May 14, 1862.   "
384. White House, formerly the residence of Mrs. Custis Washington; now the residence of Col. Lee; May 17, 1862; since burned.   "
385. Mr. Toller's House, Cumberland, Virginia, May, 1862.   "
386. Ruins of Bridge on the Richmond and York River Rail-road; burned by the Confederates.   "
387. Groups—Lieutenants Jones, Bowen, and Custer, May, 1862.   "
388. Groups of Officers of General McClellan's Staff, May 20, 1862.   "
389. Group of General Andrew Porter's Staff, May 20, 1862.   "
636. Group at Cumberland, May, 1862.   "
637. Group at Mr. Toller's Farm, Cumberland.   "
638. Group—English Officers, Camp Winfield Scott, near Yorktown, May, 1862.   "
428. Lieutenant Washington, a Confederate prisoner, & Capt. Custer.   "
429. General Barry and friends.   "
430. Camp Lincoln, near Richmond, June, 1862.   "
431. Gibson's Battery of Horse Artillery, near Fair Oaks.   "
432. Group—Gibson and staff.   "
433. Benson's Battery of Horse Artillery, near Fair Oaks, June '62.   "
434. Group—Brigade Officers of Horse Artillery, near Fair Oaks.   "
435. Captain Tidball and Staff near Fair Oaks.   "
436. General Stoneman & Staff at his Headquarters, near Fair Oaks.   "
437. General Stoneman.   "
438. Generals Stoneman and Nagley and Staff, near Richmond, June, 1862.   "
440. Group—Major Robertson and friends.   "
441. General Caldwell and Staff, at Fair Oaks, June 1862.   "
442. General Kearney's Brigade Hospital.   "
444. Group—Prince's Servants.   "
445. General Stoneman and Staff, near Richmond, June 1862.   "
447. View of Ravine at Yorktown, where a large number of Confederate magazines were situated.   "
455. Confederate Fortifications, Yorktown, Va.   "
458. Confederate Fortifications, Yorktown, Va.   "
460. Water Battery, Gloucester, Mounting 15 Heavy Guns.   G. N. Barnard
462. Moore House, Yorktown, where Cornwallis signed the capitulation, 1862.   "
468. Savage Station, Va, June 27, 1862.   "
471. Front View of Old Frame House, Orchard and Well, at Seven Pines. Over 400 were buried here after the battle of Fair Oaks. In the distance, Sickles' Brigade, in line of Battle.   "
475. Ft. Richardson, near Quarles House, Fair Oaks Station, 1862.   "
479. House Fair Oaks Battlefield used as a hospital by Hooker's Division.   "
482. Hundred-pounder Gun on Rebel Steamer "Teazer."   "
483. The Teazer, Confederate Gun Boat, Captured by the Maritanza, July 4, 1862. This view shows the destruction caused by the bursting of 100 pound rifled shell.   "

486.	The Original "Monitor" after her fight with the "Merrimac."	James F. Gibson
488.	Iron-clad Gun-boat "Galena" showing the effect of Rebel shot.	"
489.	Military Bridge across the Chickahominy, built by the 15th NY Engineers, Colonel Murphey.	"
490.	Crew of the Original "Monitor" on her deck.	"
640.	First New York Battery, 20-pound rifled guns, near Richmond, June 1862.	"
642.	Major Robertson's Battery of Horse Artillery, near Richmond, June 1862.	"
652.	Deck view of the iron-clad gunboat Galena, showing the effect of the fire from Fort Darling.	"
658.	Group, Officers on Monitor, July 9, 1862.	"
659.	Deck view of "Monitor" from stern.	"
*	Military Bridge across the Chickahominy, June 1862, #1.	D. B. Woodbury
*	Military Bridge across the Chickahominy, June 1862, #2.	"

ILLUSTRATIONS OF GENERAL POPE'S CAMPAIGN IN VIRGINIA.—Mounted as stereographs and album cards.

500.	Panoramic view from the center of Battlefield of Cedar Mountain. Union camps in the foreground; the mountain in the distance.	T. H. O'Sullivan
501.	Battle-field of Cedar Mountain. House where General Winder was killed, riddled by cannonballs.	"
502.	Battle-field of Cedar Mountain. House in which General Winder was killed.	"
503.	Battle-field of Cedar Mountain. House in which General Winder was killed. Family group.	"
504.	Battle-field of Cedar Mountain; west view.	"
506.	Battle-field of Cedar Mountain; panoramic view; the mountain in the distance.	"
507.	Confederate Hospital at Cedar Mountain.	"
508.	Parson Slaughter's House, on Slaughter's (or Cedar) Mountain. Site of a Confederate Battery.	"
509.	Group of Officers of the Tenth Maine, on the Battle-field of Cedar Mountain.	"
510.	Dead Horses on Battle-field of Cedar Mountain. First position of the Confederate forces, from which they were dislodged.	"
511.	Graves on the Battle-field of Cedar Mountain, where a large number of Union soldiers are buried.	"
512.	Bridge over the north fork of the Rappahannock, near Sulphur Springs, Va.	"
513.	Bridge over north fork of Rappahannock, McDowell's Engineers at work.	"
514.	Bridge across the Rappahannock; north view.	"
515.	Erecting Bridge across north fork of the Rappahannock, near Sulphur Springs, Va.	"
517.	Rappahannock Bridge; south view.	"
518.	Fugitive Negroes fording the Rappahannock; fleeing from Jackson's army.	"
519.	Fugitive Negroes crossing Rappahannock during Pope's retreat.	"
520.	Battery fording a tributary of the Rappahannock, on the day of the Battle of Cedar Mountain.	"
521.	Hazel River, a tributary of the Rappahannock; bridge in the distance.	"
522.	Rappahannock Station.	"
523.	Culpeper Court House. Group of Confederates captured at the battle of Cedar Mountain, at the window.	"
524.	View in Culpeper. Court House in the distance.	"
525.	Street view in Culpeper.	"
526.	Scene in Culpeper; a Wounded Negro in the foreground.	"
527.	Approach to Culpeper.	"
528.	Railroad Depot and Yard, Culpeper.	"
529.	Railroad Station, Culpeper.	"
530.	Railroad Station at Culpeper; south view.	"
531.	View of Culpeper.	"
532.	Street approaching Warrenton; courthouse in the distance.	"
533.	Court House in Warrenton.	"
534.	View in Warrenton.	"
535.	Railroad Depot in Warrenton.	"
536.	Railway Approach to Warrenton.	"
537.	Hotel at Sulphur Springs, Va.; rear view.	"
538.	Officers of the Sixtieth New York Volunteers, at Sulphur Springs, Virginia.	"
542.	Hotel at Sulphur Springs, Va.; street view, south.	"
543.	East Range of Confederate Defenses at Manassas.	"
544.	Confederate Fort at Manassas.	"
545.	Fortifications at Manassas.	"
546.	View on the Orange and Alexandria Railroad.	"
547.	The New Bridge at Bull Run, built by McDowell's Engineers.	"
548.	View on Bull Run.	"
587.	Army Blacksmith and Forge, Antietam, Sept., 1862.	"
593.	Ruins at Manassas, after Jackson's raid, July 1862.	"
594.	Cartlett's Station.	"
644.	Col. Duryea, First Rhode Island Cavalry.	"
645.	Scene at Blackburn's Ford, July 4, 1862.	"
646.	Headquarters General McDowell, formerly General Beauregard's, July 5, 1862.	"
647.	Camp of General McDowell's Body Guard, July 5, 1862.	"
648.	Confederate Barracks, Manassas.	"

649. Group of Officers First Rhode Island Battery.	T. H. O'Sullivan
650. Yellow Hospital, Manassas.	"
651. Our Special Artist at Manassas, July 4, 1862.	"
* Colonel Childs & Staff, 4th Pennsylvania Cavalry.	Alexander Gardner
* General Averill and Staff at Westover Landing, James River, August, 1862.	"
* Col. Childs and Staff, Fourth Pennsylvania Cavalry, Westover Landing, August, 1862.	"
* Col. Averill and Officers of Third Pennsylvania Cavalry, Westover Landing, August, 1862.	"

ILLUSTRATIONS OF GENERAL MCCLELLAN'S CAMPAIGN IN MARYLAND. Mounted as stereographs and album cards. Those marked + are mounted for album cards only.

550. Group of Irish Brigade, as they lay on Battle-field of Antietam, Sept. 19, 1862.	Alexander Gardner
551. A Contrast: Federal buried, Confederate unburied, where they fell, on Battle-field of Antietam.	"
552. Completely Silenced: Dead Confederate Artillerymen, as they lay around their battery, after the Battle of Antietam.	"
553. Ditch on the right wing, where Kimball's Brigade fought so desperately, at the Battle of Antietam.	"
554. He Sleeps his Last Sleep. A Confederate Soldier, who after being wounded, had evidently dragged himself to a little ravine on the hill-side, where he died.	"
555. Confederate Soldiers, as they fell, near the Burnside Bridge, at the Battle of Antietam.	"
556. Confederate Soldiers, as they fell inside the fence, on the Hagerstown road, at the Battle of Antietam.	"
557. Gathered Together for Burial: After the Battle of Antietam.	"
558. Dead Horse of Confederate Colonel; both killed at the Battle of Antietam.	"
559. Killed at the Battle of Antietam.	"
560. View in the Field, on the west side of Hagerstown road, after the Battle of Antietam.	"
561. Burying the Dead, after the Battle of Antietam.	"
562. View near Dunker Church, on the Battle-field of Antietam.	"
563. View in Ditch on right wing, after the Battle of Antietam.	"
564. Demolished Confederate Battery, near Sharpsburg, September 19, 1862.	"
565. View of Ditch on right wing, which had been used as a rifle-pit by the Confederates, at the Battle of Antietam.	"
566. Confederate Soldiers, as they fell, at the Battle of Antietam.	"
567. View on Battle-field: Group of Louisiana Regiment, as they fell, at the Battle of Antietam. The contest at this point had been very severe.	"
568. View on Battle-field of Antietam, where Sumner's corps charged the enemy; scene of terrific conflict.	"
569. View on Battle-field of Antietam.	"
570. A Lone Grave, on Battle-field of Antietam.	"
571. View on Battle-field of Antietam, near Sherrick's House, where the Seventy-ninth New York Volunteers fought after they crossed the creek; group of dead Confederates.	"
572. View on Battle-field of Antietam, where Hooker's corps behaved so gallantly; group of Confederate dead.	"
573. Dunker Church, on Battle-field of Antietam.	"
574. Ruins of Mumma's House, on Battle-field of Antietam.	"
575. Rullet's House, on Battle-field of Antietam.	"
576. General Hooker's Headquarters during the Battle of Antietam.	"
577. Captain Knapp's Battery, Pennsylvania Artillery, (Banks' corps) on Battle-field of Antietam.	"
578. Antietam Bridge, on Sharpsburg and Boonsboro Turnpike; looking upstream.	"
579. Group—Artillery Officers on Battle-field of Antietam.	"
580. General Caldwell and Staff, on Battle-field of Antietam, Sept. 21, 1862.	"
581. Picnic Party at Antietam Bridge, September 22, 1862.	"
582. Newcomer's Mill, near Antietam.	"
583. Antietam Bridge, looking across stream.	"
584. Burnside Bridge, Antietam, looking up stream.	James F. Gibson
585. Graves of Federal Soldiers at Burnside Bridge, Antietam, Sept. 21, 1862.	Alexander Gardner
586. Colonel Morehead, One Hundred and Sixth Pennsylvania Volunteers, on Battle-field of Antietam, Sept. 19, 1862.	"
587. Forge Scene at General McClellan's Headquarters, Sharpsburg, Sept. 22, 1862.	"
588. Confederate Wounded after the Battle of Antietam, at Smith's Barn; Dr. A. Hurd, Fourteenth Indiana Volunteers in attendance.	"
589. Smith's Barn, near Keedysville, used as a hospital after the Battle of Antietam.	"
590. Smith's House and Barn, near Keedysville, used as a hospital after the Battle of Antietam.	"
591. Real's Barn, burned by the bursting of a Federal shell at the Battle of Antietam.	"
592. Straw Huts, erected on Smith Farm and used as a hospital after the Battle of Antietam.	"
594. Catlett's Station.	T. H. O'Sullivan
595. Principal Street in Sharpsburg, Maryland.	Alexander Gardner
596. Lutheran Church, Sharpsburg, Maryland.	"
597. View on Antietam.	"
598. Sherrick's House, near Burnside Bridge, Antietam.	"
599. Street in Sharpsburg; Episcopal Church in distance.	"
* Antietam Bridge, looking downstream.	"

* Antietam Bridge, looking upstream.   Alexander Gardner
* Antietam Bridge, looking across stream.   "
* Burnside Bridge, looking up to stream.   "
* Burnside Bridge, looking down to stream.   "
* General Caldwell and Staff on Battle-field of Antietam, September 21, 1862.   "
* General McClellan's Headquarters Guard, Ninety-third New York Volunteers, at Antietam, September, 1862.   "
* President Lincoln and General McClellan at Headquarters, Army of the Potomac, October 4, 1862.   "
* President Lincoln, Generals McClellan, Porter, Morrell, Hunt, Humphrey, Colonel Sackett, Lieutenant Colonels Swietzer, Webb, Locke, Doctor Letterman, Captain Custer, &c., at Headquarters Fitz John Porter, Antietam, October, 1862.   "
* President Lincoln, General McClernand, and E. J. Allen, Chief of S.S., U.S.A., at Secret Service Department, Headquarters Army of the Potomac, Antietam, October 1862.   "
* Signal Tower on Elk Mountain, overlooking Battle-field of Antietam.   "
* Our Mess at Antietam. Group of Officers of Ninety-third New York Volunteers.   "
* Group—Dr. Letterman, Col. Clark, Gens. Gibbon and Buford, Lt. Cols. Colburn and Myers, Capt. Duane &c., at Antietam, October, 1862.   "
* Group—Gen. Marcy, Lt. Col. Colburn, Messrs. Garrett, Hatch, Kennedy and others, at Headquarters Army of the Potomac, near Antietam, October, 1862.   "
* Group—Mr. Coleman, Col. Clark, Lt. Cols. Colburn and Myers, Gen. Buford, Sidney Deming, &c., at Antietam, October, 1862.   "
* Group at Secret Service Department, Headquarters, Army of the Potomac, Antietam, October, 1862.   "
* Group of Guides for the Army of the Potomac, Berlin, October, 1862.   "
* Military Telegraph Construction Corps erecting line across the Potomac at Berlin, October, 1862.   "
* Group at Mrs. Lee's, near Birkettsville, Md., October, 1862.   "
* Dan Webster, General McClellan's War Horse.   "
* Pontoon Bridge across the Potomac at Berlin, October 1862.   "
600. Burnside Bridge, southeastern view.   "
601. Burnside Bridge, from the southeast.   "
602. President Lincoln and General McClellan, at Headquarters Army of the Potomac, Antietam, October 4, 1862.⁺   "
603. General Marcy and friends at Headquarters Army of the Potomac, October 4, 1862.   "
604. President Lincoln, General McClernand, and E. J. Allen, Chief of S.S., U.S.A., at Secret Service Department, Headquarters Army of the Potomac, October 4, 1862.⁺   "
605. Group—President Lincoln, Generals McClellan, McClernand and Marcy, and Messrs. Garrett, Hatch, Lamon, Kennedy, and others, previous to reviewing the troops on Battle-field of Antietam, October 3, 1862.   "
606. Group—President Lincoln, Generals McClellan, Porter, Morell, Hunt, Humphrey, Colonel Sackett, Lt. Cols. Swietzer, Webb, Locke, Dr. Letterman, Captain Custer, &c., at Headquarters, Fitz John Porter, Antietam, October 3, 1862.⁺   "
607. Bridge across the Antietam, northeast view.   James F. Gibson
608. Antietam Bridge, on the Sharpsburg and Boonsboro Pike, southeast view.   "
609. Antietam Bridge, looking downstream.   Alexander Gardner
610. Antietam Bridge, eastern view.   James F. Gibson
611. Antietam Bridge, south view.   "
612. Burnside Bridge across the Antietam, northeast view.   "
613. Burnside Bridge across the Antietam, southwest view.   Alexander Gardner
614. Burnside Bridge across the Antietam, eastern view.   James F. Gibson
615. Burnside Bridge across the Antietam, northeast view, with graves of Union soldiers.   Alexander Gardner
616. Pontoon Bridge across the Potomac, at Berlin.   "
617. A Welcome Visitor.   "
618. Group—Messrs. Allen, Hammond, Fargo, and Hall.   "
619. Can you make a Picture of my Horse this Morning?   "
626. Group—Major Myers, Lts. Stryker and Norton, Harrison's Landing, August, 1862.   "
628. General Heintzelman—Staff, Harrison's Landing, August, 1862.   "
630. Group—Colonel Crocker, Lieut. Colonel Butler, and Adjutant of the Ninety-third New York, Volunteers, Antietam.   "
631. Group—Messrs. E. J. Allen, Babcock, Moore, Bangs, Littlefield.   "
632. Group—Lieutenants Pearce, Babcock, and Rockwell, on Elk Mountain, Maryland.   "
633. Signal Tower on Elk Mountain, overlooking Battle-field of Antietam.   "
634. Group of Signal Corps Detachment, Pleasant Valley.   "
643. Gimlet, a celebrated War Horse of the Rappahannock.   "
645. Pickett Station, Blackburn's Ford, Bull Run.   "
654. Harpers Ferry Gap.   Holmes & Woodbury
655. Ruins of Harpers Ferry Arsenal, October, 1862.   "
656. Engineer Corps making Corduroy Roads.   "
657. A Negro Family coming into the Union Lines.   David B. Woodbury
658. Ruins of Bridge across the Potomac, at Berlin, destroyed by the Confederates, June, 1861.   Alexander Gardner
667. Group at Secret Service Department, Headquarters, Army of the Potomac, Antietam, October, 1862.   "

ILLUSTRATIONS OF GENERAL BURNSIDE'S CAMPAIGN IN VIRGINIA.—Mounted as stereographs and album cards.

684.	General McClellan and Staff, Warrenton.⁺	Alexander Gardner
685.	Group at Mrs. Lee's House, Birkettsville, Maryland.⁺	"
687.	Group at Medical Directors Department, Warrenton.⁺	"
689.	Group of Guides to the Army of the Potomac.⁺	"
690.	Group at Headquarters Army of the Potomac, Antietam.⁺	"
691.	Group of Signal Corps.⁺	"
692.	Group at Headquarters Medical Directors, Army of the Potomac.⁺	"
661.	General Burnside and Staff.⁺	"
662.	General Sumner and Staff.⁺	"
663.	Group—Generals Burnside, Wilcox, Couch, Park, Hunt, Farero, Patrick, Cochrane, Sturgis, Hancock, Buford, at Headquarters, Gen. Burnside, Warrenton, November, 1862.⁺	
664.	General Burnside on Horseback, November, 1862.⁺	"
665.	General Sumner at the Residence of Maj. Payne, of Longstreet's Staff, Warrenton, November, 1862.⁺	"
666.	Group at Medical Director's Department, Headquarters, Army of the Potomac, Warrenton, November, 1862.⁺	"
668.	What do I want? John Henry!⁺	"
669.	Group at Medical Director's Department, Headquarters, Army of the Potomac, November, 1862.⁺	"
670.	Captain J. B. Howard, A.Q.M., and Staff, Headquarters, Army of the Potomac, Warrenton, November, 1862.⁺	"
676.	View of Fredericksburg, from Tyler's Battery.	James F. Gibson
678.	Balloon Camp, near Falmouth.	"
*	General Burnside and Staff, Warrenton, November, 1862.	Alexander Gardner
*	General Burnside on Horseback, Warrenton, November, 1862.	"
*	General Sumner and Staff, Warrenton, November, 1862.	"
*	General Sumner at the Residence of Maj. Payne, of Longstreet's Staff, Warrenton, November, 1862.	"
*	Group—Generals Burnside, Couch, Wilcox, Hancock, Park, Farero, Patrick, Cochrane, Sturgis, Buford & Hunt.	"
*	General Heintzelman and Staff, at Arlington House.	"
*	Group—Medical Director's Department, Headquarters Army of the Potomac, Warrenton, November, 1862.	"
*	Group at Medical Director's Department, Headquarters Army of the Potomac, Warrenton, November, 1862.	"
*	What do I want? John Henry!.	"
*	Captain J. B. Howard, A.Q.M., and Staff, Headquarters Army of the Potomac, Warrenton, November, 1862.	"
*	Group of Officers of Signal Corps, Warrenton, November, 1862.	"
*	Signal Corps Detachment on Elk Mountain, Md.	"
*	Group—Cols. Sackett, Ruggles, Clarke, and Major Davies, at Headquarters, Army of the Potomac, Warrenton, November, 1862.	"
*	Lt. Colonel Colburn on Horseback.	"
*	Lt. Colonel Norton on Horseback.	"
*	Major E. J. Allen on Horseback.	"
*	G. N. Bangs on Horse.	"
*	Captain Howard and Horse.	"
*	G. Littlefield on Horseback.	"
657.	Arrival of the first Negro Family within the lines, on 1st January, 1863.	David B. Woodbury

ILLUSTRATIONS OF GENERAL HOOKER'S CAMPAIGN IN VIRGINIA.—Mounted as stereographs and album cards.

672.	Quartermaster's Department, Aquia Creek.	Alexander Gardner
673.	View at Aquia Creek Landing, from Confederate battery; looking down the Potomac.	"
674.	Aquia Creek Landing, February, 1863.	"
675.	Provost Marshal's Office, Aquia Creek Landing.	"
677.	Phillips' House on fire, Falmouth Station, near Fredericksburg, Feb. 14, 1863.	"
679.	Embarkation of Ninth Army Corps at Aquia Creek Landing, February, 1863.	"
680.	View at Aquia Creek Landing, from Commissary Department.	"
681.	View at Aquia Creek Landing.	"
682.	View at Aquia Creek Landing.	"
683.	View of Fredericksburg.	"
516.	Ambulance Train, Falmouth.	T. H. O'Sullivan
686.	General Hooker and Staff, Falmouth.⁺	"
688.	Group at Commissary Department, at Aquia Creek.⁺	Alexander Gardner
693.	Group at Headquarters Army of the Potomac.⁺	James F. Gibson
694.	A Mess at Headquarters Army of the Potomac.	"
695.	Group—Lord Abbinger and Friends, Headquarters Army of the Potomac.	"
696.	General Stoneman and Staff.	"
*	Aquia Creek Landing, No. 1.	Alexander Gardner

* Aquia Creek Landing, No. 2.   Alexander Gardner
* View at Aquia Creek Landing.   "
* Provost Marshal's Office, Aquia Creek.   "
* Quartermaster's Department, Aquia Creek.   "
* Group at Transportation Office, Aquia Creek.   "
* Group at Hospital, Aquia Creek.   "
* Group—General Barnes, Lieutenant Colonels Porter and Santelle, Commodore McGraw, Doctor Whyte, Captain Forsythe, &c., at Aquia Creek, February, 1863.   "
* Group—Lieutenant Colonel Porter, Commodore McGraw, Captains Hall and Forsythe, &c., W. S. Hall's Wagon Camp near Aquia Creek, February, 1863.   "
* Embarkation of Ninth Army Corps.   "
* Locomotive, Fred Leach, Aquia Creek.   "
* General Ward and Friends.   "
* Group of Commissary Clerks, Aquia Creek.   "
* Group—General Andrew Porter's Staff.   "
* Group—Officers of Fourth Pennsylvania Cavalry.   "
* Group—Lieut. Colonel Dickinson and Friends.   T. H. O'Sullivan
* Post Office Headquarters Army of the Potomac, Falmouth.   "
* Lacy House.   "
* Fredericksburg, No. 1.   "
* Captains Chandler, Russell and Moore, on Horseback.   "
* Pontoon Bridge across the Rappahannock.   "
* Pontoon Bridge across the Rappahannock.   "
* Captain Howard on Horseback.   "
* Fredericksburg, No. 2.   "
* General Butterfield on Horseback.   "
* General Pleasonton and Captain Custer.   "
* General Pleasonton.   "
* General Hooker and Staff.   "
* Pontoon Bridge over the Rappahannock.   "
* General Patrick and Staff.   "
* General Patrick on Horseback.   "
* Group—Officers of Seventeenth N.Y. Battery. Lt. Colonel Dickinson on Horseback.   "
* Evacuation of Aquia Creek, June, 1863.   "
* Brazilian Steam Frigate, Navy Yard, Washington, yards manned on the occasion of the President's visit.   Alexander Gardner
* Group at Fort Lincoln.   "
* Seventeenth New York Battery, Camp Barry.   "

ILLUSTRATIONS OF GENERAL MEADE'S CAMPAIGN IN PENNSYLVANIA, MARYLAND, AND VIRGINIA. Mounted as stereographs and album cards.

No.	Title	Photographer
226.	Unfit for Service, on the Battle-field of Gettysburg.	James F. Gibson
227.	Scene in a Wheat-field on the Confederate right, at the Battle of Gettysburg.	T. H. O'Sullivan
228.	Farmers' Inn and Hotel, Emmitsburg, where our special Artist was captured, July 5, 1863.	James F. Gibson
229.	All over now—Confederate Sharp-shooter, on Battle-field of Gettysburg.	Alexander Gardner
230.	Line of Breast-works on Round Top, Gettysburg.	T. H. O'Sullivan
231.	Line of Breast-works looking eastward, on Battle-field of Gettysburg.	James F. Gibson
232.	Gateway of Cemetery, Gettysburg.	Alexander Gardner
233.	Unfinished Confederate grave near the center of Battle-field of Gettysburg.	T. H. O'Sullivan
234.	Federal Soldiers as they fell, at Battle of Gettysburg.	James F. Gibson
235.	Confederate Soldiers as they fell, near the center of the Battle-field of Gettysburg.	Alexander Gardner
236.	Confederate Soldiers who had evidently been shelled by our batteries on Round Top, at the Battle of Gettysburg.	T. H. O'Sullivan
237.	The Home of a Rebel Sharp-shooter, on Battle-field of Gettysburg.	James F. Gibson
238.	Office of the United States Sanitary Commission, Gettysburg.	Alexander Gardner
239.	View in Wheat-field opposite our extreme left, at Battle of Gettysburg.	T. H. O'Sullivan
240.	Scene in the Woods on the extreme right of the Confederate line.	James F. Gibson
241.	View of Breast-works on Round Top—the hill which formed our extreme left at the Battle of Gettysburg.	Alexander Gardner
242.	Evidence of how severe the contest had been on the right at the Battle of Gettysburg.	T. H. O'Sullivan
243.	View in field on right wing at Battle of Gettysburg.	James F. Gibson
244.	Dead Sharp-shooter on the right of the Confedeate line, Gettysburg.	Alexander Gardner
245.	A harvest of death on the Battle-field of Gettysburg.	T. H. O'Sullivan
246.	Scene near the woods on Confederate center, at Battle of Gettysburg.	James F. Gibson
247.	Interior view of Breastworks on the extreme left.	Alexander Gardner
248.	View around Abraham Trossel's House, near center of Battle-field of Gettysburg.	T. H. O'Sullivan
249.	Scene in the woods at foot of Round Top, at Battle of Gettysburg.	James F. Gibson
250.	Members of a South Carolina regiment laid out for Burial.	Alexander Gardner
251.	Rocks could not save him at the Battle of Gettysburg.	T. H. O'Sullivan

252. View in Slaughter Pen, foot of Round Top, Gettysburg. — James F. Gibson
253. Scene in the woods at Slaughter Pen. — Alexander Gardner
254. Special Artist of Harper's Weekly sketching Battle-field of Gettysburg. — T. H. O'Sullivan
255. View of Breast-works on Round Top, Gettysburg. — James F. Gibson
256. View in Wheat field, on Confederate right wing. — Alexander Gardner
257. View on the left, on the Battle-field of Gettysburg. — T. H. O'Sullivan
258. A Confederate Sharp-shooter, who had been killed by a shell at Battle of Gettysburg. — James F. Gibson
259. General Meade's Headquarters during the Battle of Gettysburg. — Alexander Gardner
260. Confederate dead on center of Battle-field of Gettysburg. — T. H. O'Sullivan
261. View of breast-works on Round Top, Gettysburg. — James F. Gibson
262. Slaughter Pen on left wing at Battle of Gettysburg. — Alexander Gardner
263. Dead Confederate Sharp-shooter at the Battle of Gettysburg. — T. H. O'Sullivan
264. Breast-works thrown up on the extreme left at the Battle of Gettysburg. — James F. Gibson
265. View of Slaughter Pen at Battle of Gettysburg. — Alexander Gardner
266. View at Losser's Barn where the Ninth Massachusetts Battery was cut up. — T. H. O'Sullivan
267. View of Round Top. — James F. Gibson
268. View near the Emmitsburg road on the Battle-field of Gettysburg. — Alexander Gardner
269. Mt. St. Mary's College, Emmitsburg, Md. — T. H. O'Sullivan
270. Right wing Mount St. Mary's College, Emmitsburg, Maryland. — James F. Gibson
271. St. Joseph's Seminary, Emmitsburg. — Alexander Gardner
272. Emmitsburg, Maryland. — T. H. O'Sullivan
273. Gettysburg from the Cemetery. — James F. Gibson
274. War, effects of a Shell on a Confederate Soldier at Battle of Gettysburg. — Alexander Gardner
280. Gen. Ward, Gen. Mott, Col. Austin, Col. Brewster and Colonel Franham, 2nd Division, 3rd Corps, October, 1863. — T. H. O'Sullivan

[It is interesting to note the sequence of photographer credits in the above series of stereoviews. It seems possible that rather than determining which photographer actually took each view, the credits were arbitrarily assigned in this pattern.]

282. Group at Telegraphic Corps, HQ, Army of the Potomac. — T. H. O'Sullivan
292. General Patrick and Staff near Bealton, Va. — "
293. Ruins of Sulphur Springs Hotel, near Warrenton, Va. — "
294. Headquarters New York Herald, Army of the Potomac. — "
    * Office of Sanitary Commission, Gettysburg. — "
    * Losser's House, Battle-field of Gettysburg. — "
    * Lt. Col. Dickinson and Major Ludlow. — "
    * Lt. Col. Dickinson and Major Ludlow, Capt. Dahlgren, Capt. Rosencrantz, Count Zeppalin of Prussia. — "
    * General Meade's Headquarters, Battle-field of Gettysburg. — "
    * Gettysburg. — "
    * Effects of a Shell at the Battle of Gettysburg. — "
    * Sharp Shooter's Last Sleep at the Battle of Gettysburg. — "
    * View in field on right wing, where Gen. Reynolds fell, at the Battle of Gettysburg. — "
    * Harvest of Death at the Battle of Gettysburg. — "
    * Interior view of Breastworks at the Battle of Gettysburg. — "
    * Round Top Hill on the extreme left at Battle of Gettysburg. — "
    * Gateway to Cemetery at Gettysburg. — "
    * Unfit for Service at the Battle of Gettysburg. — "
    * Home of a Rebel Sharp Shooter at the Battle of Gettysburg. — "
    * Capt. Coxe and Staff, Commissary Department, Headquarters Army of the Potomac, Fairfax Court House. — "
    * Group—Telegraph Office, Headquarters Army of the Potomac. — "
    * Eighth Infantry, Fairfax Court House. — "
    * Fairfax Court House, Virginia. — "
    * Headquarters Generals Beauregard and McClellan, Fairfax Courthouse. — "
    * Assistant Quartermaster's Department, Fairfax Court House. — "
    * Secesh Prisoners' Headquarters, Army of the Potomac, Fairfax Court House. — "
    * View of Pontoon Bridge across the Rappahannock from Rebel Line Works. — "
    * Mount St. Mary's College, Emmitsburg. — "
    * St. Joseph's Seminary, Emmitsburg. — "
    * Office of National Intelligencer, Washington from 1818 to 1863. — "
    * Office of Sanitary Commission, Washington. — "
    * Group—Officers of Sixty-first N.Y. Volunteers. — "

ADDITIONAL PHOTOGRAPHS ISSUED AFTER SEPTEMBER 1863.

    * Colonel George Sharpe, John C. Babcock, John McEntee, 80th N.Y., H.Q. Secret Service, August 1863. — T. H. O'Sullivan
    * General Pleasonton, November 15, 1863. — "
223. Camp in woods near Culpeper, November, 1863. — "
227. Mail Wagon, Jerusalem Plank, 1864. — "

APPENDIXES

237.	Germanna Ford, Rappidan, 1864.	T. H. O'Sullivan
242.	Belle Plain, May, 1862.	
256.	Line of breastworks occupied by Union troops of North Bank of North Anna—enemies' line of works on South Bank in the distance	"
281.	General Prince & Staff, October, 1863.	"
127.	Rear View of Winter Quarters of Telegraphic Corps & Photographic Departments, attached HQ Army of the Potomac, April 1864.	"
700.	The crossing of the Rapidan River at Germanna Ford.	"
701.	The crossing of the Rapidan River at Germanna Ford.	"
702.	Troops Crossing at Germanna Ford, Rappahannock River, Va., May 4, 1864.	"
703.	Encampment of 7000 rebel prisoners in the Punch Bowl, Belle Plain, Va., May 15, 1864.	"
707.	Quartermaster's Department, Belle Plain, May 17, 1864.	James Gardner
708.	General view of Belle Plain, Va., May 17, 1864.	T. H. O'Sullivan
710.	General view of Belle Plain, taken looking eastward toward the lower landing, May 16, 1864.	James Gardner
715.	Wagon Train Crossing the Rappahannock River, May, 1864.	"
717.	Homes on Caroline St, Fredericksburg, damaged during the shelling of December 11, 1862, taken May 19, 1864.	"
721.	Scene at Mrs. Alsop's House, Spotsylvania, May 20, 1864.	T. H. O'Sullivan
722.	Confederate dead laid for burial near Mrs. Alsop's House, Spotsylvania, May 20, 1864.	"
723.	Dead Confederate soldier, near Mrs. Alsop's house, Spotsylvania, May 20, 1864.	"
724.	1st MA Heavy Artillery burying the dead at Mrs. Alsop's House. Pine forest near Spotsylvania Co. HQ after the battle of the 19th May 1864.	"
725.	Confederate Dead on the Battlefield, Spotsylvania Courthouse, May 12, 1864.	"
726.	Confederate Dead on the Battlefield, Spotsylvania Courthouse, May 19, 1864.	"
727.	View looking north from Beverly House, with the V Corps artillery reserve in the distance, May 19, 1864.	"
728.	Beverly House, near Spotsylvania Court House, the HQ of Gen. Warren, May 19, 1864.	"
729.	Massaponax Church, May 21, 1864.	"
730.	A Council of War at Massaponax Church, Va., May 21, 1864, General Grant leaning over General Meade, examining a map which had just been completed by the Topographical Engineers.	"
731.	A Council of War at Massaponax Church, Va., May 21, 1864, General Grant writing a dispatch.	"
732.	A Council of War at Massaponax Church, Va., May 21, 1864.	"
733.	Union Hospital at the Marye House, Marye's Heights, Fredericksburg, May 19, 1864.	"
735.	Outbuildings adjacent to the Marye House, Fredericksburg, May 19, 1864.	"
736.	The Baptist Church, Fredericksburg, May 20, 1864.	"
739.	Front of Sanitary Commission depot, Commerce St., Fredericksburg, May 20, 1864.	"
740.	Wounded soldiers at the Sanitary Commission depot, Fredericksburg, May 20, 1864.	"
741.	Nurses and officers of the Sanitary Commission, Fredericksburg, May 20, 1864.	"
742.	The backyard of Sanitary Commission depot, Fredericksburg, May 20, 1864.	"
744.	Bethel Church, HQ of General Burnside, May 23, 1864.	"
690.	Bethel Church, May 23, 1864.	"
746.	A Canvas Pontoon Bridge on North Anna near Jericho Mill.	"
747.	Jericho Mill, North Anna River, view from North Bank, May 24, 1864.	"
748.	Jericho Mill from South Bank of North Anna, Va., with canvas Pontoon Bridge, constructed by 50th N.Y.V. Engineers.	"
749.	Jericho Mill, North Anna River, view from South Bank showing engineers constructing road, May 24, 1864.	"
750.	Jericho Mill, North Anna, Va., Looking Up Stream from South Bank, Canvas Pontoon Bridge and Pontoon Train on Opposite Bank, May 24, 1864.	"
751.	5th Corps' Ammunition Train Crossing North Anna, Va., at Jericho Mill, on Canvas Pontoon Bridge, constructed by 50th NY Eng.	"
753.	Chesterfield Bridge on North Anna, with Cavalry crossing. Rifle Pit in the foreground, enemies' works in the distance.	"
754.	Union Supply Wagons crossing the Pamunkey River, looking eastward, May 28, 1864.	"
755.	Interior view of captured Confederate redoubt at the Chesterfield Bridge, on North Anna, captured by 2nd Corps under General Hancock, May 23, 1864.	"
756.	Line of Breastworks occupied by Union troops on North Bank of North Anna, enemies' line of works on South bank in distance.	"
759.	Quarle's Mill, North Anna River, view from South Bank.	"
760.	The corduroy bridge over the North Anna River at Quarle's Mill, from the North Bank.	"
761.	Quarle's Mill, North Anna River, view from South Bank.	"
762.	Destruction of railroad Bridge across the North Anna River, May 25, 1864.	"
767.	Pontoon Bridge at Hanovertown Ferry on the Pamunky, Constructed by the 50th N.Y.V. Engineers, May 28, 1864.	"
770.	Old Church Hotel, Va., June 2, 1864.	"
771.	Burnett's Inn, Cold Harbor, Va., June 4, 1864.	"
777.	Charles City Courthouse, June 14, 1864.	"
780.	Ruins of houses at Charles City Courthouse, June 14, 1864.	"
781.	Pontoon Bridge over the James River from North Bank, June 15.	"

783. The execution of William Johnson, Petersburg, June 20, 1864.	T. H. O'Sullivan
784. Outside of one of the forts captured by 18th Corps, under Gen. Smith, with Dunn's house in front of Petersburg, June 24, 1864.	"
785. View of Rebel Works in Front of Petersburg, Captured by the 18th Corps under General Smith, June 24, 1864.	"
786. Field telegraph, Battery Wagon and officers tent of Military Telegraph Corps, HQ, Army of the Potomac, June 24, 1864.	"
787. Cowan's independent Battery, 1st NY inside one of the rebel forts in front of Petersburg, June 24, 1864.	"
789. View of Cowan's Independent 1st NY in Rebel fort in front of Petersburg, captured by 18th Corps under Gen. Smith, June 24, 1864.	"
793. View on James River from Gen. Grant's HQ, July 5, 1864.	"
796. Docks at City Point, James River, Va., July 5, 1864.	"
798. Railroad Docks at City Point, James River, July 5, 1864.	"
801. View of bombproof works, occupied by U.S. Colored Troops in front of Petersburg, Va., August 7, 1864.	"
802. Black troops of Ferrero's Division on eastern front at Petersburg, Va., August 7, 1864.	"
804. Near view of Bombproof tent in the advance line in front of Petersburg, Va., August 7, 1864.	"
805. A bombproof tent in front of line of Petersburg, Va., August 7.	"
808. Bombproof Huts in the front line before Petersburg, August 10, 1864.	"
814. View of ruins, City Point, after the explosion of August 9, 1864.	"
823. Section of the 30-pound Parrott Battery on the right of the 10th Corps in the works in front of Petersburg, Va., September 1, 1864.	"
824. View of the officers quarters of the 1st MA Cavalry, General Meade's escort.	"
827. 1st Mass. Cavalry Camp in the woods.	"
831. The "Dictator" at its final position at Petersburg adjacent to Battery 5, September 1, 1864.	"

MEMORIES OF THE WAR: Petersburg and Richmond, Virginia.

859. Castle Thunder, Richmond, Looking up Carey Street, April 7, 1865.	Alexander Gardner
866. Pratt's Castle, Gambler's Hill, Richmond, Residence of General Heningson, April 8, 1865.	"
872. View of Ruins, Looking up Twelfth Street, from Carey Street, April 6, 1865.	"
873. Libby Prison, from Union Hotel, April 6, 1865.	"
881. Panorama of Richmond from Gambells Hill, #1.	"
882. Panorama of Richmond from Gambells Hill, #2.	"
883. Panoramic View of Richmond in Ruins, from the Old Arsenal looking down the James River, April, 1865.	"
884. Panoramic View of Richmond in Ruins, from the Old Arsenal looking down the James River, April, 1865.	"
887. Ruins of Arsenal, Richmond, Looking towards Petersburg Depot, April 10, 1865.	"
890. Graves of Union Soldiers, on Belle Isle, Richmond, April 8, 1865.	"
891. Belle Isle, Richmond, April 8, 1865.	"
894. Kerr's Tobacco Factory, on Carey and Twenty-first Streets, Richmond, used as a store house for supplies sent to Federal Prisoners and where the first Union Flag was thrown out on the morning of the third of April, 1865. Taken April 7, 1865.	"
896. Libby Prison, looking West, on Water Street, Richmond, April 6, 1865.	"
897. Castle Thunder, Richmond, Va.	"
905. View of Ruins, Richmond, from Main Street, looking down 14th Street, April 8, 1865.	"
908. Ruins of Gallago Flour Mills, Richmond, from Canal Street said to be largest mills in the country, capable of turning out 2,100 barrels of flour per day. View from Canal Street and taken on April 10, 1865.	"
909. Mechanicsville, Va., April 10, 1865.	John Reekie
910. Tomb of President Monroe, Hollywood Cemetery, Richmond, April 10, 1865.	"
911. Residence of Jefferson Davis, Clay and Twelfth Streets, Richmond, April 12, 1865.	"
912. Executive Mansion, (Jeff Davis') Richmond, April 12, 1865.	"
913. Bridge Across the Chickahominy, Mechanicsville Road, Va., April 15, 1865.	"
914. Unburied Dead on Battlefield.	"
916. View on Battle-Field of Cold Harbor, April 15, 1865.	"
918. Collecting the remains of the dead, Gaines' Mill, Va.	"
919. Washington Monument on Capitol Square, Richmond, April 14, 1865.	"
920. Elliston's Mill—Battlefield of Mechanicsville, Va, April 15, 1865.	"
921. Ballard's Hotel, Richmond, April 14, 1865.	"
922. Caisons on Stoney Creek, Destroyed on the evacuation of Richmond, April 15, 1865.	"
923. Richmond City Hall, April 14, 1865.	"
925. Residence of General Robert E. Lee, Franklin Street, Richmond, April 17, 1865.	"
930. Bridge Across the Chickahominy, Va., April 15, 1865.	"
932. Ruins of Gaines' Mill, Scene of two Battles, 27th June, 1862 and 1st June, 1864. Taken April 15, 1865.	"
938. Spottiswood Hotel, Richmond, April 15, 1865.	"

No.	Title	Photographer
951.	Union Wagon Train leaving Petersburg on Washington Street, April 10, 1865.	John Reekie
952.	View looking northwestward on Sycamore Street, Petersburg, April 10, 1865.	"
990.	Cemetery	"

VIEW OF CONFEDERATE WATER BATTERIES ON THE JAMES RIVER:

1032. Seven Inch Brooke Rifle Gun in Battery Brooke—Fort Brady (U.S.) in extreme distance over terminus of gun. — William Frank Browne

1046. Ordnance Depot at Drury's Bluff—Bird's eye view of a Ship at the dock. This view was taken from the top of the Bluff, eighty feet above the deck. — "

1051. Sling Cart for Moving Cannon. — "

1054. A three-fourths rear view of the same sling cart shown in 1053—(description seen on No. 1053). This view shows the construction of the wheels, the alternate spokes projecting from opposite ends of the hubs, and all terminating in the same plane in the rim of the wheel. — "

1062. The Union Line Before Petersburg. — "

1065. Brigade Band at Gen. Abbott's Headquarters, Fort Drury. — "

1069. View of Confederate Church at Fort Darling—Graves in the foreground—Entrance to the Fort on the right. — "

1075. Ordnance Depot at Broadway Landing. Ordnance awaiting shipment—Mountain Howitzer captured from U.S. Cavalry, and recaptured at Petersburg—Eight inch Columbiad (Confederate) used on Petersburg Heights—Armstrong's, Blackley's, and Whitworth's Projectiles on hand barrow captured at Fort Fisher, N.C.—U.S. Howitzers on left which repulsed Confederate assault on Redoubt Dutton, June, 1864—U.S. Navy Gun captured at Fort Clifton. — "

1078. The Ambulence Corps. — "

1079. Ordnance Depot at Broadway Landing. An Eight Inch Columbiad, captured from the Confederates on Petersburg Heights, slung on two Sling Carts—An Eight Inch Mortar slung on a small Sling Cart—A twenty pdr. Parrott slung on a Gin in the distance—Shipping, piles of Ordnance Boxes, &c. — "

1084. Interior of Ft. Sedgwick. — "

1130. Magazine in Battery Rodgers, on the Potomac. — "

1140. Fifteen-inch gun in Battery Rogers on the Potomac. — "

1151. Sling Cart for moving Heavy Cannon. — "

EXECUTION OF THE CONSPIRATORS:

981. The Arrival on the Scaffold, July 7, 1865. — Alexander Gardner

799. The Reading of the Death Warrant (copy). — "

982. The Drop, July 7, 1865. — "

983. The Suspension, July 7, 1865. — "

*7796. The Execution of Mrs. Surratt and the Lincoln Assassination Conspirators (Reading of the Warrant.) — "

*7797. The Execution of Mrs. Surratt and the Lincoln Assassination Conspirators (Adjusting the Noose.) — "

*7798. The Execution of Mrs. Surratt and the Lincoln Assassination Conspirators (The Drop.) — "

[The following description appeared in the War Photograph and Exhibition Company catalog, c. 1891. "These views Nos. 7796, 7797, 7798 comprise a scene of much historic interest. They were made by having three separate cameras set to photograph the scaffold. When the Warrant was being read one camera was used and that view was taken; while the ropes were being placed around their necks another camera was used and that scene taken; then when the drop was sprung the third camera was used, and so the entire scene of such tragic interest was photographed clear and distinct."] — "

*7752. Execution of Captain Wirtz, the Keeper of Andersonville Prison (Reading the Warrant.) — "

*7753. Execution of Captain Wirtz, the Keeper of Andersonville Prison (Adjusting the noose.) — "

*7755. Execution of Captain Wirtz, the Keeper of Andersonville Prison (The Drop.) — "

[The following description appeared in the War Photograph and Exhibition Company catalog, c. 1891. "These three views 7752, 7753, 7755 comprise a scene of much historic interest. They were made by having three separate cameras set to photograph the scaffold. When the warrant was being read one camera was used and that view taken; while the rope was being placed around his neck another camera was used and that scene was taken; then when the drop was sprung the third camera was used, and so the entire scene of such tragic interest was photographed clear and distinct."]

[These descriptions, written in 1891 as part of the promotional copy used to sell the photographs, are inaccurate. At the conspirators' execution Gardner used two cameras, as discussed in the text: one large format camera and one stereoview camera. A study of the photographs makes clear that once these cameras were in position, neither was moved.

There was only one camera used at the Wirz hanging. All of Gardner's photographs were taken from the same point, and all, including the postmortem view, were made with an 8 × 10 camera.]

C. ALEXANDER GARDNER STEREOGRAPHS IN THE COLLECTION OF THE KANSAS STATE HISTORICAL SOCIETY: *ACROSS THE CONTINENT ON THE UNION PACIFIC RAILWAY, EASTERN DIVISION*

This important series of more than one hundred fifty stereoviews was acquired by the Kansas State Historical Society in 1930 from Miss Crete Rose, of Lanham, Maryland. The collection had been in her family since her father's childhood and constitutes the most complete collection of Gardner's "Class D" photographs from *Across the Continent on the Union Pacific Railway, Eastern Division.* Also, many of the missing views were provided courtesy of Mr. Leonard A. Walle, Northville, Michigan.

NO.   TITLE

3. Depot of Missouri Pacific Railroad Co.
4. View on Levee, St. Louis, Mo.
5. Elevator, St.Louis, Mo.

NO.	TITLE	MI WEST OF ST. LOUIS
83.	Topeka, Kansas	
84.	State House, Topeka, Kansas (under construction)	
85.	View at Depot, Topeka, Kansas	
86.	Kansas Avenue, Topeka, Kansas	
87.	Lincoln College, Topeka, Kansas	
88.	Prairie Hunting, Topeka, Kansas	
89.	View on Kansas River, Topeka, Kansas	
90.	Pontoon Bridge at Topeka, Kansas	
90½.	View at Mr. Wetherall's, Topeka, Kansas	
91.	St. Mary's Mission, Kansas	375
92.	Pottawatomie Indians at St. Mary's Mission	
93.	Depot at Wamego, Kansas	388
94.	Lincoln Avenue, Wamego, Kansas	
95.	Depot, Manhattan, Kansas	402
96.	Manhattan, Kansas	401
97.	Poyntz Avenue, Manhattan, Kansas	402
98.	View on Kansas River at Manhattan, Kansas	401
99.	View on Kansas River at Manhattan	402
100.	Big Blue River, Kansas	401
101.	Fort Riley. No longer an Outpost, Kansas	420
102.	View on Kansas River at Fort Riley, Kansas	
103.	Monument to Major Ogden near Fort Riley, Kansas	
104.	View in Kaw Valley from Hill above Fort Riley, Kansas	
104½.	A Rare Specimen Found on Hill above Fort Riley, Kansas	
105.	Junction of Smokey and Republican River, Kansas	421
106.	Railroad Bridge across the Republican, Kansas	
107.	Depot at Junction City, Kansas	425
108.	Junction City, Kansas	
109.	Packing House, Junction City, Kansas	
110.	Stone Sawing Mill, Junction City, Kansas	
111.	Quarries at Junction City, Kansas	
112.	Trestle Bridge near Abilene, Kansas	447
113.	View on Muddy Creek, Abilene, Kansas	
115.	Loading Cattle at MacCoy's Stockyard, Abilene, Kansas	447
116.	Prairie Dog Town, Abilene, Kansas	447
117.	The Mayor of Prairie Dog Town, Abilene, Kansas	
118.	Prairie Dog In Hole at Prairie Dog Town, Abilene, Kansas	447
119.	Prairie Dog at Prairie Dog Town, Abilene, Kansas	
120.	Hotel and Depot, Salina, Kansas	470
121.	Salina, Kansas	
122.	Section Men at Salina, Kansas (The extreme distance is five miles off)	
123.	Trestle Bridge near Fort Harker, Kansas	500
124.	Fort Harker, Kansas	503
125.	View at Fort Harker, Kansas	
126.	Ranch at Clear Creek, Kansas (Formerly an overland stage station)	498
127.	Group with Tame Elk at Ranch on Clear Lake, Kansas	
127½.	Same title as 127, slightly different view	
128.	Workman's Ranch on Alum Creek, Kansas	496
129.	Devil's Bake Oven on Alum Creek, Kansas (seven miles east of Fort Harker)	496
130.	Mushroom Rock on Alum Creek, Kansas	496
131.	View at Mushroom Rock on Alum Creek, Kansas	
132.	View of Mushroom Rock on Alum Creek, Kansas	
133.	Mushroom Rock on Alum Creek	
134.	Indian Cave on Mulberry Creek	494
135.	Picnic at Indian Cave on Mulberry Creek	
136.	Inscription Rock at Indian Cave	
137.	The Escort at Indian Cave	
138.	Indian Hieroglyphic Rock on Smoky Hill River, Kansas (15 miles northeast of Fort Harker)	496
139.	Depot, Ellsworth, Kansas	508
140.	Ellsworth, Kansas	
141.	North Side of Main Street, Ellsworth, Kansas	
142.	South Side of Main Street, Ellsworth, Kansas	
143.	Walnut Street, Ellsworth, Kansas	
144.	Cattle Fording the Smoky Hill River at Ellsworth, Kansas, on the Old Santa Fe Crossing	
145.	Bull Train Crossing the Smoky Hill River at Ellsworth, Kansas	
146.	Hays City, Kansas	580
147.	Fort Hays, Kansas	
148.	U.S. Express Overland Stage Starting for Denver from Hays City, Kansas	
149.	View on the Plains, Six miles West of Fort Hays, Kansas	586
150.	View on the Plains, Kansas	585
151.	Construction Train West of Fort Hays, Kansas	
152.	"Westward, the Course of Empire Takes Its Way," Laying Track 600 miles west of St. Louis, Mo.	
153.	View at Hays City, Kansas	580

NOTES

EPIGRAPH

1. From *With Walt Whitman in Camden* (6 vols.), by Horace Traubel (New York, 1914), vol. 3, pp. 234, 346. Several references to Gardner in Walt Whitman's published correspondence indicate that they were friends, though little is known of their relationship.

CHAPTER 1

1. Don K. McCoo, "A Rare Specimen Found: Alexander Gardner, Scots American Photographer, 1821–1882" (dissertation, Glasgow School of Art, Graphics Department, June 1985), p. 10.
2. Ibid.
3. Joseph M. Wilson, *A Eulogy on the Life and Character of Alexander Gardner* (Washington, D.C.: Lebanon Lodge, No. 7, 1883), p. 8.
4. McCoo, "A Rare Specimen," p. 12.
5. Hayward Cirker and Blanche Cirker, *Dictionary of American Portraits* (New York: Dover, 1967), p. 464.
6. McCoo, "A Rare Specimen," pp. 12–13.
7. J. O. Crosby Papers, Garnavillo Museum, Iowa, in McCoo, "A Rare Specimen," p. 18.
8. 1850 Federal Census Records, Mendon Township, Clayton County, Iowa.
9. Wilson, *A Eulogy on the Life and Character*, p. 9.
10. McCoo, "A Rare Specimen," pp. 18–20.
11. *Glasgow Sentinel*, "Review of the Week: To Our Readers," 4 October 1851, in ibid., pp. 15–16.
12. *Glasgow Sentinel*, "The Glasgow Atheneum," 10 May 1851, p. 16, in ibid.
13. *Glasgow Sentinel*, 10 May 1851, p. 1, in ibid., p. 17.
14. McCoo, "A Rare Specimen," pp. 20–21.
15. *Glasgow Sentinel*, 22 September 1855, p. 4, in McCoo, pp. 24–25.
16. *Glasgow Sentinel*, 8 December 1855, p. 4, in ibid.
17. *Dumbarton Herald*, 10 January 1856, p. 2, in ibid., pp. 26–27.
18. McCoo, "A Rare Specimen," p. 27.
19. Josephine Cobb, "Alexander Gardner," *Image Magazine* (June 1958): 129.
20. *Cedar Rapids Gazette*, 5 November 1936, obituary for Mrs. Margaret S. Chapin.

CHAPTER 2

1. Floyd Rinhart and Marion Rinhart, *The American Daguerreotype* (Athens: University of Georgia Press, 1981), pp. 6–9.
2. Ibid., pp. 15–21.
3. James D. Horan, *Mathew Brady: Historian with a Camera* (New York: Bonanza, 1955), p. 4.
4. Ibid., p. 6.
5. Ibid., p. 9.
6. Ibid., p. 9.
7. Ibid., p. 10.
8. Ibid., p. 14.
9. Ibid., pp. 17–18.
10. Ibid., p. 18.
11. Ibid., p. 18.
12. Ibid., p. 19.
13. Don K. McCoo, "A Rare Specimen Found: Alexander Gardner, Scots American Photographer, 1821–1882" (dissertation, Glasgow School of Art, Graphics Department, June 1985), pp. 29–30.
14. Josephine Cobb, *Mathew B. Brady's Photographic Gallery in Washington*, vols. 53–56 (Washington, D.C.: Columbia Historical Society Records), pp. 12–13.
15. William Welling, *Photography in America: The Formative Years, 1839–1900, A Documentary History* (New York: Crowell, 1978), p. 122.
16. Horan, *Mathew Brady*, p. 27.
17. Joseph M. Wilson, *A Eulogy on the Life and Character of Alexander Gardner* (Washington, D.C.: Lebanon Lodge No. 7, 1883), p. 9.
18. Cobb, *Brady's Photographic Gallery*, p. 14.
19. Josephine Cobb, "Alexander Gardner," *Image Magazine* (June 1958): 129–30.
20. Cobb, *Brady's Photographic Gallery*, pp. 16–19.
21. Cobb, "Alexander Gardner," p. 129.
22. Dorothy Meserve Kunhardt and Philip B. Kunhardt, Jr., *Mathew Brady and His World* (Alexandria, Va.: Time-Life, 1977), p. 53.
23. Ibid., p. 55.
24. Lloyd Ostendorf, *Lincoln in Photographs: An Album of Every Known Pose* (Norman: University of Oklahoma Press, 1962), p. 35.
25. Horan, *Mathew Brady*, p. 32.
26. McCoo, "A Rare Specimen," p. 29.
27. Cobb, *Brady's Photographic Gallery*, p. 22.

28. Cobb, "Alexander Gardner," p. 130.
29. William Marder and Estelle Marder, *Anthony, An American Photographic Pioneer* (Amesbury: Pine Ridge Publishing Company, 1982), pp. 170–171.
30. Beaumont Newhall, *Image of America: Early Photography, 1839–1900* (Washington, D.C.: Library of Congress Catalog, 1957), p. 16.
31. James D. Horan, *Timothy O'Sullivan: America's Forgotten Photographer* (New York: Bonanza, 1966), p. 29.

CHAPTER 3

1. Beaumont Newhall, *The History of Photography: From 1839 to the Present Day* (New York: Museum of Modern Art, 1978), p. 67.
2. James D. Horan, *Mathew Brady: Historian with a Camera* (New York: Bonanza, 1955), p. 38.
3. Mark Mayo Boatner III, *The Civil War Dictionary* (New York: McKay, 1959), p. 99.
4. Horan, *Mathew Brady*, p. 39.
5. Don K. McCoo, "A Rare Specimen Found: Alexander Gardner, Scots American Photographer, 1821–1882" (dissertation, Glasgow School of Art, Graphics Department, June 1985), p. 34.
6. Boatner, *Civil War Dictionary*, p. 654.
7. Francis Trevelyan Miller, *The Photographic History of the Civil War*, 10 vols., vol. 8 (New York: Review of Reviews, 1912), p. 23.
8. Ibid., p. 14.
9. Roy Meredith, *Mr. Lincoln's Camera Man: Mathew B. Brady* (New York: Dover, 1974), pp. 144–145.
10. Dorothy Meserve Kunhardt and Philip B. Kunhardt, Jr., *Mathew Brady and His World* (Alexandria, Va.: Time-Life, 1977), p. 57.
11. Horan, *Mathew Brady*, p. 40.
12. James D. Horan, *Timothy O'Sullivan: America's Forgotten Photographer* (New York: Bonanza, 1966), p. 34.
13. United States Copyright Book, 1861–1868, Library of Congress, Washington, D.C.
14. Ibid.
15. Ibid.
16. Boatner, *Civil War Dictionary*, pp. 632–634.
17. William A. Frassanito, *Antietam: The Photographic Legacy of America's Bloodiest Day* (New York: Scribner's, 1978), p. 33.
18. Ibid., p. 34.
19. D. Mark Katz, *Custer in Photographs* (Gettysburg, Pa.: Yo-Mark Production, 1985), pp. 6–7.
20. Frassanito, *Antietam*, pp. 34–35.
21. Newhall, *History of Photography*, p. 68.
22. Landt and Lisl Dennis, *Collecting Photographs: A Guide to the New Art Boom* (New York: Dutton, 1977), pp. 10–11.
23. *James F. Gibson* v. *Alexander Gardner*, Case no. 842.
24. Frassanito, *Antietam*, p. 36.
25. Boatner, *Civil War Dictionary*, pp. 17–21.
26. Frassanito, *Antietam*, pp. 71–72.
27. Ibid., pp. 52–53.
28. Ibid., p. 286.
29. Dennis, *Collecting Photographs*, pp. 11–12.
30. Newhall, *History of Photography*, p. 74.
31. Josephine Cobb, "Alexander Gardner," *Image Magazine* (June 1958): 132.
32. Horan, *Mathew Brady*, p. 41.
33. Ibid., pp. 40–41.
34. Ibid., p. 41.
35. Boatner, *Civil War Dictionary*, pp. 331–339.
36. Champ Clark, *Gettysburg: The Confederate High Tide* (Alexandria, Va.: Time-Life, 1985), p. 34.
37. William A. Frassanito, *Gettysburg: A Journey in Time* (New York: Scribner's, 1975), pp. 24–26.
38. Ibid., pp. 29–32.
39. Ibid., pp. 32–34.
40. Ibid., p. 27.
41. Ibid., p. 26.
42. Ibid., p. 29.
43. *War of the Rebellion: Official Records of the Union and Confederate Armies*, vol. 28, pt. 1, p. 191.
44. Frassanito, *Gettysburg*, p. 39.
45. Ibid., pp. 224–226.
46. Ibid., pp. 187–192.
47. Ibid., pp. 216–217.
48. Frassanito, *Antietam*, p. 284.
49. William A. Frassanito, *Grant and Lee: The Virginia Campaigns* (New York: Scribner's, 1983), p. 19.
50. Josephine Cobb, "Notes and Documents, Photographs of the Civil War," *Military Affairs* 26, no. 3 (Fall 1962):132.
51. Frassanito, *Grant and Lee*, pp. 35–38.
52. Ibid., pp. 39–119.
53. Ibid., pp. 119–120.
54. Ibid., pp. 120–220.
55. Ibid., pp. 216–221.
56. Ibid., p. 220.
57. Ibid., pp. 292–293.

58. Ibid.
59. Letter written by Alexander Gardner recommending T. H. O'Sullivan for the position of photographer for the Treasury Department, October 23, 1880.
60. Frassanito, *Grant and Lee*, pp. 342–343.
61. Ibid., pp. 378–418.
62. *War of the Rebellion: Official Records of the Union and Confederate Armies*, vol. 66, pt. 1, p. 664.
63. Francis B. Heitman, *Historical Register and Dictionary of the United States Army*, vol. 1 (Washington, D.C.: U.S. Government Printing Office, 1903), p. 708.
64. Joseph M. Wilson, *A Eulogy on the Life and Character of Alexander Gardner* (Washington, D.C.: Lebanon Lodge, No. 7, 1883), p. 9.

CHAPTER 4

1. Lloyd Ostendorf and Charles Hamilton, *Lincoln in Photographs: An Album of Every Known Pose* (Dayton, Ohio: Morningside, 1985), pp. ix–x.
2. Ibid.
3. Ibid., p. 77.
4. James D. Horan, *Mathew Brady: Historian with a Camera* (New York: Bonanza, 1955), p. 35.
5. Ostendorf and Hamilton, *Lincoln in Photographs*, p. 77.
6. *Anthony's Photographic Bulletin*, no. 2, 1882.
7. Horan, *Mathew Brady*, p. 36.
8. Ostendorf and Hamilton, *Lincoln in Photographs*, pp. 358–359.
9. Ibid., p. 86.
10. Roy Meredith, *Mathew Brady's Portrait of an Era* (New York: Norton, 1982), p. 105.
11. William A. Frassanito, *Antietam: The Photographic Legacy of America's Bloodiest Day* (New York: Scribner's, 1978), p. 275.
12. Transcript of telegram, courtesy of Mr. Paul E. Keller, Berea, Ohio.
13. Frassanito, *Antietam*, p. 275.
14. D. Mark Katz, *Custer in Photographs* (Gettysburg, Pa.: Yo-Mark Production, 1985), p. 9.
15. Ostendorf and Hamilton, *Lincoln in Photographs*, p. 134.
16. Ibid., p. 142.
17. Ostendorf and Hamilton, *Lincoln in Photographs*, p. 147.
18. Dr. John K. Lattimer, *Kennedy and Lincoln, Medical and Ballistic Comparisons of Their Assassinations* (New York: Harcourt Brace Jovanovich, 1980), p. 6.
19. Ibid., p. 218.
20. *Lincoln Lore*, Bulletin of the Louis A. Warren Library and Museum, no. 1700 (October 1979), Lincoln Life Insurance Company, Fort Wayne, Indiana.
21. Ostendorf and Hamilton, *Lincoln Photographs*, pp. 228–229.
22. Dorothy Meserve Kunhardt and Philip B. Kunhardt, Jr., *Mathew Brady and His World* (Alexandria, Va.: Time-Life, 1977), p. 30.
23. *Washington Morning Chronicle*, 5 May 1865.
24. *Lincoln Lore*, no. 1700 (October 1979).
25. *Washington Morning Chronicle*, April–May 1865.
26. Ostendorf and Hamilton, *Lincoln in Photographs*, p. 203.
27. Mark E. Neely, Jr., *The Abraham Lincoln Encyclopedia* (New York: De Capo, 1982), p. 272.
28. Ostendorf and Hamilton, *Lincoln in Photographs*, p. 210.
29. See "Booth's First Attempt," *Incidents of the War Magazine* 1 (Spring 1986): 8–11.

CHAPTER 5

1. "Some Incidents in the Trial of President Lincoln's Assassins," a paper read by General Henry L. Burnett at a meeting of the Commandery, State of New York, Military Order, Loyal Legion, December 5, 1888.
2. Robert H. Fowler, *Album of the Lincoln Murder: Illustrating How It Was Planned, Committed and Avenged* (Gettysburg, Pa.: Gettysburg Publishing Company, 1965), p. 10.
3. Dorothy Meserve Kunhardt and Philip B. Kunhardt, Jr., *Twenty Days: A Narrative in Text and Pictures of the Assassination of Abraham Lincoln and the Twenty Days and Nights that Followed* (New York: Castle, 1965), pp. 40–53.
4. Fowler, *Album of the Lincoln Murder*, p. 30.
5. Theodore Roscoe, *The Web of Conspiracy: The Complete Story of the Men Who Murdered Abraham Lincoln* (Englewood Cliffs, N.J.: Prentice-Hall, 1959), p. 185.
6. Louis J. Weichmann, *A True History of the Assassination of Abraham Lincoln and of the Conspiracy of 1865*. Floyd E. Risvold, ed. (New York: Vintage, 1965), pp. 218–219.
7. Robert L. Keesler, "More on That Surratt Picture," *Surratt Society Newsletter* (June 1983).
8. Roscoe, *Web of Conspiracy*, pp. 204–205.
9. As of 8 December 1986, this letter was in the possession of dealer Robert Batchelder, Ambler, Pennsylvania.
10. Keesler, "That Surratt Picture."
11. *War of the Rebellion: Official Records of the Union and Confederate Armies*, ser. 1, vol. 46, pt. 3, Correspondence (Washington, D.C.: U.S. Government Printing Office, 1894), pp. 843–848.
12. Roscoe, *Web of Conspiracy*, p. 237.
13. Ibid., pp. 238–239.
14. Ibid., pp. 243–250.
15. Ibid., pp. 260–264.

16. Fowler, *Album of the Lincoln Murder*, pp. 42–48.
17. Roscoe, *Web of Conspiracy*, p. 402.
18. *War of the Rebellion: Official Records of the Union and Confederate Armies*, ser. 1, vol. 46, pt. 1, pp. 1320–1322.
19. Osborn H. Oldroyd, *The Assassination of Abraham Lincoln: Flight, Pursuit, Capture, Punishment of the Conspirators* (Washington, D.C., 1901), pp. 78–79.
20. Ibid., p. 79.
21. Roscoe, *Web of Conspiracy*, p. 415.
22. Weichmann, *A True History*, p. 211.
23. Roscoe, *Web of Conspiracy*, p. 416.
24. Transcript of the letter provided by Lloyd Ostendorf.
25. Philip Van Doren Stern, "The Unknown Conspirator: Did the Mysterious Portuguese Sea Captain Help Plot Lincoln's Assassination, or Was He an Informer?" *American Heritage* (February 1957): 54.
26. Josephine Cobb, "Alexander Gardner," *Image Magazine* (June 1958): 136.
27. Roscoe, *Web of Conspiracy*, pp. 415–416.

CHAPTER 6

1. Louis J. Weichmann, *A True History of the Assassination of Abraham Lincoln and of the Conspiracy of 1865*. Floyd E. Risvold, ed. (New York: Vintage, 1965), pp. 233–244.
2. Robert H. Fowler, *Album of the Lincoln Murder: Illustrating How It Was Planned, Committed, and Avenged* (Gettysburg, Pa.: Gettysburg Publishing Company, 1965), pp. 54–59.
3. Dr. John K. Lattimer, *Kennedy and Lincoln: Medical and Ballistic Comparisons of Their Assassinations* (New York: Harcourt Brace Jovanovich, 1980), p. 116.
4. Ibid., pp. 117–118.
5. Harlowe R. Hoyt, *Town Hall Tonight* (Englewood Cliffs, N.J.: Prentice-Hall, 1955), n.p.
6. Weichmann, *A True History*, pp. 280–281.
7. Ibid., p. 285.
8. Unless otherwise noted, all quotes in this section (pp. 182–188) are from Hoyt, *Town Hall Tonight*, n.p.
9. *War of the Rebellion: Official Records of the Union and Confederate Armies*, ser. 1.
10. Naomi Rosenblum, *A World History of Photography* (New York: Abbeville, 1984), p. 200.
11. James D. Horan, *Mathew Brady: Historian with a Camera* (New York: Bonanza, 1955), p. 65.
12. Mark Mayo Boatner III, *The Civil War Dictionary* (New York: David McKay, 1959), p. 942.
13. Francis T. Miller, *The Photographic History of the Civil War*, 10 vols., vol. 7 (New York: Review of Reviews, 1911), pp. 177, 179.
14–18. Horan, *Mathew Brady*, pp. 65–67.
19. Copy of the letter in the possession of the Western Reserve Historical Society.

CHAPTER 7

1. Swann Galleries, Photographic Auction Catalog, 13 November 1986, lot no. 281.
2. William C. Darrah, *The World of Stereographs* (Gettysburg, Pa.: Darrah, 1977), p. 74.
3. Ibid., p. 96.
4. Karen Current, *Photography and the Old West* (New York: Abrams, 1978), p. 48. Published in association with the Amon Carter Museum of Western Art.
5. William A. Bell, *New Tracks in North America*. 2 vols. (London: Chapman & Hall, 1869), pp. xvi, 1.
6. William Jackson Palmer, *Report of Surveys Across the Continent, in 1867–68, on the Thirty-fifth and Thirty-second Parallels, for a Route Extending the Kansas Pacific Railway to the Pacific Ocean at San Francisco and San Diego* (Philadelphia: Selheimer, 1869).
7. Current, *Photography*, p. 50.
8. Chronology of William Reddish Pywell, compiled by Marshall Pywell, Washington, D.C.
9. Robert Taft, "Additional Notes on the Gardner Photographs of Kansas," *Kansas Historical Quarterly* 6 (May 1937): 175.
10. Robert W. Richmond, "Alexander Gardner and the 1867 Kansas Expedition," *American West* 2, no. 3 (1965).
11. Robert Sobieszek, "Conquest by Camera: Alexander Gardner's Photographs Along the 35th Parallel," *Image Magazine* 14 (1971): 8.
12. Current, *Photography*, p. 51.
13. Ibid., p. 52.
14. Sobieszek, "Conquest by Camera," p. 8.
15. James E. Babbitt, "Surveyors Along the 35th Parallel: Alexander Gardner's Photographs of Northern Arizona, 1867–1868," *Arizona: The Journal of Arizona History* 22, no. 3 (1981):327.
16. Josephine Cobb, "Alexander Gardner," *Image Magazine* (June 1958): 136.

CHAPTER 8

1. Paula Richard Fleming and Judith Lusky, *The North American Indians in Early Photographs* (New York: Harper & Row, 1986), pp. 22–23.
2. Ibid., p. 23.
3. Ibid., p. 24.
4. David Nevin, "The Soldiers." The Old West Series (New York: Time-Life, 1973), pp. 135–138.
5. Raymond J. DeMallie, "Scenes in the Indian Country: A Portfolio of Alexander Gardner's Stereographic Views of the 1868 Fort Laramie Treaty Council," *Montana Magazine* 31 (1981): 44–45.
6. Ibid., pp. 45–46.

7. Ibid., p. 47.

8. Ibid., p. 48.

9. D. Mark Katz, *Custer in Photographs* (Gettysburg, Pa.: Yo-Mark Production, 1985), pp. 146–149.

10. DeMallie, "Scenes in the Indian Country," p. 48.

11. Ibid., p. 43.

CHAPTER 9

1. Josephine Cobb, "Alexander Gardner," *Image Magazine* (June 1958): 124–127.

2. Ibid., p. 127.

3. Josephine Cobb, *Mathew B. Brady's Photographic Gallery in Washington*, vol. 53 (Washington, D.C.: Columbia Historical Society, 1956).

4. William Welling, *Photography in America: The Formative Years, 1839–1900* (published by William Welling, 1978), p. 206.

5. Cobb, "Alexander Gardner," p. 136.

6. Joseph M. Wilson, *A Eulogy on the Life and Character of Alexander Gardner* (Washington, D.C.: Lebanon Lodge No. 7, 1883), p. 206.

7. *100th Annual Report to Policyholders*, Acacia Mutual Life Insurance Company, Washington, D.C., March 3, 1969, p. 3.

8. Ibid., p. 5.

9. Wilson, *A Eulogy on the Life and Character*, pp. 12–14.

10. Ibid.

11. Ibid.

12. Ibid.

13. Alexander Gardner, *The Assessment Plan for Life Insurance* (Washington, D.C.: Beresford, 1880), p. 19.

14. Wilson, *A Eulogy on the Life and Character*, pp. 12–13.

15. Ibid., pp. 12–14.

16. Ibid., p. 19.

17. Ibid. p. 20.

18. Ibid., pp. 21–22.

19. Ibid., pp. 22–23.

20. *The Philadelphia Photographer* 20, no. 231 (1883): 92.

CHAPTER 10

1. Walter Prescott Webb, "A Texas Buffalo Hunt with Original Photographs," *Holland's Magazine* (October 1927).

2. D. Mark Katz, "William Frank Browne: Custer's Photographer," *Incidents of the War Magazine* 2 (Spring 1987): 1.

3. John Dowling, "George N. Barnard, Pioneer Photographer," *News Photographer* (1987).

4. William Welling, *Collectors' Guide to Nineteenth-Century Photographs* (New York: Collier, 1976), pp. xiv–xv.

5. Paul Vanderbilt, *Guide to the Special Collections of Prints and Photographs in the Library of Congress* (Washington, D.C.: Library of Congress, 1955), pp. 19–22.

INDEX

PHOTO CREDITS

A NOTE ON THIS BOOK

This edition of Witness to an Era *was set in Linotron Walbaum by PennSet, Inc., Bloomsburg, Pennsylvania. Design was by Mary Wirth of Beth Tondreau Design. The book was printed on 113 gsm Moorim Matte paper and has a Smythe sewn binding. Color separations were by Strine Printing Company of York, Pennsylvania. Printing and binding were done in the Republic of China through Regent Publishing Services.*